August

MISSION HISTORY OF ASIAN CHURCHES

This book succinctly deals with the mission history of the Asian church and the Asian missionary movement in six Asian nations and Indochina nations. This book is unique in three aspects. First, it provides the mission history of the Asian church and Asian missionary movement up to the present. Secondly, the authors are all Asians who relate their Asian perspective of the Asian church and of Asian missions. Thirdly, it provides new opportunities and challenges for the Asian missionary movement for the twenty-first century. I strongly recommend the book as a textbook for history of the Asian church and history of Asian missions courses at theological seminaries.

—BONG RIN RO, THD
professor of Church History and Missions, Hawaii Theological Seminary

The Edinburgh Conference in 1910 focused on the missionary movement from the "Christian" West to the "non-Christian" world, or what we term the "majority world" today. But the great new fact of our time is that the Christian missionary movement from the majority world is vital, growing, and far outnumbers the movement from the West. This book brings together important research on that movement and will be an encouragement to all who are committed to the fulfillment of the Great Commission.

—PAUL E. PIERSON, PHD
dean emeritus and senior professor of History of Mission and Latin Studies, Fuller Theological Seminary

This remarkable collection of essays is further evidence that Christianity is a world movement, and that mission is integral to vitally authentic faith. As missions "from the West to the rest" recede with the ebbing tide of Christendom, Christian faith communities across Southeast Asia "cannot help speaking about what [they] have seen and heard." Emil Brunner's axiom that the church exists by mission as a fire exists by burning is nowhere better illustrated than in this informed, heartening, and essential book.

—JONATHAN J. BONK, PHD
executive director Overseas Ministries Study Center, editor of International Bulletin of Missionary Research

We've all heard about the rise of the mission movement in the global South. In *Mission History of Asian Churches*, we get a glimpse of what this burgeoning movement looks like in its Asian context. Written by national and regional mission experts, this book offers a fascinating look at the history, development, and present status of these mission movements. I can't think of a better introduction to what God is up to in building a powerful sending movement across Asia. Every story is unique, each reflecting the awkward relationships between human frailty and divine power, as well as Western approaches and non-Western alternatives. Underneath it all, one can see the continuing thread of God's purpose to bring every people to Himself. A compelling and encouraging read.

—**DAVE DATEMA**
general director of the U.S. Center for World Mission

MISSION HISTORY OF

ASIAN CHURCHES

Timothy K. Park, editor

WILLIAM CAREY
LIBRARY

Mission History of Asian Churches
Copyright © 2011 Timothy K. Park

All Rights Reserved. No part of this work may be reproduced or transmitted in any form or by any means—for example, electronic or mechanical, including photocopying and recording—without prior written permission of the publisher.

The publisher does not maintain, update, or moderate links and/or content provided by third-party websites mentioned in the book.

All scripture quotations, unless otherwise indicated, are taken from the Holy Bible, New International Version®, NIV®. Copyright © 1973, 1978, 1984 by Biblica, Inc.™ Used by permission of Zondervan. All rights reserved worldwide. www.zondervan.com

Scripture quotations marked "NKJV™" are taken from the New King James Version®. Copyright © 1982 by Thomas Nelson, Inc. Used by permission. All rights reserved.

Published by William Carey Library
1605 East Elizabeth Street
Pasadena, CA 91104 | www.missionbooks.org

Francesca Gacho, editor
Renee Robitaille, graphic designer
Rose Lee-Norman, indexer

Cover photos: (Top) Sorae Church, Sorae, North Korea–first Protestant church built by Korean Christians (ca. 1895). Photo from *Fifteen Years among the Topknots: Life in Korea* by Lillias H. Underwood, American Tract Society, 1908 p. 124; (Bottom left) Union Evangelistic Hall (1914), photo provided by Timothy K. Park; (Bottom right) The Korean church's first Protestant missionaries in Shantung, China, photo provided by Timothy K. Park.

William Carey Library is a ministry of the
U.S. Center for World Mission
Pasadena, CA | www.uscwm.org

Printed in the United States of America
15 14 13 12 11 5 4 3 2 1 BP1000

Library of Congress Cataloging-in-Publication Data

Mission history of Asian churches / editor, Timothy K. Park.
p. cm.
ISBN 978-0-87808-470-8
1. Missions--Asia--History. I. Park, Timothy Kiho, 1948- II. William Carey Library.
BV2100.M57 2010
266.0095--dc22

2010025059

Dedicated to

DR. RALPH D. WINTER

(1924–2009)

A friend of the Asian Society of Missiology

Contents

Preface xi

Chapter One: New Christianity in the Twenty-first Century: Asian Mission as a Major Force in Mission
David J. Cho, PhD 1

Chapter Two: A Mission China: An Analysis of Its Ten Affecting Factors
Thomas Lee, PhD 21

Chapter Three: The Emergence and Expansion of Indian Mission Movement from 1947–2009: A Study into the Successes and Failures
K. Rajendran, PhD 45

Chapter Four: Mission History of Indochina
Chansamone Saiyasak, DMin, PhD 91

Chapter Five: A Mission History of Indonesian Church
Purnawan Tenibemas, PhD 121

Chapter Six: Missionary Movement of the Korean Church
Timothy K. Park, PhD 153

Chapter Seven: The Church and the Missionary Movement in Singapore
Violet James, PhD 175

Chapter Eight: The Rise of the Filipino Missionary Movement: A Preliminary Historical Assessment
Tereso C. Casiño, ThD, PhD 195

Index 225

Preface

While attention is usually focused on the West as the major source of missionaries in the world, there is a growing missionary movement by Asian churches that have begun more than a century ago. National churches in Asia have contributed immensely to the Great Commission and are to be reckoned corporately as the new force in world mission.

The book aims to reveal the mission mind-set of Asian churches through a brief survey and assessment of the cross-cultural mission agenda of select Asian countries. The authors are not only experts, but are also eyewitnesses and participants in mission in their respective countries. Thus, firsthand assessments are made from the perspective of learned and qualified individuals who are also immersed in the history, culture, language, and experiences of their own countries.

The articles in this book were presented at the Second International Forum of Asian Society of Missiology in Semarang, Indonesia on March 16–20, 2009. I acknowledge the members and staff of Gereja Isa Almasih Jemaat Pringgading and their senior pastor, Dr. Indrawan Eleeas, for hosting the forum. Special thanks to ASM Mission History Forum Committee members: Rei V. Eusebio, David Hartono, Paul Y. Jeong, Greg Y. Paek, and Sam Sikitari. I am grateful to Ttokamsa Home Mission

Church (THMC), Elder Do Won Chang and his wife Jin Sook Chang of THMC for their generous financial contributions, and to my friend and colleague, Rei V. Eusebio, the project coordinator, who helped edit the materials and managed the whole process of publishing this book. Although thorough checks have been made of the sources cited in the articles within this book, many sources are only available in their original languages. We have attempted to remain faithful to the original papers by the authors and now present them here.

—TIMOTHY K. PARK, PHD
editor

1

New Christianity in the Twenty-first Century: Asian Mission as a Major Force in Mission

DAVID J. CHO, PHD

Take a Good Look at the Changing World

After the dissolution of the International Missionary Council (IMC) at New Delhi in 1960, a new force in mission sprung up in Asia, Africa, and Latin America. The non-Western world and the non-Western force became stronger than the Western forces in missions.

Not only did the contrary wind of world mission blow harder from the East, but the center of Christianity had already shifted from the Western hemisphere to the East and South in the twenty-first century. Ultimately, Western Christendom collapsed in the face of the overwhelming power of secular nationalism. Western scholars have claimed that we are living in the new age of post-Christendom.[1] For instance, the demographics of religion indicate the decline of Christianity in

1 Douglas John Hall, "Confessing Christ in Post-Christendom Context," *Ecumenical Review* 52 (2000): 410–17.

Western Christendom. In Europe, 90 percent of the Christian population is not attending church.[2]

The era of Western Christianity has passed in our lifetime, and the day of new Christendom in the non-Western world is dawning. In Asia, Africa, and Latin America, new indigenous independent denominations are arising. The traditional Western denominations do not represent the whole picture of churches in the non-Western world, and it has been proven that traditional Western-institutionalized church order was inadequate for their changing new society.

According to the *World Christian Encyclopedia*, there are over 200 million Bible-believing Christians outside traditional Christianity in Asia and Africa. In India, there are over twenty-five million unchurched Christians among Hindustanis. In Africa, there are fifty-two million Bible-believing Christians outside the denominational churches. In China, there are seventy million Bible-believing House-Church Christians outside the official Chinese Three-Self Churches. Thus, new Christianity is arising in the non-Western world.[3]

Arising De-Westernized New Christianity and Indigenous Missionary Movement

The process of expansion outside of the Western world is the new type of Christianity that has thrived most successfully in the Global South. The new type of Christianity in the non-Western world is very different from the Western form of Christianity of Europe and America.

In 1982, when a tough statement of "de-Westernization of Asian Christianity" was made in my keynote address at the Third

---

2 John Stewart and Edna Vaktz, eds., *Mission Handbook, 1998–2000* (Monrovia, CA: MARC, 1997), 32.

3 David Barrett, George Kurian, and Todd Johnson, *World Christian Encyclopedia* (New York: Oxford Press, 2001).

Triennial Convention of the Asia Missions Association in Seoul, Korea, many participants thought that I had gone too far. Even Dr. Ralph D. Winter was wondering and doubtful about my thoughts of de-Westernization of Asian Christianity then.

At the end of the convention, however, all participants reached consensus on "the need for appropriate de-Westernization in order to allow for a Christian fulfillment of Asian selfhood."

Some Western missiologists, including Winter, also began to express their concurrence for de-Westernization of Christianity lately at the end of the twentieth century.[4] The process of de-Westernization of Christianity in Asia, Africa, and Latin America as the new type of Christianity is very different from the Western form and is more enthusiastic and much more concerned about the immediate workings of the supernatural through prophesy, visions, ecstatic utterances, and healing.

Indigenized Denominations

In Korea, one of the largest churches is the nondenominational independent church in Seoul. The world's largest Presbyterian churches and Methodist churches are in Seoul, Korea. However, Korean Presbyterian and Methodist denominations are not the same as the traditional Western form, but have a solely indigenized way of belief and worship of their own.

Many Presbyterian and Methodist churches are independent and do not have a "mother-and-daughter" relationship with their Western counterparts. Their way of prayer and worship are more Pentecostal and ecstatic.

In the Philippines, the El Shaddai movement is one of the striking examples. Founded in 1984,[5] this wildly successful group looks like a classic Pentecostal church, but it is firmly rooted

4 See, for instance, Philip Jenkins, *The Next Christendom: The Coming of Global Christianity* (New York: Oxford University Press, 2002).

5 http://www.chanrobles.com/elshaddai.htm.

within Roman Catholicism. It is in fact a lay charismatic group designed to combat Protestant penetration in the Philippines.

In Brazil, as in most of Latin America, the Pentecostal and charismatic churches have grown greatly in number to 75 percent of all Protestants. Autonomous Pentecostal movements like Brazil for Christ (Brazil Para Cristo), God is Love, and the Four Square Church have grown over the last twenty years. The Assemblies of God in Brazil alone have over twelve million members.[6]

Spontaneous Indigenous Missionary Movements

Missionary movements in the non-Western are spreading like wildfire in every nation of the third world.

According to the report at the end of 2008 by Korea World Mission Association, 20,503 Korean missionaries are working in 168 countries. They analyzed the numbers of missionaries classified according to the regions of each continent as following:

CONTINENTS	REGIONS	COUNTRIES	MISSIONARIES	RATIO
ASIA	South Asia	4	1,069	5.2%
	Northeast Asia	7	5,353	26.1%
	Southeast Asia	11	3,377	16.5%
	Central Asia	10	1,730	8.4%
	Subtotal	32	11,529	56.2%
EUROPE	Western Europe	20	992	4.8%
	Eastern Eurasia	23	996	4.9%
	Subtotal	43	1,988	9.7%
AMERICA	Latin America	17	807	3.9%
	North America/ Caribbean Sea	6	2,317	11.3%
	Subtotal	23	3,124	15.2%

6 Kenneth D. MacHarg, "Brazil's Surging Spirituality," *Christianity Today*, December 21, 2000.

CONTINENTS	REGIONS	COUNTRIES	MISSIONARIES	RATIO
AFRICA/ARAB	Southeast Africa	20	823	4.0%
	West Central Africa	21	355	1.7%
	North Africa/Middle East	18	729	3.6%
	Subtotal	59	1,907	9.3%
OCEANIA/ PACIFIC	South Pacific	11	713	3.5%
	Subtotal	11	713	3.5%
OTHERS	Non-Residential		140	0.7%
	Sabbatical		279	1.4%
	Home Base		823	4.0%
	Subtotal		1,242	6.1%
GRAND TOTAL		168	20,503	100%

These demographics are indicating that missionaries from Korea are working in almost every corner of the world and dealing with many cultures.[7]

Emil Jebasingh, an advocate of Indian missionary movement, initiated the "Bless India Gathering" for VISION 2020 movement of India towards a goal of converting 20 percent of the country to Christianity by 2020. Their Vision Statement was "[to evangelize and disciple by 2020, all the people (groups) of India by providing mature transformable leadership towards VISION 2020 (20 percent India, Christian India) . . . To identify and bring together churches and missions committed to the Great Commission [and] take and enable them to work together with strategic plans to develop qualitative (that protects standards of excellence and upholds Biblical values) leadership that results in healthy, reproducing, disciple churches in all geographical units within the different people and social groups in India, with measurable goals towards VISION 2020."[8]

7 KWMA Report, January 2009.
8 Keynote Address of Emil Jebasingh at Bless India Gathering.

The Follow-up Committee reported, "Out of the 375 organizations who attended Bless India Gathering, a total of 1,600 mission organizations researched to serve as 'ready organizations.'" Missionary movements in India are very enthusiastically setting their goals.[9]

In Africa, indigenous missionary movements are radical and smartly innovative. Reuben Ezemadu is one of the well-known leaders of Movement for African National Initiative (MANI) as well as all the other missionary movements in the continent. MANI has forty years history with thirty-seven African countries. The aim of MANI is to be a catalyst, mobilizing the resources of the body of Christ in Africa to fulfill the Great Commission. The consultation of indigenous missions in Africa was held on March 2003.

The first Africa-wide meeting of MANI was held in Nairobi, Kenya in March 2006. Reuben Ezemadu, Continental Coordinator for MANI said, "MANI is envisioning and focusing the church in Africa on her role in global missions and the potential that God has given Africa to be blessing in the world." He [Ezemado] is enlarging his initiatives beyond the African continent to the African diaspora who went as slaves to North and South America since 2008.[10]

Another country that is particular to me is Indonesia. In 1972, the Korea International Mission, Inc. (KIM) which I organized began a cooperative partnership with Indonesia Missionary Fellowship (IMF). The target field was Kalimantan Island. KIM sent over twenty missionaries to IMF to work with their missionaries in Kalimantan. It was a very effective partnership development to train Indonesian nationals in church planting in the island.

---

9 Ibid.

10 Handbook of Consultation on Indigenous Missions In Africa, March 2003, http://www.maniafrica.com.

I chose Indonesia as a target country to be a mutual partner of missionary movement because it is the largest Islamic country in Asia, with the largest Christian population among the Islamic countries of the world. I have dreamed of recruiting the missionary resources of Indonesia to input its many unevangelized islands and to make a model of building partnership missions among Asian churches.

Since 1973, I have invited over twenty missionary candidates from Indonesia and other Asian nations to Korea to undergo training at the Summer Institute of World Mission (SIWM) and at the East-West Center for Missions Research and Development (EWCMRD) I established in Seoul. Thirty-five years later, these missionaries grew up as important mission leaders in Indonesia and in other parts of Asian nations as well. Jacob Nahuway, the Chairman of AMA, who was invited to be the distinguished speaker of the greeting address for this ASM Forum, is one of them. He studied for two years at the East-West Center for Missions Research and Development in Korea.

We are here in Samarang, a city of Java Island, Indonesia, to share our mutual burden for the advancement of Asian missionary movement through sharing the history of missionary movements of each one's own country.

Our Liability in the Study of Mission History

I am observing the history of Christian expansion as a part of the history of the world. In world history, the powers of state and religion interact continuously. Jacob Burckhardt of Germany said,

> State, culture and religion coexist in the world and have powers with different function and forces restricting each other. The religion and culture co-exist in the world, however, they can-

> not mingle together essentially as water and oil in a vessel could not be mixed.[11]

Therefore, to study mission history is not to just introduce the story of missionary activities, but also to examine the facts realistically. Our liability to study mission history is to anatomize and to unveil the realities of hidden mistakes, offense, digression, and inhuman activities of missions in history. Through these anatomies of the history of missions, we have to find out how to justify our missionary service in the future of world history with the various conditions and restrictions of the power of cultures, religions, and states.

I would like to indicate three essential factors to study missions:

The first factor is the anatomical study. Anatomical study of mission history means digging out every fact of the past carefully, searching even minor symptoms within mission history and the secular history of the world. If we justify without anatomizing the history of Christian mission, our activities could confuse the missionaries. They would believe, without critical thinking, the activities, weaknesses, or mistakes of mission history, or even overstate the achievements of mission history, on the other hand.

Through rethinking and examining mission history as a part of world history by analyzing the connection among the ruling power, the nation, culture, and religion, we have to anatomize the history of expansion of Christianity of two thousand years very carefully. We must search for a way to remove obstacles and justify what should succeed in the future of mission, particularly to find accurate relationships between state and religion, as well as between nation and culture.

Therefore, accurate study of mission history needs to attempt an analysis of the power encounter among Christian religions,

---

11 J. Burckhardt, *Welteschichtlich, Betrachtungen* (Korner, 1969).

Roman Empire, and papacy until the Reformation era. The changing power encounter or relationship of church and history during the Reformation and Revolutionary Age in Western Christendom are to be anatomized.

The second factor is the clinical study of mission history. Clinical study involves observing and testing the facts and realities of the environment and actual matters of mission history. Without checking and testing the environment and actual matters of mission history, we will commit wrong judgment and wrong estimation.

The third factor is the diagnostics study of mission history. In all kinds of illness, distress, and disability, facts and proper and accurate diagnosis is needed. In mission history, there are many facets of illness and distress that need diagnostic study to cure the symptoms. Thus, to have an accurate and proper study of mission history, we should diagnose to cure the failures, mistakes, and illnesses of past missions.

To introduce anatomical, clinical, and diagnostic study of mission history, let me introduce some case stories to find hidden facts about double faces of well-known missionaries from Western Christendom.

EAST INDIA COMPANY AND MISSIONARIES

From AD 1600 to 1900, the East and the West encountered colonialism and Christian mission of Western Christendom. Since the beginning of the sixteenth century, the peak of colonialism, Christian mission, and the commerce of Western Christendom in the East continued until the early half of twentieth century.

ENGLAND COMES TO INDIA

In AD 1600, Queen Elizabeth I issued a special authority or license to the East India Company. In the same year, Shakespeare was still alive and continued his writings. In 1611, the Bible was translated as King James Version. In 1608, John Milton was born. The political revolutions of John Hampton and Oliver Cromwell were breaking out.

Thus, "noble and cruel" coexisted in England, influencing each other and were undividable.

Jawaharlal Nehru, a great leader of India and the first Prime Minister of a liberated new India said, "The noble England did not come to India but only barbaric crown law with brutal inhuman acts and feudal system with reactionary behavior."[12]

Colony, commerce, and Christendom often combined in Africa and Asia. The missionaries, like Carey and many others, were often caught between the goals of their nations and their own goals as missionaries, frequently leading to conflicts. For example, it was not until the British Parliament had a number of strong evangelicals as members that Carey was able to get a law passed outlawing the practice of *suttee*, the burning of young widows with the bodies of their husbands. The East India Company refused Carey passage on its ships to India and denounced him in Parliament. It also denied Morrison passage on its ships to China. It is ironic that later, both Carey and Morrison had to be employed by the company in order to support themselves. But as they did so, they evangelized and translated the Scriptures. Carey and his colleagues translated part or all of the Bible into thirty languages. After fourteen years, Morrison ordained the first Chinese Protestant pastor. That is why he is known as "the father of the (Protestant) church" in China.

Therefore, anatomizing these three factors [Colony, commerce, and Christendom] simultaneously when we research the mission history of the former colonies of Western Christendom is essential.

---

12 Jawaharlal Nehru, *The Discovery of India, Korean edition* (Seoul: Hangilsa, 1981).

CHINA AND AMERICA: IMMIGRATION OF CHINESE WORKERS AND MISSIONARIES FROM AMERICA

Tens of thousands of Chinese from South China immigrated to America in the second half of the nineteenth century to escape the Taiping Rebellion. The governor of California wrote to President Andrew Johnson in 1885: "Without Chinese workers, it would be impossible to complete the western portion of the great national enterprise within the time required by Congress."[13]

Thus, the Central Pacific Railway depended on Chinese workers to construct the transcontinental rail. However, the history shifted as follows:

> From later part of 1800s, however, America's Wild West was on a rampage against Chinese . . . Thousands of Chinese fled the white peril and went home to China . . . The bloodbath reached a climax . . . In one town, mobs hacked 28 Chinese residents apart [and] burned others alive, while the town's proper ladies stood by clapping and laughing . . . In America, laws and ordinances against Chinese were becoming so universal that Congress began to set limit on Chinese immigration—the first time that America had ever restricted the entrance of a particular nationality to its shores.
>
> The response in China was bitter. Small mobs stormed American and European missions . . . This distortion allowed the Western Powers to bring new pressure on the weak imperial government in Peking . . . Under diplomatic pressure, Peking issued proclamation calling on all Chinese

13 Sterling Seagrave, *The Soong Dynasty* (New York: Harper & Row, 1986), 21.

> to "live in peace with Christian missionaries."[14] No similar effort was made by Washington to control yellow peril mobs in America.

The American missionaries in China protested strongly against that policy.

The following story is a case of American missionaries in China behaving inappropriately as missionaries. John Allen was the first missionary from Southern Methodist Mission Board. According to Sterling Seagrave's report,

> Dr. Allen was a man who had no doubts about his own superiority. Although an American, he had come to China as many Englishmen had over the years, setting themselves up in Oriental ivory towers, orchid houses of the mind. Dr. Allen had arrived as a missionary before the American Civil War, only to have the conflict cut off all his funds from the home church. To support himself, he found a job teaching and translating at Chinese institution connected to Shanghai's imperial arsenal, where he could deal exclusively with the privileged elite. In his case, the term 'missionary' was misleading. He was a high priest in the tradition of Jesuit emissaries. He did not have it in him to preach Western religion to the unwashed eastern masses, or to coerce ordinary Chinese into caring about the virtues of Christianity. He considered himself rather a missionary to Chinese intelligentsia, rationalizing that if he could impress the elite with Western science they would be more

14 Ibid., 44–45.

> receptive to Western culture, and to the subtler nuances of Christian ideology.[15]

Allen was not typical of Western missionaries in China. Many led the fight against the practice of foot binding, established medical clinics, hospitals, nursing and medical schools, schools and universities, and evangelized in the remote areas. Men and women of the China Inland Mission conformed as closely as possible to the Chinese lifestyle. Because they were so vulnerable, over one hundred missionaries and family members were killed in the Boxer Rebellion.

WESTERN MISSIONARIES IN THE YI DYNASTY OF KOREA

Robert J. Thomas (1839–1866) was a missionary sent by the Congregational Church to China. He sailed to Taedong River of Pyongyang, Korea through the armed commercial ship with a Chinese Bible and was killed by the armed Korean navy. It was written that he was the first martyr of Western missionaries in Korea.

I have researched carefully about him and found that he had not come to Korea as a missionary, but as a commercial attaché of the Royal British Empire in China and come to persuade in opening the port of Pyongyang, Korea. Even though he was carrying a Bible, he had already resigned a year before he came to Korea and had switched his job to be a diplomatic officer of the British government.

Horace Allen, the first American Protestant missionary to Korea, came in 1884 as a part of the American embassy because that was the only way he was allowed to enter the country. Because he saved the life of a member of the royal family after an assassination attempt, permission was given for Appenzeller, a Methodist, and Underwood, a Presbyterian, to come as the fist two ordained

15 Seagrave, *The Soong Dynasty*, 47.

Protestant missionaries the following year. Underwood was the founder of Yonsei University as well as a church planter, and was greatly respected by Korean Christians and non-Christians alike. His wife, Dr. Lilias Horton Underwood, was the first woman physician in Korea, and worked with the poor as well as the royal family. Samuel Moffett, who came in 1890, was another famous Presbyterian missionary from America. He was a church planter and seminary professor, greatly respected by fellow missionaries and Koreans.

There are, however, untold stories of inappropriate behaviors of a few Western missionaries. One of them was widely believed to have acquired a huge amount of ill-gotten wealth through the trades of gold mining in Woonsan. Another man had alleged ill-gotten wealth as a lumber merchant of Baikdu Mountain and Yalu River. Still another engaged as an exclusive trader of petroleum in Korea and became a contractor of Kyong-In Railroad and Telephone Company.[16]

No missionary was perfect. Many believed Western culture to be Christian and superior, and it took time for them to see the values in other cultures. A few took advantage of their situation to enrich themselves, but they were a tiny minority in comparison with those who served sacrificially, and often died young and, at times, buried their children there. Appenzeller, one of the first two ordained missionaries, only lived a few years before being drowned as he went to a meeting on Bible translation. But their accomplishments were remarkable. At a time when it was not considered possible nor advisable for girls to study, Mrs. Scranton, a Methodist, established the first school for girls in Korea, now Ehwa University, the largest women's university in the world. The first medical school was also established. And in 1907, only twenty years after Underwood's arrival, the Presbyterians

---

16 David J. Cho, *50 Years History of Korean Church from 1874 to 1924*, Korean edition (Seoul: DCMI, 2004).

ordained the first seven Korean Presbyterian pastors, encouraging Koreans to take leadership in the growing church.

As the missionary movement grows from Asia, Africa, and Latin America, we have much to learn, both from the positive achievements of the Western missionaries, as well as from their excessive identification with their culture and their insensitivity to the values of non-Western cultures. Fortunately, we recognize that God uses even imperfect people and movements for his glory.

Through research and anatomizing the hidden facts in history, we could learn what should not be done and how to behave appropriately as a servant of God in the mission field.

The Need for Analytic Thinking

Analytic thinking on the history of mission means to look critically at understanding, not only the achievement of missionaries, but also the failures, mistakes, faults, offenses, and violation the laws. The capacity to look critically at underlying promises, postulates, and precepts in history manifests because the uncertainty ahead inhibits our ability to foresee the pitfalls of evil that will appear in the mission fields.

Asian mission leaders, who are planning and developing the strategies of mission, need to think deeply and be aware of where they are, where they are heading, and what they should and should not do.

Be Creative and Develop Asian Strategies

Do not copy the Western model of mission and imitate their ways without careful examination of their motives and historical background. Many Asian missionaries are following the ways that they have observed from Western missionaries in their mission fields without questioning. Therefore, they are falling into the same mistakes that Westerners had committed.

Ralph D. Winter, at the ASM Bangkok Conference in 2007, made a serious warning to Asian missionaries:

> Asian missionary leaders face the danger of making some of same mistakes of Western leaders made. One of problems is the Western leaders may not know what their mistakes are, and thus cannot warn Asian leaders of what Western leaders did wrong.[17]

We, the Asian mission leaders, should be creative to create our own strategies and methodologies to avoid the same mistakes that Western mission leaders had committed. We are not the same as the white Westerners. We should distinguish ourselves as Asian and create an Asian approach of mission. We have our own unique resources that Westerners do not possess. Ideally, Asian mission leaders would develop a set of strategies that can be kept in the shelves for use when situations demand.

Perhaps it will cause uncertainty about the future, which will prohibit this degree of sophistication, but at least it should be possible to develop alternative scenarios of Western strategies in future global affairs.

Be Flexible and Change the Way of Thinking

Many Western missionaries had difficulties changing their lifestyles in the mission fields. They were less flexible to follow native cultures, and even though the Western missiologists created their own curriculum as Cultural Anthropology, they did not create "adaptology" to change the lifestyle.

We should be more flexible to adapt to the different lifestyles and learning styles. Without adaptation of learning styles of the people, there would be no way to communicate properly with them.

---

17 Timothy K. Park, ed., *Asian Mission: Yesterday, Today and Tomorrow* (Pasadena, CA: IAM, 2008).

Therefore, a change of the way of thinking is very much needed. Because any mission strategy reflects specific cultural and social environment of the mission field, no strategy of mission can meet the requirement of every international culture and social system.

Many Asian missionaries copied Western mission strategy and adopted it as our own. The global systems, external and internal conditions, and environment are rapidly changing today.

The ability to make mission strategy innovation requires the change of mind-set of Asian mission leaders. In theory, Asians can modify policy and strategy. In reality, however, policy and strategy renewal does not take place overnight. Although outmoded ideas can be instantly discarded, the act of creating suitable replacement is time consuming, taking months or years when major intellectual refinement is needed. Thus, newly emerging Asian missiologists are advised to be advanced in their thinking as much as possible.

Epilogue

The correct and accurate understanding of the value of the history is the key of observation and study of the history. I have presented the facts of the appearance of a de-Westernized new Christianity of the changing world in the twenty-first century. In addition, I introduced the newly emerging indigenous missionary movement of the non-Western world in the twenty-first century that became a major force of Christian mission today. I have emphasized the importance of research of the history of Christian mission and the liability of the study of mission history of the past.

I have introduced three essential factors of the methods of history study and emphasized the need of deep thinking of Asian mission leaders. Those were the need of creativity of thoughts and development of Asian mission strategies. I also strongly emphasized the need of change of intellectual style. I have limited my presentation as I have summarized above.

The remaining important matters are how to make the new history of Asian mission, as well as how to write and teach the history of Asian mission. All of these important tasks are entrusted to all of you who are participating in this forum. You will find very creative, appropriate ways at the group discussion. I expect and trust that this historic forum of Semarang will achieve the task of creating the future of research of mission history.

Bibliography

Barrett, David, George Kurian, and Todd Johnson. *World Christian Encyclopedia*. New York: Oxford Press, 2001.

Burckhardt, Jacob. *Welteschichtlich, Betrachtungen*. Korner, 1969.

Cho, David J. *A Historical Anatomy of the Power Encounter of the Christian Mission with the Nations: A Paradigm for the Future*. Korean edition. Seoul, Korea: The Star Press, 1991.

Cho, David J. ed. *The Third Force: The Official Report of the Third Triennial Convention*. Seoul '82 of the Asia Missions Association. Seoul, Korea: EWC/mrd, 1982.

Cho, David J. *50 Years History of Korean Church from 1874 to 1924*. Korean edition. Seoul: DCMI, 2004.

Ezemadu, Reuben. MANI Brochure. Ibadan, Nigeria, 2008.

Hall, Douglas John. "Confessing Christ in Post-Christendom Context." *Ecumenical Review* 52 no. 3 (July 2000): 410–17.

Handbook of Consultation on Indigenous Missions In Africa, March 2003.

Jenkins, Philip. *The Next Christendom: The Coming of Global Christianity*. New York: Oxford University Press, 2002.

Jebasingh, Emil. Keynote Address to Bless India Gathering, Chennai, India, 2006.

"Korean World Mission Association Report." January 2009.

MacHarg, Kenneth D. "Brazil's Surging Spirituality." *Christianity Today*, December 4, 2000.

Nehru, Jawaharlal. *The Discovery of India*. Korean edition. Seoul: Hangilsa, 1981.

Park, Timothy K. ed. *Asian Mission: Yesterday, Today and Tomorrow.* Pasadena, CA: IAM, 2008.
Seagrave, Sterling. *The Soong Dynasty*. New York: Harper & Row, 1986.
Stewart, John and Edna Vaktz, eds. *Mission Handbook, 1998–2000.* Monrovia, CA: MARC, 1997.

About Dr. David J. Cho

David Cho was born in 1924 near the Yalu River at the Korea-China border. He fled to South Korea from the Communist rule of North Korea, where he attended and graduated at the Presbyterian Theological Seminary with an honor in Theology. He came to the United States to pursue studies in mission and evangelism. He received a ThM in Mission from Asbury Theological Seminary in Wilmore, Kentucky and earned his PhD at the William Carey International University in Pasadena, California, where he serves as professor and director of Korean Studies. He established the International School of Mission (ISM) in Seoul, Korea in 1963, which later expanded to the East-West Center for Missions Research and Development, the first missionary training and research institute in the non-Western world.

2

A Mission China: An Analysis of Its Ten Affecting Factors

THOMAS LEE, PHD

The ten factors that may contribute in making a Mission China:

1. The population of Christians in China,
2. The training of leaders in Three-Self Church and House Churches,
3. The development and cooperation of the urban and the rural churches,
4. The development of the administrative structure of the China Church,
5. The improvement of the political situation,
6. The economic growth and the financial strength of the believers,
7. The mission awareness of the China Church,
8. The mission training and sending ministry,
9. The growth of the intellectual Christians,
10. The Christian literatures and their contributive strengths.

Introduction: God's Steadfast Love to China

According to China Church history, the evangelion of Jesus Christ knocked on China's door four times. First, during the Tang dynasty, the Nestorians came to the ancient capital Xian and stayed for 244 years from AD 635 to 879.[18] Second, the Catholic monks came during the Ming dynasty in AD 1289 and influenced some intellectuals in the capital city of Peking, but vanished during the end of the dynasty. The third time was in the Manchurian dynasty by Catholic monk Mateo Ricci in the year AD 1583, but he later clashed with the Chinese culture and was forbidden to stay on. Only in the fourth time in 1807 were the Protestant missionaries[19] able to build lasting influences. The influx of Protestant missionaries after 1807 contributed to the building of the modern China Church and more local leaders were trained to continue the ministry in their land.

Before the Communists took over China in 1949, four nationwide mission movements were called in China: the first nationwide Mission Conference was held in 1877. This movement emphasized mission to the unreached inland provinces and urged the training of more local pastors to take over the ministry.[20] The second Mission Conference in 1918 was mainly a Chinese pastor-oriented meeting, called to evangelize the most remote provinces in west China. The third was the "Five-Year Revival Movement"

18 The Nestorians flourished and established churches almost at all the cities in China and even won the favors of the Emperor, but vanished due to the excessive influence of Buddhism and inability to train the locals to take up the ministry. Later, in AD 1279, Nestorians came again and spread among the Mongolians, but they encountered the same fate and vanished once the Mongolians were chased out of China. For best references in China Church history, go to Su Wen-Fung, *China Church History,* in Chinese (San Francisco: Hua Suen Pub., 2005), or Wen Mu, *China Church History,* in Chinese (Hong Kong: Global Chinese Bible Institute, 1999).

19 This was the period in which some well-known Protestant missionaries like Robert Morrison (AD 1807), and Hudson Taylor (AD 1853) established their works in China.

20 During the AD 1877 Mission Conference, only four Chinese pastors appeared among the nine hundred foreign missionaries, while in the follow-up meeting to this conference in AD 1890, the local pastors (1,657 persons) have outnumbered the foreign missionaries (1,296 persons).

aimed to double the believers from 1929–1934. The fourth was a nationwide "Three Years Mission Movement" organized between 1946–49, which culminated with a numerical count of 834,909 Christians and 6,500 churches in China.

Those four incoming works of foreign missionaries and the four mission movements by the local pastors confirmed, on one hand, the unceasing love of God to China for 1,400 years, even though it seemed that the first three incoming works of foreign missionaries were unfruitful. On the other hand, the ability of the local church in China to organize nationwide mission works as well. I believe that the church in China will be capable to start any mission movement in this country, and even in the near future, to send missionaries out of China and make China a Mission China.[21]

Below, I present several factors that will affect the China Church in becoming a Mission China in the coming future. I purposely arranged these factors according to their weight of impact in the making of a Mission China.

I want to confess that it is not easy to gather good resources to write about the China Church. I gathered data from many China yearbooks, China dailies, published books, articles from journals or the Internet, and my previous articles on the same topic.

---

21 "A Mission China" is a popular hymn sung by the Chinese Christians for the last ten years, and many verses in this hymn arouse and revive the hearts of Chinese believers: "There is love like summer crickets sound unceasingly, while silk worms threw their silk as long as they live. There is a calling asking me to march out bravely, while the Holy Spirit leading my heart ahead. Moving out towards Jerusalem, no matter snow or rain, stand firm to preach the name of the Lord, and making victory for the Kingdom of God. With calling I step ahead, awakening the sleepy China, and I will not return even blood shedding. With vision I march ahead, build together a Mission China, and spread the gospel to all the corners of the earth" (Translation mine, 2009).

The Population of Christians in China

There are 1.32 billion people in China in 2007, and it is expected to rise to 1.45 billion by 2020.[22] This estimate is based on the one-child policy launched in 1967. Similarly, the growth rate of the Christian population in China is fast.

The growth and population of the Christians in China are decisive factors for Mission China. The complexity of counting the number of Christians in China is always a disputable matter. There are "high," "low," and "middle" views about the numbers. By 2007, the "high" may expect 80–100 million (6–7.5%), the "low" may count at 40–50 million (3–3.8%), and the "middle" view may provide the number 60–70 million (4.5–5.3%).[23]

The China Church is growing fast. We have the record of 834,909 Christians and 6,500 churches in 1948. After 1978, churches grew everywhere in China, especially in the central and coastal provinces. Interpolating on the official data (1990), Tony Lambert's survey (1989), and a magazine in Hong Kong (1990), the reported number of Christians in China is 40 million.[24] In addition, "the growth rate of the Christians in Henan and Anhui provinces is very high, comprising 5–10% of the population of these provinces."[25]

By 1990, there were 2,700 churches (with proper buildings, mainly in the urban areas) and twenty thousand congregations (mainly in the villages) in the Three-Self Church.[26] Usually,

---

22 China Government Year Book Department, *2008 China Year Book*, in Chinese (Beijing: Han book, 2008), 352–54. Usually, most of the social workers do not believe that this number is an exact number due to many born girls are not reported caused by the one child policy and the Chinese culture insists that only boy is the real successor of a family.

23 Alan Hunter and Chan Kim Kwong, *A Strong Movement in the Making: Protestants in China, 1990*, in Chinese (Hong Kong: Tien Dao, 1992) has the best report in this area in 1990, 6–8.

24 Ibid., 11.

25 Ibid., 8.

26 The Three Self Church is obviously controlled by the United Political Front (UPF), either from Beijing or local city. The purposes of UPF are clear: "to abolish the Christian Church, to against any foreign interception to the Chinese Church, and to install government/communist policy into the Church." Ibid., 23–28.

China leaders would count the House Church as being ten times more than the Three-Self Church, so in 1990, we estimated about 250,000 churches in China.[27] If on average, each church has one hundred Christians, then there will be 25 million. The growth rate was high in the 1990s, a simple calculation of three times increment after fifteen years. Then in 2005, the projected number is estimated at 75 million Christians in China.

The author's view is that there are 60 to 80 million Christians and 600,000–800,000 churches/congregations in China in 2005, and an estimate of more than 100 million Chinese people have heard the gospel of Jesus Christ for the past twenty-five years. This is a good number for the China Church to become a Mission China. However, it also depends on how the church is moving ahead.

The Training of Leaders in Three-Self Churches and House Churches

The China Church never stops providing trainings to believers. Since the arrival of foreign missionaries, a Bible school was built in Malacca (next to the Malacca Strait) by Robert Morrison in 1815.[28] After 1889, treaties were signed between China and the West that enabled foreign missionaries then to start many Bible schools in China. By the year 1920, there were thirty-four seminaries and more than three hundred Christian schools in this

27 Ibid., 15.

28 Robert Morrison came to China in 1807. In 1815, he built the first Bible School in Malacca. A graduate, Leung Fa, returned to China and built the first seminary in China in 1828. After 1850, more than twenty Bible schools existed in China. China Government abolished the ancient Feudal Exam System in 1893, then many westernized Christian schools and colleges were welcomed and built in most of the big cities. Between 1890 and 1950, more than ten well-known universities in China were built by foreign mission organizations.

country.[29] Undoubtedly, the education planted by foreign missionaries greatly contributed to a modern China.[30]

After the Communists took over China in 1950, many seminaries moved to Hong Kong and continued in their training ministry for the overseas Chinese churches. Those that remained in China were closed down by the government, and then were in idle position for more than thirty years. Nevertheless, after the modernization policy in 1978, both the Three-Self Church (government-approved churches) and the underground House Church restarted their training ministry widely. By 1998, there were eighteen seminaries belonging to the Three-Self Church; by 2007, there were thirty-seven of them. In the same manner, the House Church operated its training ministry extensively almost all over the country, especially in the villages.[31]

Because training stopped for more than thirty years, a Hong Kong-based journal rightly portrayed the pastoral situation in China: "The lack of pastors in China is so serious that one hundred Churches could not even have a pastor."[32] *Pei Suen* (training of Christian workers) in the 1980s and 1990s were so extensive among the House Church that this term has become a proper noun today. Almost all the House Church groups have their own training ministry, and some obtained help from overseas Chinese churches or seminaries. Most of these were intensive classes providing basic biblical, theological, and pastoral teaching. We had estimated that by the year 1998, there were more than four hundred theological training centers in the Three-Self Church, and

---

29 Milton T. Stauffer, *The Christian Occupation of China: A general survey of the numerical strength and geographical distribution of the Christian forces in China between 1901–1920,* in Chinese (Beijing: China Social Science Pub., 1987), 34.

30 See Chou Lian-Hua, *The Role and Contributions of Christian Universities in China,* in Chinese (Taipei: Song of Song Pub., 1995), 24–28.

31 The most extensive report in this area is by Yan Siu-Lin, *The Training of Pastors among the House Church in the 1980's,* unpublished thesis in Chinese (Hong Kong: China Bible Seminary, 2000).

32 Se Xien, "Where have all the pastors gone?" in *Jiao Journal 34,* in Chinese (March–April 1989), 7.

more than two thousand among the House Church, either intensive or long term.[33] Most of these trainings are rigid. Students woke up in the early morning with one or two hours of prayer and devotion before they went into seven or eight hours of classes in the day. It was only in 2000 that some larger groups were able to establish proper and long-term seminary training.

The theological training in the Three-Self Church is done openly, but its curriculum is more restricted and controlled by the government. On the other hand, the trainings among the House Church were done in secret and followed a full curriculum. For example, the largest theological training school in China in 2008 has 124 full-time seminaries and 594 pastoral training centers (intensive) with a student population of 132,500.[34]

From what we observe, the theological training in China in the past decade was not as adequate as in overseas. It was just to meet the current needs of the China Church.[35] Most of the church groups, mainly belonging to the House Church, accelerated their theological education only after 2003, with much help from overseas seminaries. The number of training institutions is not enough to meet the rapid growth of the church in China. I believe that simply feeding the need will continue until 2012 or even later, depending on how well and how much these schools or classes can train leaders. I also believe that unless the China Church has a strong leadership foundation and a good supply of pastors, the expansion to start foreign mission works or cross-cultural training is still too early to talk about now.

---

33 Thomas Lee, *Theological Training in China*, essay to Hong Kong Pin An Church, in Chinese (Hong Kong, 1998).

34 Data is from Global Chinese Bible Institute, based in Hong Kong.

35 Comments on this issue, see Heng Fuk-Zhang, "Theological Education and China Church Leadership" in *China Church Development* no. 10 (November 2000), in Chinese, 20–21.

The Development and Cooperation of the Urban and Rural Churches

"Jesus went through all the towns and villages, teaching in their synagogues, preaching the good news of the kingdom and healing every disease and sickness" (Matt 9:35).

By the year 2007, 728 million people lived in 2,467,000 villages (55.1%), while 593 million people lived in the 655 cities and 19,249 towns (44.9%).[36] The annual growth rate of the urban population is 5.17%, which is five times faster than the rural population growth. Predictably, by 2015, half of the population (700 million) will live in cities and towns, while the other half will live in rural areas.[37] It is not easy to feed the 1.32 billion people and keep everyone warm, and the Communist Party is always proud of accomplishing this. It is obvious that the modernization policy since 1978 has changed the face of social structure in China, and more people moved to the cities, especially in the costly areas.

We can see cities growing rapidly. Cities are clustered together and are so huge that those who inhabit them are satisfied with everything provided, and they never have to leave their own city.[38] The rural areas are neglected, and only the very young and very old people are left behind.

The pastors of China churches are always keen on evangelizing the neighboring villages, like Jesus went through all the cities and villages. In 1996, the House Church leadership meeting (a strictly underground meeting, named "Jerusalem Meeting")

---

36 China Government Year Book Department, *2008 China Year Book*, 482, 964.

37 Ibid., 482–83.

38 You can see cluster of cities formed in Beijing-Tianjing, Shanghai-Suzhou, Guangzhou-Shenzhen-Chuhai, etc. The population in the cluster of cities is so huge that it sometimes reaches 40 million, like Chongching.

declared the strategy "No Empty Village Mission Strategy," which aims every village to have a church by 2010.[39]

The same phenomena occurred in the China churches, and we observed the following situations:

1. The rural churches seem to be "left behind" and have been growing weak in many spheres of ministry. This is in comparison to ten years earlier when the rural churches are the major force in China Church. Many voices had risen to request the growing richer urban churches to help the rural churches. However, it seems that the two are growing more and more apart.

2. The younger pastors are reluctant to stay in rural churches and tend to move to city churches. Hence, many unevangelized rural areas are neglected.

3. The city pastors are more equipped and gifted compared to the rural pastors. However, according to the development of the China Church, the churches in villages have been established since the 1980s while the urban churches were only established in the 1990s. Even today, rural churches or pastors significantly outnumber those that are in the cities. In addition, the rural pastors are more mission minded, while the gifted urban pastors tend to stay in their own churches. I believe that for the next five or ten years, we need these rural pastors to become missionaries to where we can send them out, but we know they are not the best.

39 The next "Jerusalem Meeting" intended to meet on December 5, 2000, but since November 28, the government soldiers started bombing the churches nearby until December 3, and finally eighty-four house church buildings were destroyed. The meeting was cancelled and some leaders escaped to Shanghai and met for only a day.

> A mission church needs many gifted and mission-minded pastors.[40]

The fifty-five different minority tribal peoples, even though they comprise more than 120 million and mostly live in the western and remote areas, are being deprived of the gospel. Missionaries are aware of the needs of the minority tribal peoples and are expecting that these people groups should be evangelized before China Church moves out into the west, such as Central Asia and the Middle East.

Unless awareness is promoted by teaching and guidance to the urban church leaders, we cannot bring the far-reaching two nearer and together in one heart. They need to cooperate to advance the gospel in this country, and then out of this country. A Mission China is possible in the coming future but it depends on how aware we are about this present situation and how able we are to help the urban and the rural churches in China to harness their best capacities.

The Development of the Administrative Structure of the China Church

Leaders in China churches are more of a "charismatic type" than that of formally trained pastors. China Church leaders rose up because they could overcome many persecutions and have exemplary devotional life. These "fathers" or "uncles" are growing old and it is time that they pass what they built to the younger leadership. Some churches are so huge that sometimes they consist of more than one thousand congregations or meeting points. It is not easy to maintain unity by just looking at the founding leaders. For the younger leaders to work smoothly, a proper administrative structure has to be drawn out. Right

---

40 Thomas Lee, *Back to Jerusalem Movement: Its Past, Present and Future*, in Chinese (Hong Kong: BJM-Intl., 2007), 12.

now, everyone feels "trapped" inside the structure. In recent years, many bigger groups set up departments to write their own church manual or handbook and operate from what is laid down in the handbook. For example, the qualifications on how to ordain a pastor are spelled out in the church handbook, and accordingly, only those ordained are allowed to perform the sacraments.

In addition, different kinds of ministry such as Sunday schools, youth fellowships, sister fellowships, Bible schools, and outreach ministries are in almost all the bigger groups. Proper management structure has to be set up to maintain the expansion of these various ministries.

A recent article titled "The Two Crossroads of China Churches"[41] illustrated that China churches come to two crossroads: the theological education and the ordination of pastors. Whether they want it or not, decisions have to be made in order to move on. We need the administrative structure in the church to move on, and we also need real spiritual leaders to run the structure well. If not, everyone will be "trapped" in the structure like those high churches without good leadership. This factor also contributes to a Mission China.

The Betterment of the Political Situation

In September 1997, the Communist Party in their fifteenth General Central Representatives Meeting, while drawing for the twenty-first century national plan, confirmed that "only Teng Siu Ping modernization theory [the modernization ideas laid down since 1978] can decide the fate and future of this socialist country."[42] By November 2002, during the sixteenth General

41 Thomas Lee, "The Two Crossroads of China Churches," in Chinese, in *Bi-monthly Prayer Bulletin* Mar–Apr. 2009.

42 On Jie-Ming and Zhang Xi-Ping, *The Situation and Trends of China Development*, in Chinese (Beijing: Central Party Pub., 1998), 253.

Central Representatives Meeting, the Communist Party bravely changed their leadership composition to a younger generation. By October 2007, during the seventeenth General Central Representatives Meeting, we observed that a more "liberal" power was being installed in the Central Party. From this time onwards, foreign observers dared to believe that China was moving ahead with their political betterment.

However, no matter how reformed the political situation is today, we still observe many restrictions to liberal social movements, human rights, and religious freedom. Compared to ten or twenty years ago, however, there are fewer occurrences of confinements and imprisonments.[43] We hope that by 2012, in the eighteenth General Central Representatives Meeting, the whole nation will be more open and, thus, will even recognize the millions of House Churches movements.[44]

In the past, the house churches were always working discreetly or "underground." Many church activities such as evangelism, church plantings, leadership and theological trainings, printing of literatures, Sunday school classes, Christian youth fellowships, university Christian activities, and even mission sending were strongly restricted. The recognition of the House Church by the Chinese government is a vital factor for the emergence of a Mission China.

There are two views about the format of recognizing the House Church by the Chinese government: a "sudden recognition" and a "gradual recognition." It does not matter much how the House Church is recognized. The House Church has been used to working under the suppressed situation for many years,

43 There are contrary and pessimistic voices toward the political reform in China. Criticisms always circled around that the reform is only something to cover the weaknesses and corruptions of the Communist ruling. See Wang Chun-Siu, *The End Road of China Reform* (Hong Kong: Harfield, 2008).

44 Thomas Lee, *House Churches and Mission in China,* a sermon preached in the 2008 Guangzhou City Church Pastor Mission Conference (August 2008).

and in-country mission works were never diminished all this time, even though persecutions occurred frequently. The betterment of the political situation, however, could contribute to the birth of a Mission China.

There is always a viewpoint that if the Chinese government recognizes the House Church, then it would stimulate the Three-Self Church to move out to mission works as well, due to the many "bondages" that could have been released from them. We are observing the hand of God moving among many political figures in the country, and believe that he is in control and has the best *kairos*.

The Economic Growth and the Financial Strength of the Believers

The economic growth in China for the past twenty years is a miracle. In 2007, the gross domestic product (GDP) is 11.4 percent, while even in 2009 the country tries to maintain 8 percent GDP even though the world economy is in great recession. The gross national product (GNP) in 2007 is 240 trillion RMB (Renminbi) (about US$34 trillion).[45] Everywhere in China, you can see and feel the movement of the booming economy. The performance of China in the 2008 Olympic Games made many hearts around the world tremble. However, the booming economy plus the one party government inevitably causes many corruptions.[46] I would say one could find corruption in all spheres of the society and government. As the slogan cries, "Everyone is involved in corruption."

Indeed, the economic progress benefits almost all the people in China, either farmers or city dwellers. Until 2009, we can no longer say that China is a poor country. Anywhere you go, you can see modern high-rise buildings, luxurious cars, big restaurants,

---

45 China Government Year Book Department, *2008 China Year Book*, 402.

46 Many comments on the corruptions in China and the government know that this has become a "time-bomb" in the country. I would not want to illustrate the details here.

expensive clothing, and branded electrical equipment. China companies make multibillion acquisitions in the international market. Christians in China have started making, offering, and paying for their own pastors and ministries. The city churches are getting richer and are able to support, not only their local needs, but also other ministries.[47]

We believe the economy will continue to grow in China in the future, even though the world financial market suffers lately. We can expect the financial strength of China churches to grow as well and be able to support more ministries in and out of China. Thus, this financial strength is an important factor for a Mission China.

The Mission Awareness of the Church in China

For the past thirty years, the church in China has always been enthusiastic in evangelism, especially to its own neighboring villages. Evangelism is the way the China Church expands herself to other parts of the country. Some of the well-known groups are: China Gospel Fellowship, Henan (which at the highest point reached 30,000 churches, led by Brother Shen); FangCheng, Henan (claimed to have 10,000 churches, led by Brother Zhang); the Crying Church, Henan (claimed to have 3,000 churches, led by Brother Hsu); the XuChang Church, Henan (1,100 churches, led by Brother Guo); the YinShang Church, Anhui (about 3,000 churches, led by Brother Cheng); the BunPu Church, Anhui (1,150 churches, led by Brother Cheng); the HuaiBei Church, Anhui (about 400 churches, led by Brother Zhang); the HuoQiu Church, Anhui (850 churches, led Brother Wang), the ChangFeng Church, Anhui (400 churches, led by Brother Yu); the Wenzhou City Church, Zhejiang (about 800, led by Brother

47 Take an example, the Great Commission Seminary in Beijing. Its 2008 annual budget is one million RMB, and now able to collect about one fifth from tuition fees and local supports, while ten years ago it relied totally from foreign aid.

Huang); the YueChing Church, Zhejiang (about 1500, led by Brother Miao); the RuiAn Church, Zhejiang (450 churches, led by Brother John Hsu); the ChangZhi Church, Shanxi (1,400 churches, led by Brother Jing); LinFeng Church, Shanxi (500 churches, led by Brother Wang); the Southwest Fellowship, Chongqing (3,500 churches, led by Sister Soo and Sister Wang); the Western Fellowship, Xichuan (1,000 churches, led by Brother Liu); the WuHai Church, Inner Mongolia (450 churches, led by Brother Wang); the WeiFang Church, Shandong (500 churches, led by Brother Chou); and the PingYuen Church, Shandong (600 churches, formerly Jesus Family, led by Brother Soon).

The author has the list of more than 2,600 large church groups and the contact of the leaders in China. The number is growing and will likely reach one million churches in 2010. We have no doubt about the zeal of local missions by the local churches.[48]

After 1990, the vision of the Back to Jerusalem Movement (BJM) rekindled in China Church, and some larger church groups became interested in this movement and trained some pastors. Though not fully trained and only according to their simple curriculum, they later sent out some missionaries to the Middle East with the help of one or two foreign sending agencies. Most of these missionaries returned and others left their mission field to go into business. China churches are still very much inspired by BJM, however, they are not very aggressive about cross-cultural mission works.

We hear clamors that we should first concentrate in our local mission works since there are still billions of people waiting for the gospel in the country. Recently, some groups have sent missionaries into the minority tribal peoples and have planted over one thousand churches among them.[49]

---

48 Thomas Lee, *Mission Strategies in the Early 21st Century in China* (Hong Kong: Global Chinese Bible Int., 2002), 22.

49 Thomas Lee, *China Minority Tribal peoples and their Mission Strategy*, Great Commission Bi-monthly, issue 78 (February 2009), 6–10.

There are many reasons the China Church did not perform its cross-cultural mission in the past:

1. Cross-cultural mission awareness and capabilities are insufficient.
2. Traditional leadership has no international experience and is reluctant to see afar.
3. Lack of financial ability.
4. Existing political constraints.

I believe that unless there is mission awareness among China's churches, Mission China will not come as soon as it is expected.

The Mission Training and the Sending Ministry

In the past, there have been many mission trainings in China, but none of them were formally structured. The main reason was that China Church had no experience in mission training, much less in sending missionaries. Marching into the twenty-first century with help from foreign mission experts, we see some mission schools beginning to emerge in China. There are at least three major sources of mission training in the past eight years:

1. The Korean style of mission training: Korean missionaries have been in China since the 1980s and have established Bible schools. Later, some mission schools appeared in Beijing, Qingdao, Shanghai, Xian, Qunming, and Guangzhou. The Korean style of mission schools uses a combination of Bible and mission courses in the curriculum. After graduating from the mission schools, students are sent out by the schools to western China, usually with financial support from the Korean churches. I would say that there are no obvious results from these types of mission trainings in China. Today, we still see Korean

style of mission trainings in Beijing, Qingdao, Qunming, Shanghai, and Urumqi.

2. The overseas Chinese mission organization style of mission training: Overseas Chinese mission organizations came to China in 1997. They started mission schools in Beijing, Shanghai, Chengdu, Qunming, and a few other cities. It was only in 2007 that they founded the first cross-cultural mission school in Chengdu. In 2008, another cross-cultural mission school appeared in Beijing.
3. The Westerners style of mission training: After we evaluated the results from the two full programs of cross-cultural mission schools, our greatest difficulties are that we were unable to recruit very capable, qualified, and professional students, as they were unable to catch up with the foreign languages. These difficulties discouraged the China churches to send their missionaries out of the country.

So far, we know there are two types of mission sending: one to the minority tribal peoples in western China, and another out of the country in Central Asian or Middle Eastern countries. Most of the graduates from mission schools were sent to do mission works and church planting among the minority tribal peoples, especially to the Muslims (Uyghur, Kazakhs, Dongxiang, Kyrgyz, etc.), the Tibetans, and the Mongolians. The others are sent out to other countries.[50]

These three sources of mission training provide the China churches mission experiences and resources in training cross-cultural

---

50 Until 2008, there are more than few hundred missions and church planting works among the minority tribal peoples and good results have obtained. While we find some missionary sending to Kazakhstan, Pakistan, Uzbekistan, Egypt and I know more are going to Kuwait, Jordan, Israel, UAE, etc.

missionaries, but this might take many years before cross-cultural mission becomes fully developed. The Back to Jerusalem International Organization has good strategies and plans in helping different groups to perform cross-cultural mission training in China.[51] I expect to see a good future, if these sources can join forces together in mission training and sending. We still need foreign agencies to help the China Church in training and sending. This is the most important factor for the making of a Mission China.

The Growth of the Intellectual Christians

Since the modernization policy was inaugurated in 1978, the Chinese government has invested heavily in education. Tertiary education is one of the major areas in this investment. There are more than 27 million students in 2,321 universities in China, and every year they produce millions of graduates.[52] For instance, in 2008 there were 4.7 million university graduates.[53] Presently, there are 18 million students in these universities. University campuses have become a special phenomenon in the city. Once you enter the university areas, you can feel you are going to a "different world" in China: it is energetic, cybernetic, and usually, a place where there is freedom of speech.

Many articles have been written about the multimillion graduates and their impact on the present society. Thousands of University Christian Fellowships (UCF) exist. A survey informed us that there are more than three thousand established UCFs, and probably another six thousand operated discreetly, around the university areas.[54] It is estimated that millions of university

51 Since the second *Back to Jerusalem Movement International Consultation* (2006) has laid down the four strategies in its Declaration: Mobilization & Recruiting, Training, Sending, Field Support. See BJM II & BJM III Declaration Papers, BJM-Intl.org website.

52 China Government Year Book Department, *2008 China Year Book*, 738.

53 Ibid., 739.

54 Thomas Lee, *University Christian Fellowships Movement and Its Contribution in the Present and the Future in China* (Papers read in the 2006 National University Christian Fellowship Leaders Convention).

students have heard the gospel and many have turned to Christ. A survey tells us that there are more than two million Christians in or already graduated from the universities in the past twenty years. About 200,000 of the Christian graduates have become influential intellectuals in their own sphere of society. We found well-known Christian artists, writers, professors, medical doctors, businesspersons, scientists, and others. However, this figure is still too small to make any real and significant impact on such a huge Chinese society.

In recent years, many church leaders have become aware of the importance of these Christian graduates and started programs to train the Christian intellectuals. One difficulty is the academic background of China Church pastors or leaders. They are unable to cope or communicate with the Christian intellectuals. Most of the pastors or leaders have only lower secondary school background. I believe we have to wait for more well-educated and capable pastors to come out in the future to take care of the needs of Christian intellectuals in the country, and I believe these Christian intellectuals play a very important role in a Mission China.

The Christian Literatures and their Contributive Strengths

The publication and printing of Christian literatures have always been forbidden or restricted in China. With government approval, the Three-Self Church is able to print a limited number of Bibles every year. The underground church has always been cleverly printing Bibles, spiritual books, and training materials since then. You can always find numerous Christian literatures transferring from here and there secretly.

There are few big printing sources, mainly around Wenzhou and Shandong areas. Wenzhou is well known for its Christian calendars and pirated theological books. Shandong is known for printing spiritual books and training materials. The largest underground printing source recorded that they have printed more than 10 million books in the past twenty years. Another source announced that they print half a million booklets every year. With others Christian printers, I believe, each year the House Church secretly produces more than two million books. Recently some Christian publishers were able to obtain official ISBN (registered book numbers) and print theological books. Most of these theological books however are not the best for Christians. The contents of these books belong to liberal or social theology. On the other hand, we found many smaller printing sources outside the House Churches, and they contribute much to the Christian population.

In 2001, the China Christian Literature Society (CCLS) was formed and since then has gathered most of the Christian writers (forty of them) and publishers (about thirty underground publishers) and held a consultation every year.[55] Presently, CCLS has the largest group of active printers and publishers among China House Churches, making strong contributions to the Christian population at large. Many Christian magazines circulate among the House Churches. Among them are *Life Magazine* (80,000 copies quarterly), *Golden Lampstand* (25,000 copies bimonthly), *Great Commission* (15,000 copies bimonthly), *The Seed* (40,000 copies quarterly), *Eyes* (16,000 copies quarterly), *The Ways* (10,000 copies quarterly), *Stream* (25,000 copies quarterly), *The Shepherd* (12,000 copies quarterly), *The Bible* (30,000 copies quarterly), and more. More Christian magazines or bulletins exist, but are distributed only internally within their own groups.

Even though there are such printing activities in China, because of the restrictions and the dangers, Christian literatures have not yet influenced both the China Church and

55 This China Christian Literature Society stopped its consultation for the last two years because during the 2007 consultation more than one hundred members of the police stormed them.

society. We are praying for more freedom of speech, though this may not be a reality in the near future. Christian literature has the potential to become a valuable medium for promoting a Mission China. Much effort has to be put into this ministry. I hope foreign partners could come in to provide more help especially in this period.

Conclusion

We have seen the ten factors for building a Mission China. Every factor is decisive and contributive. Thus, a quote from Nehemiah 2:20, "Then answered I them, and said unto them, The God of heaven, he will prosper us; therefore we his servants will arise and build: but ye have . . . portion, right, memorial, in Jerusalem [a Mission China]."

Bibliography

China Government Year Book Department. *2008 China Year Book* in Chinese. Beijing: Han book, 2008.

Chou Lian-Hua. *The Role and Contributions of Christian Universities in China,* in Chinese. Taipei: Song of Song Pub., 1995.

Heng Fukl-Zhang. "Theological Education and China Church Leadership." *China Church Development 10*. Chinese edition. 2000.

Hunter, Alan, and Chan Kim Kwong. *A Strong Movement in the Making: Protestants in China, 1990.* Hong Kong: Tien Dao, 1992.

Lee, Thomas. *House Churches and Mission in China.* Sermon preached in the 2008 Guangzhou City Church Pastor Mission Conference, August 2008.

———. "The Two Crossroads of China Churches." Chinese edition. *Bi-monthly Prayer Bulletin,* Mar–Apr 2009.

———. *Back to Jerusalem Movement: Its past, present and future*, in Chinese. Hong Kong: BJM-Intl., 2007.

———. *China Minority Tribal Peoples and their Mission Strategy.* Great Commission Bi-monthly 78 (2009):6–10.

———. *Mission Strategies in the Early 21st Century in China.* Hong Kong: Global Chinese Bible Int., 2002.

———. *Theological Training in China.* Essay to Hong Kong Pin An Church, in Chinese, 1998.

———. *University Christian Fellowships Movement and Its Contribution in the Present and the Future in China.* Papers read in the 2006 National University Christian Fellowship Leaders Convention.

Jie-Ming, On and Zhang Xi-Ping. *The Situation and Trends of China Development*, in Chinese. Beijing: Central Party Pub., 1998.

Se Xien. "Where have all the pastors gone?" *Jiao Journal* 34 (March–April, 1989): 7.

Stauffer, Milton T. *The Christian Occupation of China: A general survey of the numerical strength and geographical distribution of the Christian forces in China between 1901–1920.* Chinese edition. Beijing: China Social Science Pub., 1987.

Su Wen-Fung. *China Church History.* Chinese edition. San Francisco, CA: Hua Suen Pub., 2005.

Wang Chun-Siu. *The End Road of China Reform.* Hong Kong: Harfield, 2008.

Wen Mu. *China Church History.* Chinese edition. Hong Kong: Global Chinese Bible Institute, 1999.

Yan Siu-Lin. *The Training of Pastors among the House Church in the 1980's,* Unpublished thesis in Chinese, China Bible Seminary, 2000.

About Dr. Thomas Lee Yip-Mun

Thomas Lee has been the principal of more than two hundred full-time Bible schools and seminaries and 590 pastoral training centers in China. He received his BS in Mathematics and BD from Manchester University, and a MTh at Glasgow University and a PhD in Theology at Edinburgh University. He is currently the principal of Global China Bible Institute, China Great Commission Seminary, and China Great Commission Mission School among others. He serves on the Board of Child Evangelism (HK), *Golden Lampstand* Christian Literature, and International Christian Concern (a ministry in Cambodia).

3

The Emergence and Expansion of Indian Mission Movement from 1947–2009: A Study into the Successes and Failures

K. RAJENDRAN, DMISS

Introduction

In 2008, India celebrated its sixty-first year of independence. India has moved from where it was and so have the Indian Christian missions. Looking at the history of Indian missions, there is a need to measure our achievement and evaluate the past and present to prepare us for today's challenges.

Western-pioneering Protestant missionaries gave the foundation for many of the successes on which Indian missionaries now build. Growth has been spectacular over the past fifty years. Indian missionaries have grown from 543 in the year 1972, to 12,000 missionaries in 1994, and perhaps 100,000 spread across the country in 2009.[56] India is the foremost among Two-Thirds World missionary-sending countries.

56 India Missions Association's 230 members themselves have nearly forty thousand workers until 2009.

In the next fifty years, missionaries and activities will increase, but it may have a different face and methodology. We will need more planning and direction, more pastoral care and contact, more training of leadership, and more varied evangelism. Mission leaders will be stretched. They must plan for growth. Some will be bitterly disappointed that they did not prepare themselves and their followers.

Despite the growth, many missionaries suffer inadequate salaries, poor health care, inadequate education for their children, and lack of pensions and housing plans on retirement. We need bold steps to counter these problems. Missionaries, mission leaders, and all Christians need to solve them. Even theologically trained missionaries on the field may lose motivation and direction. Many hit dry patches when they face opposition, lack of growth in their work, and relationship problems. These lead some missions to arrange refresher courses once a year for their missionaries.

Several other pressing needs demand discussion and action. These include mass conversion versus individual conversions, integration of converts into the life of the church, contextualization, conflicts between evangelism and social work, the means to evangelize, accountability of missionaries and mission leaders, the place of laypeople in missions, short-term missions, cross-cultural adaptations, and comity.

Mission bodies must plan strategically for corporate ownership, measure evangelism results, build trust for Indian and international partnership, provide and hold to standards for mission and missionary welfare. They must educate the church for missions, prompt continuous education for missionaries, initiate more women's work, prepare Indian missionaries for-global ventures, draft and train future leadership and funding for missions.

Early Endeavor and the Impact of Missionaries

To begin, we need to study briefly the positive contributions and limitations of the early foreign missionaries to apply them to us now as well as in the future.

Protestant missionaries arriving in India in the late eighteenth century precipitated revolution by preaching the gospel, winning people for Christ, discipling, establishing churches, advocating social change, and even impacting the freedom movement by influencing the fathers of the new India.

Impact on Secular India

By the indirect influence of the missionaries, India remains today a secular rather than a sectarian nation. They campaigned against *sati*,[57] female infanticide, and the class of Thugs. They worked to alleviate the condition of Hindu widows and temple prostitutes and raised the acceptable age of marriage.

Christian missionaries and their teaching influenced raja Ram Mohun Roy's Hindu reformation. William Carey, the father of modern missions, worked against those when he introduced modern journalism and published both Bengali and English newspapers and magazines. He stimulated a renaissance of Bengali literature. Carey's inquiry and his personal example led to a major revolution in outlook and outreach of the Christian church.

Christian Friedrich Schwartz is another example. A German missionary at Tranquebar, Trichinopoly, and then Tanjore, he had much to do with the kings of Tanjore, and was reputed to be of high integrity and widely trusted. He influenced Tulasi Raja and taught the raja's adopted son, Serfogee Raja. Even Hyder

57 In *sati* a Hindu widow was burnt along with her deceased husband. Although not practised by all Hindus, the gruesome practice was perpetuated by many as religious fanaticism. It was outlawed in 1829 by the British Viceroy William Bentinck through the efforts of William Carey and Raja Ram Mohun Roy.

Ali, a Muslim ruler, had high regards for Schwartz. He brought peace between the English and French rulers and resolved their misunderstandings. He helped preserve the throne of Tanjore by rescuing Serfogee and becoming his effective guardian. When Schwartz died, Serfogee recorded his gratitude in an inscription at Tanjore, and wished for more "missionaries who should resemble the departed Schwartz!"[58]

Years later, a large number of Western Christians became associated with the Indian freedom movement. Allan Octavian Hume was the first president of the Indian National Congress. CF Andrews, Stanley Jones, Fred B. Fisher, Clifford Manshardt, and Samuel Evans Stokes, Jr. went a long way towards changing the popular misconception that Christianity was the other side of the imperialist coin. Stanley Jones vocally supported the Indian freedom movement, struggling at times with the ruling British government. Jones was willing to receive the nationalists to his gatherings. However, Jones never lost sight of introducing Christ to the people of India. Because of his influence, Ralph T. Templin formed the Krishtagraha movement,[59] which was similar to the Satyagraha movement started by Gandhiji. The ideology of the Krishtagraha movement was to reorient Christianity away from being pro-Western and toward achieving a soul of its own, tied in closely to Mother India. Jones, as a frontline missionary, sought to understand and interpret Gandhi sympathetically from within the orthodoxy of the Christian church.

Waskom Pickett, an American Methodist bishop, associated with Mahatma Gandhi, Jawaharlal Nehru and Indira Gandhi.[60] After independence, Pickett took part in sorting out national

---

58 Stephen Neill, *Builders of the Indian Church* (London, Westminster: The Living Stone Press, 1934), 79.

59 Richard W. Taylor, *The Contribution of E. Stanley Jones* (Madras: CLS, 1973), 18–19.

60 Bishop J. W. Pickett, *My Twentieth Century Odyssey* (Bombay: Gospel Lit. Service, 1980), 150–51.

problems when there were community clashes between Sikhs and Hindus.[61] When Bishop Pickett and Dr. Ambedkar, a leader of Indian civil rights movement and champion of the "untouchables," become friends, Ambedkar took many Christian books from Pickett and distributed them to many of his colleagues. After two years, Ambedkar asked him to baptize him secretly while he continued to be a politician. He wanted Pickett to train and baptize one thousand of Ambedkar's candidates, but they would not come under the authority of the church and its discipline. Pickett refused to baptize him unless it was publicly announced.[62] Khushwant Singh called missionaries the helpers of the nation.[63]

Impact on the Growth of the Church in India

In 1934, Stephen Neill wrote euphorically of Indian church growth: "In almost every corner of the country, the Christian Church has touched every stratum of society."[64] Singh agreed "By 1921 the Protestants constituted 1.5 percent of the population of India, more than half of whom owed their Christianization to American Missionary zeal."[65]

Ziegenbalg and others were known for training successors. Missionaries influenced Christians who carried on the beacon of evangelization.

John P. Jones, a thinker and a strategist who served with the ABCFM[66] in Madurai for thirty-six years (1878–1914), habitually accompanied his Indian disciples in all evangelism, demonstrating how to explain the gospel to people. He said,

---

61 Ibid., 26.
62 Ibid., 32–33.
63 Khushwant Singh, *India: An Introduction* (New Delhi: Vision Books) 1992, 75.
64 Neill, *Builders,* 11–12.
65 Singh, *India*, 75–76.
66 Harriet Wilder, *A Century in the Madura Mission-South India 1834–1934* (New York: Vintage Press, 1961), 16. ABCFM—The American Board of Commissioners for Foreign Missions worked in Madura, Tamilnadu.

"A mission at best is a temporary thing. It should constantly aim to so nourish and strengthen the native Church as to make it unnecessary."[67]

Many pioneers saw the good in their followers and discipled them to carry on the task of evangelization as "Jesus saw His disciples not as what they were but what they were to become."[68]

Impact on the Marginalized

Early missionaries worked hard to lift the poor, the downtrodden, the outcasts, and the marginalized who were the victims of the Hindu philosophy of Varnashrama Dharma.[69] William Goudie, a Scottish Methodist missionary, was one. He gathered outcasts by scores and hundreds and provided shepherding and instruction for them.[70] In this way, many foreign Christian missionaries did a great deal for India in general and not just for Christians.

Impact on Indian Literature and Literacy

The contribution to Indian literacy by pioneering missionaries was exceptional. Missions started schools long before the government took a hand. Until a few years ago in many parts of India, ordinary schools were not open to the low castes.[71] In Tranquebar, the school predated the church.[72] "American missionaries compiled and published the earliest grammars and

---

67 John P. Jones, *India's Problem Krishna or Christ* (New York: Fleming H. Revell, 1903), 223.

68 Chacko Thomas, former director of M.V. Doulos, OM. Lecture, (Lucknow, October 1988).

69 *Varnashrama Dharma* philosophy holds to four upper castes and does not allow backward castes and the untouchables into full society. This practice has kept untouchables in poverty, illiteracy, ignorance and three thousand years of bondage.

70 E.W. Thompson, *The Call of India* (London: The Wesleyan Methodist Missionary Society, 1912), 155.

71 Swami John D. Theerthan, *Choice Before India: Communism–Catastrophe; Sarvodya–Christ.* Trichur: Mission to Hindus, [n.d.], 16.

72 Stephen Neill, *Under Three Flags* (New York: Friendship Press, 1954), 76.

dictionaries of Punjabi, Hindi, Urdu and Marathi."[73] S. H. Kellogg pulled together more than a dozen dialects to create *A Grammar of Hindi Language*, which is still in use.[74] In South India, the Strict Baptist missionaries produced, alongside other literary work, a Tamil dictionary and grammar.[75] Lucknow Christian College was the first institution in India to teach shorthand in English, Urdu, and Hindi.[76]

J. Z. Hodge, a secretary of the National Christian Council of India, Burma, and Ceylon before the Indian independence, wrote, "Allied to education is that other outreach of influential missionary endeavour, the ministry of Christian literature."[77] Missionaries gave an enormous boost to mass education first in Bengal by teaching in the regional language.[78] In fact, this is true for almost all India.

Impact on Women's Education

In 1834, Caroline Atwater Mason wrote that only one percent of the Indian women could read and write:[79] "Reading and writing were practically confined to *nautch*[80] girls and not for respectable women."[81] Despite local disbelief and pessimism, the missionaries believed that the girls could be educated and transformed. By the 1994 census, women's literacy rate had grown to 39.42% compared to the men's at 63.86%.[82] Missionaries had contributed to and inspired this progress.

---

73 Singh, *India*, 75.

74 Ibid., 269.

75 John K. Thorpe, *"Other Sheep" of the Tamil Fold: The Centenary Story of the Strict Baptist Mission 1861–1960* (London: S.B.M. Publications, 1961), 34–36.

76 Pickett, *Odyssey*, 138.

77 J. Z. Hodge, *Salute to India* (London: S.C.M., 1944), 98.

78 Moni Bagchee, "Christian Missionaries in Bengal," in [n.a.], *Christianity in India* (Madras: Vivekananda Prakashan, 1979), 191.

79 Caroline Atwater Mason, *Wonders of Missions* (London: Hodder & Stoughton Limited, 1922), 264.

80 The term *nautch* translates to "dancers."

81 C. B. Firth, *An Introduction to Indian Church History* (Madras: CLS, 1983), 192–93.

82 Vasantharaj A., *A Portrait of India* (Madras: CGAI, 1995), 2.

The Protestant missionaries' report of December 28, 1707, at Tranquebar, said their Girls' School was the first Christian school for Indian girls, in all of India.[83] Hannah Marshman opened a school for girls at Serampore in 1800.[84] In 1870, Isabella Thoburn started a college on her veranda at Lucknow. Even the fathers of the girls said it was easier to teach their cows than their women. Thoburn persisted and eventually her graduates spread all over India, Burma, and Sri Lanka.[85] The college was probably the first women's college in all of Asia. With her came Clara Swain, the first woman medical missionary of any society, and the founder of the first hospital for women in Asia.[86] Dame Edith Brown did likewise at Ludhiana, Punjab. For years, while other communities refused to let their girls become nurses, Anglo-Indians and Christians made up almost the entire nursing profession in India.

Rajaiah D. Paul recalled the time when a hundred percent of the women employed as schoolteachers were Indian Christians.[87]

The Limitations of Foreign Missionaries

Alongside many achievements by missionaries, there were human frailties. Studying this may help the present missionaries avoid the same mistakes.[88]

Limited Access to Information

If all the Western missionaries of the past had all the anthropological knowledge, information, communication, information

83 Arno Lehmann, *It Began at Tranquebar* (Madras: CLS, 1956), 103.

84 Mason, *Wonders of Missions*, 265.

85 Margaret Carver Ernsberger, *India Calling* (Lucknow: Lucknow Publishing House, 1956), 2.

86 James K. Mathews, "The Mission to Southern Asia," in *The Christian Mission Today*, ed. James A. Engle and Dorcas Hall (New York: Abingdon Press, 1960), 133.

87 Rajaiah D. Paul, *The Cross Over India* (London: SCM Press, 1952), 91.

88 Roger E. Hedlund, *Evangelisation and Church Growth* (Madras: CGRC, 1992), 217.

technologies, and care that the present-day missionaries have, the earlier missionaries would have done far better and would have avoided many blunders. Some of them did not even have newspapers and radios, let alone satellite television, telephones, pagers, cellular phones, or computers.

Disunity and Competition

In early 1600, the Jesuits had some hope of winning Jehangir, son of Emperor Akbar of the Moghul dynasty. However, he was unhappy with the wrangling between the Portuguese Roman Catholics and the Protestant English ambassadors, Captain Hawkins and Thomas Roe.[89] In 1627 the Emperor Jehangir died. With him died hopes of Christianizing India by converting its ruler. No ruler of any princely state ever accepted the Christian faith.[90]

Disunity between the representatives of the Christian faith was endemic. The historian Stephen Neill observed, "The missionaries say that they have come just to preach Christ. All that they really want is to get people into their own little cages (after which) they will not even allow them to receive the Holy Communion together."[91] Obvious division in Christianity damaged the offer of Christ to Indians who were already filled with divergence and rifts.

Exaggerated or Caustic Reports

Missionaries reporting to their constituency were often both emotive and informative to raise concern, prayer, and finance. At times, they were condescending, lacking in empathy for their hosts—harsh, caustic, colorful, and only partly factual.[92] The following is an

89 Singh, *India*, 75.
90 Ibid., 75.
91 Neill, *Call to Mission*, 37–39.
92 Mason, *Wonder of Missions,* 71.

example of a missionary's report to his compatriots: "It is observed that children in heathen lands are like 'wild asses, colts,' ungoverned, ungovernable, idle and dissolute. Missionaries in contrast to pagan parents, govern and educate their children, make them learned, and can fit them also to be missionaries in their turns."[93]

Even if the above was true in only some situations, this attitude made missionaries feel and act superior, and thus annoyed the ones to whom the gospel was taken.[94] Bluntly, Neill put it, "Christian history has been written far too much from the side of the operators, and far too little from that of the victims."[95] Stanley Jones wrote, "Christianity must be defined as Christ, not the Old Testament, not Western civilization, but Christ Himself. Christ must not be seen as a Western Partisan but a Brother of Men."[96] This positive change of attitude helps the missionaries to build rapport with the nationals and learn from each other.

Struggle with Host Cultures

Missionaries seldom identified with local cultures. Khushwant Singh observed that "many Christians continued bearing high sounding English names; their women wore a comical mixture of European and Indian dress. Their hymns translated sung to outlandish tunes (which) evoked more derision than reverence."[97] Stephen Neill wrote in 1934, "Missionaries wished their converts to become as much like Englishmen as possible. Christianity in India today presents itself as an alien religion."[98] He also said the Sunday service in the South Indian churches is exactly as it is in England.[99] Jack C. Winslow, a friend of Gandhi, wrote,

---

93 R. Pierce Beaver, *All Loves Excelling* (Grand Rapids, MI: Eerdmans, 1968), 50.

94 Ibid., 50–51.

95 Gerald Anderson, *The Future of the Christian World Missions,* ed. William Danker (Grand Rapids, MI: Eerdmans, 1971), 139.

96 Jones, *The Christ of the Indian Road*, 16.

97 Singh, *India,* 76.

98 Neill, *Builders*, 63.

99 Ibid., 63–64.

"Missionaries with the Gospel brought unessential Western accompaniments."[100] Keshab Chandra Sen, deeply influenced by Christianity, founded Prarthana Samaj[101] but he felt the missionaries were not presenting the Asian Christ.[102] As far back as 1903, John P. Jones was distressed that modern Christianity was a product of Western thought, interpretation, and life.[103] Rajaiah D. Paul in 1952 tried to redefine the Christian message in thought forms and in language that our compatriots would understand.[104] A Christian from Karnataka said a civilized Christian groom could not be married without a suit and a tie!

Indian Workers as "Agents"

Many missionaries treated their workers and evangelists well. However, the term used for the workers was "agents."[105] Reports said some agents were mere hirelings, whose objects were monthly pay and pleasing their European masters.[106] According to Stephen Neill, "Missionaries in the nineteenth century had to some extent yielded to the colonial complex . . . Western man was the leader, and would remain so for a very long time, perhaps for ever."[107]

"Holy" People in Mission Compounds

The strength of missionary preaching was the call to Christianity. However, according to Bishop Lesslie Newbigin, "Converts were called upon to separate themselves radically from the society.

---

100 Winslow, *The Eyelids of the Dawn*, 77.
101 *Prarthana Samaj* means a society of prayer.
102 Stephen Neill, *The Christian Church in India and Pakistan* (Grand Rapids, MI: Eerdmans, 1970), 121. Quoted from the original translation by O. Wolff, *Christus Under den Hindus-Christus der Asiat*, 62–67.
103 Jones, *Krishna or Christ*, 296.
104 Paul, *The Cross Over India*, 106.
105 Lewis, *William Goudie*, 48.
106 Houghton, *Dependency*, 163.
107 Stephen Neill, *A History of Christian Missions* (London: Penguin Books, 1990), 220.

But the 'churchly' society was rather a transplanted version of the medieval 'Christendom.'"[108] Newbigin further reiterated that because of the church as a transplanted version of medieval Christianity, the missionaries made the mistake of not teaching the newer Christians to differentiate what is good and what is harmful in a society into which they carried the gospel. So he said, "Missionaries, unable to distinguish in Hindu culture what was religious and what was social, taught the Christians to reject every Hindu custom indiscriminately."[109] This attitude made the church dependent of the Western missions and alienated it from the mainstream of Indian life.[110] In some cases, new converts were extracted from their culture of necessity because their high caste families had threatened their lives. However, extracting people from the community to the mission compound stopped people group movements to Christ. Becoming a Christian, especially a mission compound person, created a new mixed Christian culture,[111] and cultural changes were dominated by the majority caste from which the converts came.

In some ways, "the mission station approach encouraged insincere inquirers. The mission compound culture was perpetuated and nurtured by many of the missionaries who genuinely felt that the Christian community was "holy" or "separated," and thus their lives ought to be different in morality and in all other aspects of life.[112] Some missionaries consciously created compounds where they recreated and nurtured their own culture, housing, and other habits to remind them of the nation from which they came. To maintain such status, they had to employ

---

108 Lesslie Newbigin, *The Good Shepherd* (Madras: CLS, 1974), 86.

109 Richard, *Christ-Bhakti*, 56–57. Quoted from *The Harvest Field* 39, no. 6, (June 1918): 236–37.

110 Houghton, *Dependency*, 247.

111 Subash Samuel, Pastor of the local Church in Katihar. Personal Interview at Lucknow, UP. June 1994.

112 Stock, *Punjab*, 22.

and train people. New converts became workers in the mission as cooks, waiters, teachers, and Catechists.

Mission compound culture has its negative repercussions until today.[113] A comparable situation is also found among some Indian and other Asian missionaries.[114] Thus, "the mission station approach created an artificial world of almost total dependence upon the missionaries." [115]

Mission compound protection of converts made the non-Christians feel that Christians were traitors of the nation because Christians are related to Western missionaries. Thus, the local Christians were misunderstood as collaborators with the crushing colonizers: "The most unfortunate result of the separation of converts from their families was that this blocked the most effective channel for evangelism."[116] According to Houghton, "this proved to be an impediment to its (the gospel's) advance and plan to capture the heart of India."[117]

Phil Parshall, a former missionary to Bangladesh, said that the remaining mission compounds should be dismantled to allow missionaries to move into the community and share their incarnational testimony.[118]

Exclusivism and Non-Patriotism

H. L. Richard, a researcher of Indian culture says, "Too often in the process of preaching Christ, missionaries were involved in public ridicule of Hinduism."[119] This caused problems at times in preaching the gospel since "missionaries generally share four

---

113 Suresh S., former Pastor of AOG Church, Bettiah, Bihar. Interview at Kurukshetra, Haryana, June 1994.

114 S. S. Bhargava, Interview at Gorakhpur, June 1994.

115 Stock, *Punjab*, 22.

116 Ibid., 23.

117 Houghton, *Dependency*, 247.

118 Phil Parshall, "God's Communicator in the 80's," in *World Christian Movement*, ed. Ralph Winter, Steve Hawthorne, et. al. (Pasadena, CA: William Carey Library, 1988) 478.

119 Richard, *Christ-Bhakti*, 12.

things with colonial government agents: common nationality and culture, common race, administrative authority, and a position of privilege."[120] Many a young missionary-minister with little or no experience in the pastorate had been appointed a district superintendent at his first annual field conference. Privilege was seen in the material possessions and salary.[121] Houghton attributed this to "the presupposition fashioned in large measure by Englishmen in the service of the British raj, that their Indian workers were an inferior order of beings, not fit for positions of trust and responsibility."[122] The display of a sense of superiority by the missionaries strengthened the belief of Hindus that Christianity was the religious side of the propagation of colonial power. Houghton summarized the attitudes of some of these missionaries as "officialism," with a sense of a master to his employee; a spirit of "masterfulness," with a relationship of superior to inferior; and some missionaries were more "self-seeking" than their calling allowed for.[123] Richard commented, "[M]issionary history in India is inextricably tied to colonialism, a stigma that mars the work of Christ to this day."[124] Winslow, who struggled with superiority and identification said, "I must become an Indian to the Indians."[125] Because of his right attitude, he was a tremendous blessing. His Indian colleagues accepted him because of his humility and identification with his Indian counterparts.[126]

Treating locals as less mature or less than equal still occurs among the Indian missionaries. Ralph Winter advises four stages

---

120 Ibid., 19.
121 Ibid., 24–25.
122 Houghton, *Dependency*, 246.
123 Ibid., 220–221.
124 Ibid., 12.
125 Winslow, *The Eyelids of the Dawn*, 74–75.
126 Ibid., 74.

of a missionary—pioneer, parent, partner, and participant.[127] Present missionaries must practice all of these four stages for the church to grow.

Misunderstood Missionaries

Thus, in spite of all the contributions of missionaries to Indian communities, they were still misunderstood.[128] This showed particularly in suspicion regarding their social service. Arun Shourie, a journalist and an Indian politician, accused all Western missionaries of being an arm of the Colonial East India Company.[129] He interpreted missionaries' actions of goodwill and education as the consolidation of the British rule. [130] Vishal Mangalwadi refuted this in his book, *Missionary Conspiracy: Letters to a Post-modern Hindu*, as an unfair statement.[131] Some missionaries who collaborated with the business-minded colonialists were called the "political Padri."[132] Given this stigma, some people concluded that Christianity was foreign, or more precisely Western, and much more precisely British.[133] Neill stated, "Hindus considered that missionaries, united with the colonial Government, desired at any cost to make India Christian."[134] Some Indians held such misgivings about the missionaries. Thus, with all the good done, the Indian Christians are still in the process of undoing the past misunderstandings of the non-Christians.

---

127 Ralph D. Winter, "The Long Look: Eras of Missions History," in *Perspectives on the World Christian Movement—A Reader, ed.* Ralph Winter, Steve Hawthorne et. al (Pasadena, CA: William Carey Library, 1981), 170–71.

128 Otto Waack, *Church and Mission in India* (Delhi: ISPCK, 1997), 415–16.

129 Arun Shourie, *Missionaries in India* (New Delhi: ASA Publications, 1994), 56–57.

130 Ibid., 58–60.

131 Vishal Mangalwadi, *Missionary Conspiracy: Letters to a Post-modern Hindu* (Mussoorie: Nivedit Books, 1996), 16.

132 [n.a.], "Missionaries in India: Focus on Madhya Pradesh," in [n.a.], *Christianity in India*, (Madras: Vivekananda Kendra Prakashan, 1979), 182. Excepts from "Report of the Christian Missionary Activities Enquiry Committee, Madhya Pradesh." Published by All India Arya (Hindu) Dharma Sewa Sangh, PO Sewa Sanga, Sabzi Mandi, Delhi.

133 Neill, *Colonialism,* 98.

134 Ibid., 67.

The Emergence and Building of Indigenous Mission Organizations

Four Independent Indian Indigenous Missions Prior to 1947

The indigenous Marthoma Church of Kerala formed Marthoma Evangelistic Association in 1888, sent Malayalee missionaries out to several parts of India, and established Christian ashrams through indigenous funds. It was the first evangelistic association initiated by Asians. Then the Indian Missionary Society (IMS)[135] and the National Missionary Society (NMS) were established successively in 1903 and 1905. Zoram Missionary Fellowship was a mission from Mizoram in North Eastern India. These were the only four national indigenous Indian missions prior to Indian Independence in 1947.

Modern Indian Indigenous Missions

THE DISCONTINUITY OF MISSIONS

Indian Independence and the departure of many foreign missionaries forced Indians to consider mission endeavor seriously. They no longer felt dominated by foreign missionaries.[136]

THE CONTINUITY OF MISSIONS

After Indian Independence (1947), denominational foreign missions, which were operated fully by their own overseas leaders, funding, and plans, had to close it down, as they had consciously not developed local leadership. Thus, the Indian church struggled for Indian leadership.

---

135 In February 1903, Bishop Vedanayagam Samuel Azariah helped to form the Indian Missionary Society of Tirunelveli, a landmark in church and mission planting. J. Edwin Orr, *Evangelical Awakenings in Southern Asia* (Minneapolis: Bethany Fellowship, 1975), 127.

136 Houghton, *Dependency*, 216–18.

Nevertheless, there were other foreign missions such as Operation Mobilization (OM), Christian Literature Crusade (CLC), Every Home Crusade (EHC), Youth With A Mission (YWAM), Campus Crusade for Christ (CCC), Union of Evangelical Students in India (Indian IFES), Youth For Christ (YFC), and a few others. Although originating from abroad, they consciously trained Indian leaders, so when missionary visas were refused, the foreign personnel left, but the work carried on as good leadership was already in place. This is an interesting lesson for the missionaries of today, not to wait to train local leaders until they are kicked out of the country.

Thus, the missionary organizations continued. It is acknowledged today around the world that these above movements actually gave the leadership for the emergence of the modern movements in India. In India, it is recognized that a large number of newer mission organizations were birthed and led by the former members of OM, YWAM, and other organizations mentioned. Ralph Winter wrote in *Perspectives in the World Christian Movement* that when the interest in mission was decreasing, it was OM and YWAM that gave new vision for evangelization by mobilizing the churches and young people across the world.[137]

BIRTH OF NEW INDIAN INDIGENOUS MISSION ORGANIZATIONS[138]

New missions blossomed with fresh visions and strategies, each with a distinctive nature depending upon the burden and the areas where it wanted to work. Indigenous mission endeavor and consciousness grew. Sam Lazarus writes positively, "the last two

137 *Perspectives in the World Christian Movement* First Edition.

138 The Indigenous missions have several different interpretations. For some modern Indians, "indigenous" missions mostly mean fully Indian personnel, Indian funds, and Indian personnel. For many others, it is fully Indian personnel and not beyond that. The dependency, paternalism, globalism, Christian brotherhood, and many other factors are involved in this discussion.

decades, namely the 70's and 80's, have witnessed an unprecedented growth in the area of mission work and cross cultural evangelism resulting in 'mushrooming of Missions.'"[139] On the negative side, with a proliferation of new missions, the churches are confused about the genuineness of missions, not knowing which to support.[140] The Indian church had to grapple and come up with its own answers, which worked in its categories.

Denominational Missions. Then, new denominational missions came into being, such as the Nagaland Missionary Movement, the Zoram Evangelical Fellowship, the Presbyterian Synod of Mizoram,[141] and others, including the forty-five Pentecostal Missions.[142] PT Abraham, an active leader of the Sharon Pentecostal Fellowship says, "The Pentecostal-Charismatic Mission Agencies emerged largely in the decades of 1970 and 1980. In the decade 1970, twenty-one, and in the decade of 1980 another twenty-four more agencies were started."[143]

Interdenominational and Faith Missions. Following the denominational missions came the "non-denominational" or "inter-denominational" and "indigenous" "faith" missions. Some of the best known of these are Friends Missionary Prayer Band (FMPB) founded in 1962, Indian Evangelical Mission (IEM) in 1965, Church Growth Missionary Movement (CGMM), and Gospel Echoing Missionary Society (GEMS) founded in 1970. There are many others. They were more independent and moved to the neediest areas.

139 Sam Lazarus, "Preface," in *Proclaiming Christ*, ed. Sam Lazarus (Madras: CGAI, 1992), iii.

140 Findings in Church-Mission consultation, held at ECC, Whitefield, Bangalore, January 20–22, 1998.

141 The Presbyterian Synod of Mizoram has approximately six hundred missionaries.

142 PT Abraham, "Pentecostal-Charismatic Missionary Outreach," in *Proclaiming Christ*, ed. Sam Lazarus (Madras: CGAI, 1992), 101.

143 Abraham, "Pentecostal Outreach," 101.

Grouping for Cooperation—Associations and Networks Emerge

As missions developed, they saw a need to strengthen each other by cooperating to meet their common goals and purposes. Associations, national federations, and networks provided partnership, accountability, and exposure to each other. A mission's credibility often depended upon the association or network to which it belonged. For credibility, many missions joined hands, forgoing minor philosophical or policy differences, bolstering cohesion and growth.

Associations became a necessity to set standards, provide united testimony, leadership development, equal care for the missionaries, standard health care, retirement benefits, development of the missionaries, missionary children's education, recognition of comity arrangements on the mission fields, a voice, and a representation of missions to the government. The networking sets common goals and cooperation until a job is done. It is time and purpose oriented.

Evangelical Fellowship of India (EFI)

EFI was born in 1951, in the same year as the World Evangelical Fellowship.[144] Its stated purpose was, "to provide fellowship among evangelical Christians and be a means of unified action directed towards spiritual renewal in the Church, active evangelism, effective witness to and safeguard of the evangelical faith in the Church."[145]

India Missions Association (IMA)

IMA began in March 1977 with six mission groups that agreed to work together. Since then, IMA has grown to be the largest

---

144 Siga Arles, "Evangelical Movement in India: An Evaluation," in *Pilgrimage 2100*, ed. Siga Arles and Ben Wati (Bangalore: Center for Contemporary Christian, 1995), 32.
145 Ibid., 32.

missions' association in the world, with 230 member missions hosting more than forty thousand workers across India and the globe.[146] It is continuing to grow.

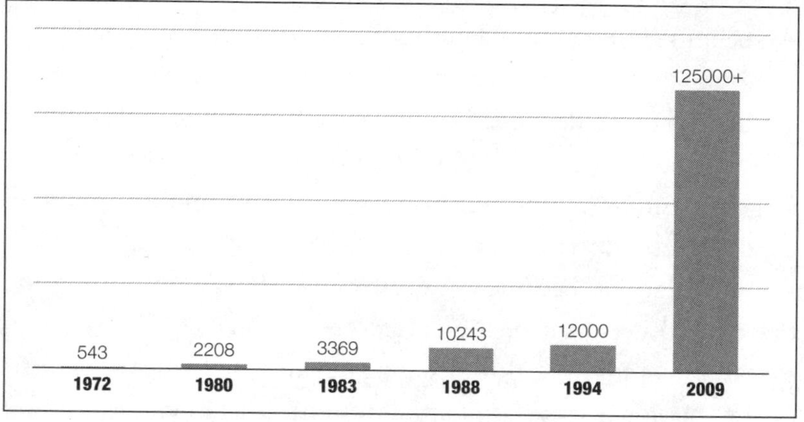

GROWTH OF INDIAN MISSIONARIES

Becoming a member of the India Missions Association assures credibility, for it requires openness to examination and verification of deed documents and board. IMA grants membership when it is satisfied with the credibility of a mission. Membership in IMA also qualifies a mission for advice to enable it to do its job better—leadership development, consultation on management, encouraging missions to become nation conscious in reaching "all" peoples for Christ, and helping donors to make choices of where they could invest their funds and resources. IMA has a vital role in encouraging mission agencies to develop, help, provide, facilitate, call for consultations, and link with one another.

Stan Nussabaum, training director at Global Mapping International remarked, "It remains clear to us that IMA is in the front door to serving a broad cross-section of Mission organizations and researchers in India, and we would like to come in

146 Refer to www.imaindia.org.

the front door."[147] IMA has indeed become the central point of national evangelism and setting general directions for missions and leadership.[148]

IMA has developed the following networks to keep the missions focused: Youth Ministries Network; Urban Ministries Network; BiG Partners/Tent-makers Network; Muslim Neighbours' Network; Bandhu (Hindu) Seva Network; Children's Network; Serve-A-Peoples Network; Board Members Network; Member Care Network; Missionary Training Network; Research Network; and Overseas Workers' Network.

Several appropriate leadership trainings, think tanks,[149] and other consultations are held to enhance and speed evangelization and mobilization of ministries in strategic ways.

Other National Associations

Other associations and federations have specific functions: National Council of Churches in India (NCCI); Pentecostal Fellowship of India (PFI); Federation of Evangelical Churches of India (FECI); Emmanuel Hospital Association (EHA); Christian Medical Association of India (CMAI); Indian Christian Media Association (ICMA); Evangelical Trust Association of North India (ETANI) and Evangelical Trust Association of South India (ETASI); National Association for Christian Social Concerns (NACSC); India Association of (Itinerant) Evangelists (IAE); Evangelical Literature Fellowship of India (ELFI); and All India Association for Christian Higher Education (AIACHE). Each has scores (some hundreds) of organizations in its federation representing thousands of staff workers spread all over India.[150]

---

147 E-mail of Stan Nussabaum, Training Director, Global Mapping Internationa to Sunderaj, IMA. April 9, 1997.

148 Rajendran, *Which Way Forward*, 82–88.

149 Think tanks are held for mission leaders to think on a particular issue to break through some areas which would enhance missions strategies. See www:imaindia.org

150 Sunder Raj and Team (eds.), *Management of Indian Missions* (Chennai: India Missions Association, 1992), 136.

Networks

Many networks are formed for different emphases of evangelism. Some of them are as follows: AD 2000 and Transformation Movement (formerly Beyond Movement); North India Harvest Network;[151] Council On National Service (CONS); Discipling A Whole Nation (DAWN); The FORUM for Evangelism and Missions (NFEM);[152] Evangelical Literature Fellowship of India (ELFI); Grass Roots Church Planters Training Network (GRCP),[153] and several others.

Supporting Agencies

Over the period of the emerging national missions, many groups came into being as support agencies. They are not networks. They provide assistance to missions in several areas such as the Cell for Assistance and Relief to Evangelists (CARE/IMA), Christian Aid, Advancing Native Missions (ANM). Partners International/Christian National Evangelism Commission (CNEC) are some of the supporting agencies, as well as Church Growth Association of India (CGAI),[154] Missionary Upholders Family (MUF), Missionary Upholders Trust (MUT),[155] and several others.

Christian Social Action Units

Evangelical Fellowship of India Commission on Relief (EFICOR), World Vision, Inter Mission, Nava Jeevan Seva Mandal (NSM), and others were set up to help the missions in

---

151 Raju Abraham, "Networking and Mobilising the Church for North India." Paper at IMA-NCE, Hyderabad, September 1996.

152 A Report in FORUM at Nagpur from April 16–18, 1997.

153 S. D. Ponraj and Sue Baird, eds., *Reach India 2000* (Madhupur, Bihar: Mission Educational Books, 1996), 20–21.

154 Vasantha Raj, Interview, Chennai, December 20, 1996.

155 Nirmala David, "The Birth of a MUF Group." in *Mission and Vision, Who and What?* eds. J. J. Ratnakumar and Krupa Sunder Raj (Bangalore: MUT Publishers, 1996), 26.

their field of service.[156] Eventually, the primarily socially concerned agencies joined and formed the National Association for Christian Social Concern (NACSC). They expected to train candidates for social action to help evangelists and the missionaries to serve the people where the missionaries and churches worked. However, this training has not picked up momentum yet.[157]

Thus, the associations, networks, and supporting agencies have added much to the credibility and planning of Indian missions.

Issues in Mission Organizations

There are several other issues raised as the Indian indigenous mission organizations progressed in the past forty years. Here are some of them highlighted.

Ambiguity: Concepts and Missionary Actions

In missions, there are many ambiguous terms, meanings, philosophies, personalities, directions, and focuses. Therefore, there is a need for clarity in definition for missions to go forward. Each mission has its own interpretations, depending upon its theological outlook; accordingly, their direction is set for their mission. However, good things can happen. [158]

Roberta Winter illustrated a classic example of how confusion in theology kept Christians from being involved in evangelism:

> A little after AD 300, Constantine (whose mother was a Christian) won control of the Roman Government. Through a series of miracles, he liberated the Christians from persecution.

---

156 EFI, "To God Be the Glory: 1951–1991," 39. Quoted in Harris, "The Theological Pilgrimage," 155.
157 Sunder Raj, Interview, Chennai, August 1997.
158 Rajendran, *Which Way Forward*, 60–63.

> They immediately set about to copy and recopy the Bible and other key Christian documents . . . The believers discovered a new problem. They found that they differed in theology and sought to clarify what was correct. Their argumentation replaced evangelization, so no one was sent to tribal peoples beyond their borders, except for the heretics who were driven out of the Empire.[159]

The theology and the biblical basis of mission determine the direction of mission work. Apart from the spiritual opposition from the evil unseen powers,[160] differences over interpreting terms and meanings have caused havoc in missions.

To understand the disagreements, Peter E. Gillquist used an unusual fiction about the beginning of the world's first two denominations:

> Two blind men healed of Jesus were sharing notes. One said that he was sitting on the road to Jericho and shouted to Jesus to heal him. Jesus came to him and healed him. But the other started arguing that it was not possible to have happened that way because Jesus needed mud to heal the blind. In his case, Jesus first spit in His hands and took some mud, mixed it and applied it on the blind man's eyes and then he asked him to go to a pool and wash the mud. So folks, this is how these world's first two denominations started. The "Mudites" and the "Anti-Mudites."[161]

---

159 Roberta Winter, "The Kingdom Strikes Back," in *Inheriting God's Perspective*, ed. Ralph Pluddemann (Bangalore: Mission Frontiers, 1996), 30–31.

160 "Finally, my brethren, be strong in the Lord and in the power of His might. Put on the whole armour of God, that you may be able to stand against the wiles of the devil" (Eph 6:10–12, NKJV).

161 Peter E. Gillquist, *Let's Quit Fighting about the Holy Spirit* (London: Lakeland, 1971), 86–87.

Similar to the story of "Mudites" and "Anti-Mudites" there came many misunderstandings that caused unnecessary divisions among Christians. Divisions arose on methods of work, the people to be reached, the initiatives and areas for new work,[162] accountability structure,[163] the direction,[164] the church government, the strategy, the cooperation, and the understanding of the basis of mission. These caused much confusion.

There were confusions about evangelism, evangelization, mission, nation,[165] holistic gospel, reached and unreached peoples, "Win the winnable," gospel to the poor, social justice, and many other issues.

Philosophical confusion reflects adversely in missions. Personality conflicts in missions come about because of individual temperaments, spiritual views, ethos, upbringing, vision and drive.

The Understanding of the "Unreached" Peoples

Christian missions overemphasized the "civilized" as reached peoples, and the "uncivilized" illiterates and the poor as the unreached peoples. This mind-set and the biased theology neglected the actual mission challenges in India. For example, there are less than two hundred workers among the 150 million Muslims, very little adaptation to contextualize the gospel to the open minded "popular Hindus," very little work among the most responsive women,

---

162 Some never bothered about bringing people to Christ, reasoning that God has already chosen the ones who are supposed to come to him anyway.

163 Accountability structure has to do with answering to the church or mission. Some claimed that the missions should spring out only from a church. When a mission organization recruited people and appealed for funds, some churches objected and claimed missions should originate from the church as in the Acts 13. This caused strife on where missions should originate. The discussion between church and parachurch, each trying to establish their authority, is an ongoing issue.

164 The concepts of "win the winnable," gospel to the poor, the holistic and the social service emphasis, and social justice were some on which the mission was built around.

165 David Samuel, Director TAFTEE, interview, Bangalore, IEM Campus during IMA Training Committee, September 6, 1997.

almost nothing done among the youth (65 percent of the Indian population). Work in the cities (40 percent of the Indian population) is not considered, as most missions went to the villages. The migrants to different cities who are open to the gospel across India are neglected: the literates, the middle and upper-middle class, and the influencers of the government. The powerful diaspora Indians are untouched,[166] and the neglect of the fast grown missionaries with little or no care.[167]

There is a need for sharper analysis to avoid confusion, training in Bible seminaries, in mission stations, among missionaries, and in local churches. We need pastors trained to help congregations to understand missions.

Missions must pause and consider strategy before action, planning anew to avoid outdated methods.

Social Work and Evangelism—Balance!

Joshi Jayaprakash in his *Evaluation of Indigenous Missions of India*, exactly ten years back, said that 57.17 percent of the missionaries were involved in church planting and only 7.17 percent were doing development work.[168] Currently in 230 IMA member missions, approximately 75 percent of all the work is the presence evangelism through the means of serving people in one way or other uplifting their standards as "holistic" approach in evangelism, thus practically expressing the love of the Lord Jesus Christ among the people where they work.

Contextualization—to be applied!

For many Christians and missionaries, the cathedral is synonymous with Christianity: "There is sometimes a tendency to forget the wide difference between the two and to think that to

166 Rajendran, *Which Way Forward*, 33–47.
167 Ibid., 97–127.
168 Jayaprakash, *Evaluations of Indigenous Missions of India*, 20b.

introduce Christianity means also introducing Western ways of life."[169] When Christians are diverted from the finality of Christ, they became sidetracked with their goals and purposes and evangelism is neglected.[170]

The famous Jesuit, Francis Xavier (1506–1552), who worked in India, followed the thinking of the medieval missionary church that everything in non-Christian life and systems should be abolished before Christianity could be introduced. Of course, he changed his mind when he reached Japan, where he saw a culture superior to that of the West.[171] Frederick W. Norris called this abolishing act as a "Radical Displacement," where Christianity with its entire Western (or whatever the national culture of the missionaries) cultural baggage was transplanted completely, and ethnic religion was brushed aside as valueless.[172] Such an iconoclastic mind-set seemed to have deterred the contextualization of Christ's teachings to the cultures in India.

Frederick Norris said some useful things to consider in contemplating contextualization. According to him, there are six ways to contextualize. First, the radical displacement of the culture, where the old host culture is completely shelved. Second, the discontinuity theory, where the Christian superiority feels no comparison with the local culture. Nevertheless, it seeks to adapt itself to the cultural forms of the people. Third, the uniqueness theory, where both religions are recognized as unique, but Christianity assumes to be superior. Fourth is the legitimate borrowing theory, where the commonality from both religions is accepted and borrowed to be truly indigenous. Fifth is the

---

169 Soltau, *Mission at the Crossroads*, 120.

170 K. Rajendran, "Understanding the Finality of Christ and its effect in the Mission field." Unpublished paper written for SAIACS requirement for the course on the Finality of Christ, SAIACS (Bangalore, 1996).

171 Harold Fuller, *Mission-Church Dynamics* (Pasadena, CA: William Carey Library, 1981), 13.

172 Frederick W. Norris, "God and the gods: Expect Footprints," in *Unto the Uttermost*, ed. Doug Priest (Pasadena, CA: William Carey Library, 1984), 55–56.

fulfillment theory, where the gospel of Christ is accepted as the fulfillment for people's quest in that culture. Last, the theory of relativistic syncretism, which accepts that all religions contain different truths that lead to the ultimate Truth.[173]

John P. Jones (1878–1914) challenged Indians in three extraordinary books to make Christianity their own in the Indian culture.[174] Stephen Neill considered, "It was never the purpose of the wiser missionaries to reproduce in India a pale, dependent copy of their own form of Christianity; they foresaw a Church living an independent life, Indian in thought and worship and leadership."[175]

Ralph Winter at the Global Consultation On World Evangelism (GCOWE) conference in South Africa in August 1997, challenged people to de-Westernize Christianity to accommodate mass movements to Christ without a hangover of Western imperialism attached to the message.

To the question of why Christianity did not root in India, Khushwant Singh observed, "Christianity did not make strong impact on India. The chief reason for this was that Christianity was never able to erase the taint of being alien to the soil of India. Efforts made to Indianize Christianity had a limited success."[176]

Soltu, in his book *Mission at the Cross Roads*, commented, "As the Gospel enters the lives of the people, it will naturally change many of their customs, but it must be understood that it is the Gospel that is making the change and not the Western [or any] missionaries."[177]

---

173 Frederick W. Norris, "God and the gods," 56–57.

174 Books written by Dr. John P. Jones are, [a] *India Its Life and Thought* (New York: The Macmillan Company, 1908). [b] *The Modern Missionary Challenge* (New York: Fleming H. Revell, 1910). [c] *India's Problem Krishna or Christ* (New York: Fleming H. Revell, 1903).

175 Neill, *Builders*, 15.

176 Singh, *India*, 76.

177 Soltau, *Mission at the Cross Roads*, 120.

There have to be more innovative ways for contextualization. However, they have to be done in the midst of the traditionalists in the church itself. If contextualization is not applied, the Indian majority will reject Christ. Much thought needs to be given on this issue.

Missionary Welfare and Future Recruiting!

Many Indians joined missions as God called them, especially in the scenario of the departure of foreign missionaries, and as a better understanding of missions dawned in the churches.

In the new Indian missionary scene, this cost includes deficient medical care, insufficient salary, and inadequate schooling facilities for children, meager retirement benefits, complete lack of housing for the future, and no provision for decent insurance and pastoral care in many areas.

1. Pastoral care: There is also a great need for missionary pastoral care as the number of missionaries increase under the mounting personal pressures and the strain of sharing Christ to those who do not understand evangelism. The lack of adequate teams for pastoral care, the absence of able administrators, and the incompetent leadership in some missions have to be addressed for the effective work of the missionaries. Several missionaries face pressures from their own organizations in the form of difficult relationships with coworkers, poor leadership, clan-ruled authority structures, unorganized plans, and inadequate training for accomplishing the task. In the organizational structure, too much accountability is expected of some missionaries while others enjoy favoritism.
2. Medical needs: When missionaries fall ill, there are inadequate medical facilities and there is no

medical insurance. There are also many missionary casualties. Most missions do not settle the family members of the missionaries.

3. Child care: The missionaries' children study in hostels, at times a thousand kilometers away. Most of them meet once a year during holidays. After the holidays when the children and the missionaries are just about to adjust to each other, they separate. Some missions are insensitive to lay undue burdens for the children and parents to be separated in distant conditions, as it was cheaper for missions to support the children in some of the prescribed schools. Thus, the missionaries were not able to bear the expenses for the children to study in the nearby schools within a hundred kilometers, where the parents could meet them frequently. This angered children and some missionaries. Ironically, though, many funds have been employed on giving scholarships to non-Christian children, and much social work is being done for others, but when it comes to meeting the expenses of the missionaries, missions and donors shy away as though the missionary is destined to suffer!

4. Inadequate salary to meet genuine needs: Modern Indian indigenous missions do not have sufficient money to do the best for their missionaries.[178] Individual missionaries struggle for their survival. Several missionaries who were interviewed agreed that missionaries and Christian workers were the ones who did not have much in savings, any health insurance, retirement benefits, or death relief

178 Winston Consultant, interview, Chennai, August 1997.

schemes. One missionary's wife became mentally ill, and the mission could not treat her because of lack of funds. Eventually the missionary also died while his wife was left behind homeless on the streets.[179] It is observed that many Indian missionaries did not speak about this for fear of being branded as "unspiritual," but quietly suffered insecurities.[180] Missionaries endured much in the name of "true spirituality" and "faith."

5. Pension and retirement housing: The missionary's self-worth has to be strengthened by planning for their housing and pension after their retirement. Some mission policies make the missionaries feel guilty to speak about such "earthly" things. This perpetuates insecurity both in the person and in his family members.

All the above issues weakened the efforts of the missionaries and have become factors for missionary attrition and future recruiting of missionaries. If the needs of the missionaries are not cared for, the missions in India will diminish.

IMA spends much time on the following five areas of member care, trying to help each mission carefully consider the following: (1) care for mission leaders, (2) care for missionaries, (3) care for missionaries' families, (4) care for missionaries' children, and (5) care for the welfare of the missionaries. Several training programs and consultations on the above have heightened the consciousness of caring for the missionaries, which becomes the strength of the mission organizations.

---

179 Shyam Winston, IMA Management Consultant, personal interview, Chennai, September 1997.

180 David and Grace Shunmugam, ex-missionaries to North India, personal interview, Chennai, July 1997.

Indian Funds, Foreign Funds, and Partnership

There has been much discussion on indigenous and local funds. Some, especially foreigners, would like to know when the Indian church is going to be entirely responsible for the evangelization of India, in terms of resourcing total work. It is a much-debated issue known as dependency vs. self-funding.

In the growing Indian missions, much is done indigenously. Notable amounts of money, labor, leadership, and strategies are acquired from within India. The ways to self-funding are ongoing issues continuously discussed and improved in the missions. Several issues of IMA quarterly magazines have highlighted this and IMA has had many seminars to help missions move forward.

Preparing Future Leaders!

The Indian Missions have come of age in their first generation. Most of the pioneering leaders in the evangelical mission organizations are retiring. Their missions have grown in number of churches and workers. It has been noticed that missions have woken up to this reality and thus are preparing the next generation of leaders. Conscious searching and a sense of multiple mentoring over a period should lead them to find and install the next generation of leadership. The boards have to become the positive influence in placing the new leaders to the future.

Mission and Strategy

After the challenging stages of recruitment and orientation, missionaries arrive on the mission field shocked, confronted by issues previously only theoretical. They must find solutions. Some problems have no solutions, and solutions that work in the church based in South India may not work elsewhere.

"You cannot have water from my tap," said Arun's neighbour. Arun and his coworkers were surprised that all of a sudden his

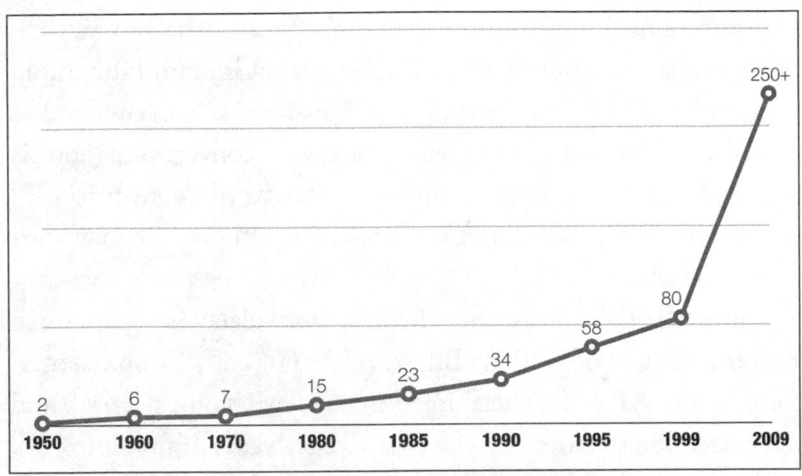

GROWTH OF MISSIONARY TRAINING INSTITUTIONS

neighbor, whom he had known for several months, refused to give them drinking water from his tap. This was because the team was associating with lower caste people in the town. Therefore, there have to be several plans to work among different people groups in India.

Mass Movement versus Individual Conversion

Much argument goes on among the mission agencies about mass movements as opposed to individual conversions and numerical growth against qualitative growth. Mission views are tinted by the theological color of individuals. This seems more of a problem in the newer evangelical churches than in the mainline churches, since personal conversion and piety are emphasized more in the evangelical churches.

The question of mass movement or individual conversion resurfaced with the Homogenous Unit Principle (HUP) of Donald McGavran. It was not that McGavran was against individual conversion, but he wanted a whole group brought to Christ first and then discipled one-by-one, as part of the group.[181] In other words, they were eventually discipled. Graham Houghton, principal of South Asia Institute of Advanced Christian Studies (SAIACS), believes that in the process of conversion, more is changed than is usually implied by the word "conversion."[182] Conversion is a process, not just an event, although it may start with an event.

Several other mass movements took place in the North Eastern States of India, Bihar, UP, Gujarat, Maharashtra, Punjab, and AP.[183] Of the Punjab mass conversion Frederick and Margaret Stock wrote, "In the first twenty years of mission work in Punjab, the problem of caring for converts became increasingly acute. In this way the mission station became the centre for the new band of believers."[184] The presence of Christians in Pakistan was attributed to the mass movements of people to Christ in the mid-1800s to early 1900s.[185]

The way forward on individual or mass conversion lies with balance and good follow-up. In missions today, in the midst of the vehement debates, many individuals and large groups become Christian believers. A balance is needed to include both mass and individual conversions.

Integration of Converts in the Church: The Struggle

When Gandhi was in South Africa, one of his close friends tried to persuade him to confess Christ. As he considered this, Gandhi went to a famous church and was evicted. For years, he never went inside any church. In later years, he occasionally went into churches.

---

181 Donald McGavran, Seminar at the Allahabad Seminary in 1974. Donald A. McGavran, "The Bridges of God," in *Perspectives*, eds. Ralph Winter, Steve Hawthorne et. al. (Pasadena, CA: William Carey Library), 285–86.

182 Dr. Houghton in discussion, SAIACS, Bangalore. September 2, 1997.

183 Stephen Neill, *The History of Christian Missions* (London: Penguin Books, 1990), 308–309.

184 Stock, *People Movements in the Punjab*, 21–22.

185 McGavran, "The Bridges of God," *Perspectives*, 286.

Worship in public was not common in Hinduism, but he conducted services in the open with strong similarities to Christian worship.[186]

Ashok Kumar, an award-winning former state cycle champion of Kerala, started a fellowship called Kristanugami Sangh.[187] They gathered contacts from the majority community and followed up in discipling them for Christ. In the same manner, Abubakker named his center the Fellowship for Neighbours. He gathered interested Muslim friends and taught them before they returned to their communities as witnesses for Christ.[188]

We need to teach, demonstrate, and train church people on this issue. Caste churches or homogeneous groups or missions are in a disadvantaged position if they are not open to receive any other people in their midst and disciple them. However, if they are trained, according to Bishop Waskom Pickett, "Every convert is a potential evangelist and the potentialities of many converts are enormous."[189]

Differences on How to Do the Task: Methodologies

There is much confusion about the means to use to reach India with the gospel of Christ. Many missions feel their methods are right and, in some cases, better than others'. Yet, each mission reaches a different segment of the Indian population. They complement each other. Until this is understood, there will be incidents of misunderstanding and friction between missions.

Full-time Missionaries, Tentmakers, and Lay Evangelists

In a UESI mission convention for their students and graduates in Kerala in October 1997, the caliber of the people who attended the meeting was high. Nearly one hundred professionals indicated

---

186 Pickett, *Odyssey*, 29.

187 *Kristanugami Sangh* means "An association of the followers of Christ." This is based at Cannanore.

188 John Abubakker, interview, Vellore, July 1997.

189 Pickett, *Christ's Way to India's Heart*, 108.

a desire to become missionaries in the future as tentmakers. Some mission leaders were there to encourage, direct, and recruit prospective missionaries.[190] The laypeople have an advantage . . . [to] witness in families, shops, labor unions, political centers, social clubs, and more.[191]

This is a growing trend. In the midst of a great emphasis on full-time evangelists and missionaries, the conviction grows that the ethos of tentmaking missionaries may suit well in India and South Asia. The method is promoted by several tentmaker agencies.

Short-term and Long-term Missionaries

Most Indian missions concentrate on recruiting and training long-term missionaries, allocating long-term tasks to reach specific peoples. Although this is good, very little has been done to harness others through short-term exposure to missions. Short-termers could become witnesses in their own geographical areas and become missionary uplifters.

Missionaries and Local Workers

In 1970s, there were many cross-cultural missionaries from South India to North India. Now after several churches have been planted, they acquired local workers. There has been tension about how to treat them as equals or subordinates. There were many discussions on repeating the blunders of some foreign missionaries in their treatment of Indian workers. More discussion and leadership development is being done to bring them to be the leaders, while the pioneers withdraw or become their helpers.

---

190 Shyam Winston, one of the speakers in the convention. Personal interview, Chennai October 8, 1997.

191 K. Imotemjen Aier, "A Local Church in Action," *ICGQ* 6, no. 2, April–June (1984): 29.

Tensions over Comity: Territorial Agreement

The many emerging missions need clear demarcation of their work areas. Among the early [foreign] missionaries and Christians, the denominational feeling was so rigid . . . sometimes [they] fought over the same territory. The need for comity, to settle matters between societies was felt. Comity means one accepting the ecclesiastical character of the other. In several Indian missionary conferences, the principle of comity of missions was discussed. This paved the way for agreement between missions for cooperation . . . and restricted their territories so that they would support each other.[192]

When there are such issues among the IMA member missions there is an attempt to sort them out, but at times, it is difficult to make the unassociated missions follow the comity arrangements.

IMA associated missions have to agree on following the comity agreement as they join the association:

1. They submit a list of the locations of their mission stations. They may not open a new station in a tribal or rural area within the working distance of another mission.[193]
2. If a mission or church has been in existence for five years, but has not been involved in evangelism around the area, its working distance is zero.

192 [n.a], *Missionary Conference* (Madras, 1902), 159, quoted by Harris, "The Theological Pilgrimage," 50.

193 Working distance of another mission was defined as the distance rate by which a mission station is expanding now, in its church planting work, during five years. For instance, if a mission station planted congregations in the last five years up to a radius of two kilometers, another mission should not come with four kilometers of that mission station (twice the working distance). In cities, the distance did not make any difference but the count of the people in thousands. If the working distance is a postal pin code area which has about thirty thousand people, the other missions/churches should avoid establishing similar work in that pin code area. Or if in the same pin code area two missions work among two distinct people groups, then it is accepted as a norm.

3. If there is a breach of this agreement, IMA will negotiate between the missions.
4. A missionary who leaves an organization to go to the next cannot carry his congregation to the next mission unless both the missions involved arrive at a mutual arrangement.
5. Mission agencies must check with IMA whether another mission works in the area before they start a new mission station.[194]

Sometimes the comity issues brought about the animosities and distrust missions had for each other. In such difficult situations, partnership did not work, and it became a matter of survival and not wishing the best for each other.

Partnerships

"The task of fulfilling the Great Commission is much greater than most of us estimate. A refusal to work in partnership with others comes from a wrong sense of success," said George Ninan.[195] Many missions are working in partnership, realizing the task is very big. For instance, one mission works in radio broadcasting, the other in follow-up, and the other in leadership development. Now progressively, this is becoming an encouraging message for the missions in India to work together.

One of IMA's main goals is to bring missions and leaders under one group in some consultation or other, so people get to know each other and begin different partnership ventures between Indian missions, and between Indian and overseas missions. Partnerships may legitimately change with situations. However, it has been a recognized truth that if no personal trust

194 [IMA] "Mission Field Comity Arrangement." [n.d].

195 George Ninan, South Asia Director of CCC, "Partnership," Unpublished paper, Bangalore, April 1997.

is built between the leaders, it is impossible for the organizations to work together.

Standards and Accountability

Growth in missions, though a blessing, has also resulted in unregulated proliferation of missions, ambiguity of objectives, dilution of definitions, and duplication of service leading to decline of standards. There has also been damage. Many emerging missions make mistakes out of ignorance.[196]

Many ministries started with good intentions and reputation, but ended with scandals due to a lack of accountability. One way we can counter such trends is to develop our own Standards and Monitoring Cell, so missions do not fail in the standards that will attract government action. To become members of IMA, the following minimum criteria are required, which indicate the need for accountability:

- Balanced Board of seven people who are not relatives;
- Minimum of five evangelists/missionaries in a mission;[197]
- Mission must have existed for at least three years;
- Audited accounts for three years;
- A resolution from the Board to become a member of IMA.

Moreover, the Institute of Christian Management (ICM) branched from IMA to train and equip missions with skills to run their missions. The mission quarterly of IMA, *Indian*

196 IMA pamphlet. Missions Standards Cell.

197 Raj Samuel, former IMA coordinator for MSC. Letter to E. K. Emmanuel, GS, Junglighat, Port Blair Andamans, on his enquiry to become member of IMA. July 29, 1994.

Missions, continuously highlights the need and the way forward in personal and organizational accountabilities.

Training Missionaries

A big challenge to confront is the selection of qualified people for mission: "Raising money was easier than raising quality men for many jobs in mission work."[198] Mission training involved biblical soundness, good philosophy of training, and a curriculum to suit varied stages of training to be adequate training before going to the field, and after that, continuing educational opportunities (CeO) while on the field. We need partnerships in training, proper evaluation, and accountability.[199]

Dr. Seth Anyomi, the African Chancellor for the World Link University (WLU) said learning was not confined to classrooms or lecture halls. He gave four contexts for learning and training: daily life and professions, the local church, the ministry team (in mission field), and in specialized training.[200] Rudy Giron, a Latin missionary to Russia, advises integration between the sending church, training school, and the receiving mission to give the missionary oversight and pastoral care.[201] There are three areas of training: learning the Word (know), learning ministry skills (do), and character development (be).

Firstly, training for a missionary should include mission awareness theory and practice with on-the-job training, starting with orientation. This could last one to two years. Secondly, spiritual retreats should be held under expert teachers. Thirdly, personal and group studies should be monitored on the field. Fourthly, leadership training must be provided. Lastly, specialized training

198 Discussion with Sunder Raj, Chennai, August 2, 1997.

199 K. Rajendran, "Strategic Training Partnership for effective Evangelisation of India." A paper presented in Interdev Conference at Larnaca, Cyprus on April 9, 1992.

200 Seth Anyomi, "Four Contexts for Learning and Training," in *Training for Cross-Cultural Ministries*, 96, no.2, (September 1996), 5.

201 Giron, "An Integrated Model of Missions," 1.

should be given according to the vision and spiritual gifts of each person.[202]

Many missionaries in service feel a need for more study or feel "burnt-out." For such, the missions must be open to coach, or else the attrition from field will be very high.

Global Indian Missionaries

Indian Christians have the double responsibility of reaching their own Indian diaspora and others in whose country they live. Sending Indian missionaries to other countries, particularly to economically well-off countries where the cost of living is higher, has been difficult. Apart from that, the Indian church and missions are growing to become aware of their contribution to the countries of the world.

Could we send Indian missionaries abroad? Will it work? Why not? It is reasoned that if Indian textile businesspeople can flourish in Central Asia, if MARUTI and TATA auto companies could run in Central Asian roads, why can the Indian church and missions not send missionaries to the rest of the world? Today there are unprecedented opportunities among Azeris, Kazaks, Kyrgyz, Tajiks, Turks, and Uzbeks who are spiritually hungry. Therefore, it is high time for India, a country that has been receiving missionaries for hundreds of years, to reciprocate in this new era of Christian missions. Some Indian organizations have already sent Indians as missionaries to many of the above nations. The momentum will increase.

Conclusion

Churches and missions need strategic planning or they will drift away. Strategic planning must encompass national and global

---

202 K. Rajendran, "Five Inputs—A Training Proposal for OM India." A Paper to OM Leaders at Hyderabad, September 1992.

needs, not just on the winning the winnable and leaving the rest with no opportunity to hear and respond to Christ.

Partnerships between the missions are being cultivated, aiming to overlook minor differences. The differences of modes of work, personalities, philosophies, and doctrines have to be understood in the light of the need of the nation, and in the light of the fact that all missions are pressing toward one goal of proclaiming the gospel. We need trust without fear of filching workers and donors from each other. Even if erred, openness, honesty, walking in the light, brokenness, and forgiveness can foster partnership. Prayer, collaboration, accountability, and believing in the best of each other will heal the present fears.

The depth of the mission challenges, the variety of the dilemmas, the size of the workforce, and the urgency of the gospel message all call for a comprehensive commitment to fulfill Christ's Great Commission. We need a comprehensive vision of the goal of the message, comprehensive integration of the efforts of the messengers, and comprehensive care for the messengers themselves.

Thus, the last century's history of missions in India teaches us to work with clarity and to cooperate to strengthen missions and the churches in greater collaboration with the rest of the world.

Bibliography

Abraham, P. T. "Pentecostal-Charismatic Missionary Outreach." In *Proclaiming Christ*, edited by Sam Lazarus. Madras: CGAI, 1992.

Albert, S. Vasantharaj. *A Portrait of India III*. Madras: CGAI, 1995.

Andrews, C. F. *What I Owe to Christ*. New York: Abingdon Press, 1932.

Arles, Siga and I. Benwati, eds. *Pilgrimage 2100*. Bangalore: Centre for Contemporary Christianity, 1995.

Azariah, Vedanayagam Samuel. *India and Missions*. Madras: CLS, 1915.

Boyd, Robin. *Church History of Gujarat*. Madras: CLS, 1981.

Carey, William. *An Enquiry Into the Obligations of Christians to Use Means for the Conversion of the Heathens*. ([n.Pub.], [n.d.])

Clark, M. M. *A Corner in India*. Gauhati: C. L. Centre, 1978.

Cornelius, John Jesudason, "Movements Towards Christ in India." In *The Foreign Missions Convention at Washington 1925*, edited by Fennell P. Turner and Frank Knight Sanders. New York: Fleming H. Revell Company, 1925.

Cressy, Earl H. *Christian Missions Meet the Cultures of East Asia*. New York: Friendship Press, 1948.

Engel, James F. *Contemporary Christian Communications: Its Theory and Practice*. New York: Thompson Nelson Publishers, 1979.

Ernsberger, Margaret Carver. *India Calling*. Lucknow: Lucknow Publishing House, 1956.

Firth, Cyril Bruce. *An Introduction to Indian Church History*. Madras: CLS, 1983.

Hedlund, Roger E. *Evangelization and Church Growth*. Madras: CGRC, 1992.

Hicks, David. *Globalizing Missions*. Miami: Unilit, 1994.

Hodge, J. Z. *Salute to India*. London: S.C.M. Press 1944.

Holcomb, Helen H. *Men of Might in India Missions: 1706–1899*. New York: Fleming H. Revel Company, 1901.

Houghton, Graham. *The Impoverishment of Dependency*. Madras: C.L.S., 1983.

Jayaprakash, L. Joshi. *Evaluation of Indigenous Missions of India*. Madras: Church Growth Research Centre, 1987.

Johnstone, Patrick. *Operation World*. Carlisle: OM Books, 1993.

Jones, John P. *India's Problem Krishna or Christ*. New York: Fleming H. Revell, 1903.

Jones, E. Stanley. *The Christ of the Indian Road*. Lucknow: Lucknow Publishing House, 1964.

Keyes, Lawrence E. "The New Age of Cooperation." In *Together in Missions*, edited by Theodore Williams. Bangalore: WEF, 1983.

Kurien, C. T. *Mission and Proclamation*. Madras: CLS, 1981.

Koola, Paul J. *Population and Manipulation*. Bangalore: Asian Trading Corp., 1979.

Mangalwadi, Ruth and Vishal Mangalwadi. *William Carey—A Tribute by an Indian Woman*. New Delhi: Nivedit Books, 1993.

Manikam, Rajaiah B. *Christianity and the Asian Revolution*. Madras: CLS, 1955.

Mathew, C. V. *Neo-Hinduism: A Missionary Religion*. Madras: CGRC, 1987.

Mathews, James K. "The Mission to Southern Asia." In *The Christian Mission Today*, edited by. James A. Engle and Dorcas Hall. New York: Abingdon Press, 1960.

Mason, Caroline Atwater. *Wonders of Missions*. London: Hodder & Stoughton, 1922.

Massey, Ashish. "Challenges to Mission in North India." In *Proclaiming Christ*, edited by Sam Lazarus. Madras: CGAI, 1992

McGavran, Donald. "New Mission." In *Contemporary Theology of Missions,* edited by Arthur Glasser and Donald McGavran. Grand Rapids: Baker Book House, 1983.

Misra, B. B. *The Indian Middle Classes: Their Growth in Modern Times*. London: Oxford University Press, 1983.

Neill, Stephen. *Builders of the Indian Church*. Westminster, London: Livingstone Press, 1934.

———. *Colonialism and Christian Missions*. London: McGraw Hill Book Company, 1966.

———. *The Christian Church in India and Pakistan*. Michigan: Eerdmans Publishing Company, 1970.

Newbigin, Lesslie. *The Good Shepherd*. Madras: CLS, 1974.

Paul, Rajaiah D. *The Cross Over India*. London: SCM Press LTD, 1952.

Parshall, Phil. "God's Communicator in the 80's," in *World Christian Movement,* edited by Ralph Winter, Steve Hawthorne, et. al. 473–481. Pasadena, CA: William Carey Library, 1988.

Pickett, J. Waskom. *Christ's Way to India's Heart*. Lucknow: LKO Pub House, 1938.

———. *My Twentieth Century Odyssey*. Bombay: Gospel Literature Service, 1980.

Ratnakumar, J. J. and Krupa Sunder Raj, eds. *Mission and Vision, Who and What?* Bangalore: MUT Publishers, 1996.

Richard, H. L. *Christ-Bhakti: Narayan Vaman Tilak and Christian Work among Hindus*. Delhi: ISPCK, 1991.

Shourie, Arun. *Missionaries in India*. New Delhi: ASA Publications, 1994.

Singh, Khuswant. *India: An Introduction*. New Delhi: Vision Books, 1992.

Srinivasagam, Theodore. "The Need for Effective Cross-Cultural Evangelism." In *Mission Mandate*, 1992.

Stock, Frederick and Margaret. *People Movements in the Punjab*. Bombay: Gospel Literature Service, 1978.

Sunder Raj, Ebenezer. *The Confusion Called Conversion*. New Delhi: TRACI, 1986.

Taylor, Richard. *The Contribution of Stanley Jones*. Madras: CLS, 1973.

Theerthan, Swami John D. *Choice Before India: Communism-Catastrophe; Sarvodya-Christ*. Trichur: Mission to Hindus, [n.d.].

Thomas, Juliet. "Role of Women in Christian Ministry." In *Proclaiming Christ*, edited by Sam Lazarus. Madras: CGAI, 1992.

Thompson, E. W. *The Call of India*. London: Wesleyan Methodist Missionary Society, 1912.

Thorpe, John K. "'Other Sheep' of the Tamil Fold." *The Centenary Story of the Strict Baptist Mission 1861–1960*, London: SBM Publications, 1961.

Tucker, Ruth. "William Carey Father of Modern Missions." In *Great Leader of the Christian Church*, edited by John Woodbridge. Chicago: Moody Press, 1988.

Waack, Otto. *Church and Mission in India*. Delhi: ISPCK, 1997.

Webster, John C.B. "Assumptions about Indian Woman Underlying Protestant Policies, 1947–1982." In *The Church and the Women in the Third World*, edited by John C. B. and Ellen Webster. Philadelphia: Westminster Press, 1984.

Wilder, Harriet. *A Century in the Madura Mission-South India 1834–1934*. New York: Vintage Press, 1961.

Winslow, J. C. and Narayan Vaman Tilak. *Pune: Word of Life Publications*, 1996 [third edition].

Winter, Ralph D. "The Two Structures of God's Redemptive Mission." In *Crucial Dimensions in World Evangelization*, edited by Arthur Glasser, Paul Heibert et al. Pasadena, CA: William Carey Library, 1977.

Winter, Roberta. "The Kingdom Strikes Back." In *Inheriting God's Perspective*, edited by Ralph Pluddemann. Bangalore: Mission Frontiers, 1996.

About Dr. K. Rajendran

K. Rajendran, originally from South India, has been with Operation Mobilization for over twenty-five years as a pioneer and a missionary trainer. In 1998, he finished his doctoral studies at South Asian Institute of Advance Studies (SAIACS) in Bangalore. He has worked with India Missions Association (IMA) since 1997 and serves as general secretary. He is also chairman of the World Evangelical Alliance Missions Commission (WEA-MC) and vice-chair of the Great Commission Round Table (GCR). He lives in Hyderabad with his wife Pramila.

4

Mission History of Indochina

CHANSAMONE SAIYASAK, DMIN, PHD

Introduction

Indochina, or the Indochinese Peninsula, is a region in Southeast Asia that lies east of India and south of China. In the strictest sense, Indochina comprises the territory of only the former French Indochina: Cambodia, Vietnam, and Laos. In the wider sense, it also includes Thailand and Burma. In this paper, the author will use the wider sense to describe the history of Christian mission.

Western Christian missions in the form of Catholicism formally reached the Indochinese Peninsula in the sixteenth century, beginning in Myanmar (1554), Cambodia (1555), Thailand (1567), Vietnam (1624), and Laos (1642). With trade, conquest, and migration, Christianity spread in connection with Western colonial powers. Western Protestant missions entered Indochina only after the turn of the twentieth century, starting in Myanmar (1807), Thailand (1828), Laos (1872), Vietnam (1911), and Cambodia (1922).

Beginning in the second half of the twentieth century, after these Indochinese nations had gained independence (excepting Thailand, which was not colonized), the national churches transitioned from Western control to a new Asian identity. Only after national churches came under indigenous leadership did they begin discovering their own mission and developing their own mission history. Now at the beginning of the twenty-first century, the Asian national church in Indochina has manifested its growing awareness of its missionary responsibility as well as the ongoing impact on its societies and cultures.

The missionary activities of the Indochinese national church (or churches) within its own national borders can be traced back to the start of foreign missions in the region. Its history of cross-cultural mission began with the work of missionaries sent by mission societies. After foreign missionaries gained converts, they normally formed congregations, providing an environment of new life. Afterwards, the missionaries would also serve as either organizers or catalysts in the formation of the national church, as well as influencers of its cross-cultural mission policies. Initially, the national converts would evangelize their own people groups who shared the same customs and culture. Subsequently, some percentage of national believers or churches would reach out cross-culturally to those of similar or near culture. The history of missions of the national church (or churches) beyond its national borders, however, developed as an outcome of the political state of affairs of the Indochina region, except for Thailand, whose mission activities outside the country developed primarily from educational and economic undertaking.

Burma (Myanmar)

A Brief Church History

Burma (Myanmar) gained its independence from the British in 1948. Protestant Christianity traced its beginning to Adoniram Judson of the American Baptists who arrived in 1813. The greatest conversion growth was found among the hill tribes. Six years after his first arrival in Burma, Judson finally baptized his first convert (from a tribal group) in 1819.

In 1865, the Burma Baptist Convention, the first national church body, was organized to bring together and coordinate all regional and linguistic groups of Baptist churches in Myanmar. The Karen Baptist Convention, Kachin Baptist Convention, and Chin Baptist Convention made up the main constituency of the Burma Baptist Convention.

Cross-cultural Missions of the Burmese Churches within National Borders

The mission of the churches in Burma within national borders is traceable to the work of early pioneer Baptist missionaries led by Judson who found initial mission successes among the tribal groups. One important outcome of the first Anglo-Burmese war starting in 1824 was the ceding of Burmese provinces to the British, which provided the opportunity for Christian missions to expand into unreached parts of the country.

The work of the American Baptists forms the largest proportion of Christianity in Burma. The first group to experience a people movement to Christ was the Karen. Judson's initial convert, Ko Tha Byu, a Karen, played an important role in leading the movement of the Karen to Christ and establishing the Karen national church. He became known as the first "apostle to the Karen."

By 1850, the Baptist churches had claimed approximately ten thousand converts. The Baptists' positive conversion result could be attributed to the efforts of the 131 Karen evangelists and missionaries spreading the gospel in the jungles of Burma. In 1853, the Baptists convened the first Missionary Convention in Rangoon, capital of Myanmar, where mission policy was discussed for the next half century. The emphasis was placed on doing evangelism by training ethnic pastors for every church, and ethnic evangelists and missionaries to reach out to non-Christian villages.

The Karen evangelists and missionaries also reached out cross-culturally to other Karen tribes and minority groups. The response to the gospel among ethnic minorities, with the exception of the Shans, Mons, and Rakhines, has been extremely favorable; however, the response from the Burman people has always been minimal. Today, Karen Christians in Burma account for 55 percent of the total Karen population of 1.29 million, and the Karen Baptist Churches constitute the second largest Baptist group in Burma, second to the Chin.

The Kachin was the second ethnic group who was most receptive to the gospel. The work among the Kachin began in 1877 when Baptist missionaries ventured into the Bhamaw region of Burma. Yet, it was not until 1878 that mission work among the Kachin was started. Nevertheless, the vision of a Kachin church became a reality only when the first seven Kachin converts were baptized in 1882. Seven years later, in 1890, the Kachin Baptist churches organized into the Kachin Baptist Convention.

The Kachin church had a strong cross-cultural ministry among other tribes and races and sent Kachin missionaries to evangelize and plant churches among the Rakhine people, Wa people, Shan, Palaung, Kadu, Ganan people, Gaw-ra-hka people, Kayah people, and Kachin people in China. The work of Kachin evangelists and missionaries has resulted in an estimated 36 percent Christians among 1.2 million Kachin.

The Chin, being the third group of people who responded favorably to the gospel, are found mainly in the western part of Burma in the Chin State. The gospel reached the Chin people in the late nineteenth century when two Karen missionaries, Thra Shwe Lin and Thra Bo Gale, working under the auspices of the American Baptists, labored among the Kachin for nine months. Afterwards, three more Karen missionaries, namely Thra Swa Pe, Thra Ne Hta, and Thra Ka Te, replaced them for at least four years.

In 1882, the first seven Chins turned to Christ and received baptism, thus giving birth to the first Chin church. Subsequently, the Chin believers took on the responsibility of expanding the mission work among their own people, resulting in the eventual formation of the Chin Baptist Convention in 1953. The Baptists finally were kicked out of the country by Ne Win's regime in the early 1960s, leaving the work of missions among the Chin in the hands of the Chin national church. Because of the strong missionary call of the Chin to reach their own people, Chin men and women, young and old, spent a part of their life going to the mission field, where the harvest was ready. Today, 90 percent of 1.5 million Chin are Christians.

Missions of the Burmese Churches beyond National Borders

The mission of the Burmese churches beyond national borders can be seen in its cross-cultural missionary work among the Karen Christians in Thailand and in other countries. Over the past two hundred years, the Karen have migrated from Burma eastward into Thailand because of political conflicts with the Burmans.

The Karen is the largest tribal group in Thailand, with 1.1 million Karen living in 2,132 villages in North Thailand and almost two million in other countries. Over the past 200 years, they have migrated from Burma eastward into Thailand because of political conflicts with the Burmans. Due largely to the witness of Karen Christians from Burma, the Karen immigrants in Thailand have come to the Christian faith in great number. Now the Karen churches in Thailand have formed the Karen Baptist Convention, and they are spreading the gospel and planting churches in unreached Karen villages in north Thailand.

Not only is the Burmese Karen's missionary spirit influencing the Karen in Thailand to turn to the Christian faith, but also the Karen diaspora in the United States are continuing the mission work among Karen refugees. Because of the political trouble facing the Karen in eastern Burma, where the Karen are housed in refugee camps along the Thai-Burma border, the United States government granted special waivers to thousands of Karen refugees and resettled them in several cities in the United States. There, the Christian Karen are now reaching other non-Christian Karen refugees, as well as stimulating the growth of American churches that have dwindled in membership.

The same thing can be said of the Kachin and the Chin. Today, the Kachin Christians who resettled in northern California for political reasons are actively involved in the ministries in various Burmese churches. San Francisco Karen Baptist Fellowship, for example, was started because of the need and desire to worship God in the Kachin language, to have genuine fellowship with the Bay Area Kachin, and to network with Kachin in Burma and other countries. As for the Chin, also because of the current political situation in Burma, thousands of Chin are scattered in Europe, the United States, and Southeast Asia. In all the places they resettled, they have taken the Christian faith with them and are attempting to spread to others. Hundreds of Chin are now serving as evangelists and missionaries and pastors beyond the national borders of Burma.

Cambodia (Kampuchea)

A Brief Church History

Cambodia (now Kampuchea) received independence from the French in 1953. Protestant Christian and Missionary Alliance (C&MA) entered Cambodia in 1922, but their work ended in 1965 when anti-American sentiments under Prince Sihanouk's control caused the withdrawal of all missionaries, leaving behind less than a thousand Christians in the national church, the Cambodian Evangelical Church. Church leaders were jailed, and the Cambodian church went through some hardship.

In 1970, foreign missionaries returned during the beginning of the war with the Khmer Rouge, and the church rapidly increased. From three churches in Phnom Penh when the war broke out, there were thirty churches by 1975, when the Khmer Rouge, led by Pol Pot, seized power. All missionaries were again driven out of the country, and an estimated 2.5 million Cambodians were executed or starved. Brutal persecution led to 90 percent of Christians and church leaders being martyred or escaping to Thailand.[203] Only ten thousand Christians and fourteen Cambodian church leaders stayed behind in Cambodia. Thousands escaped to refugee camps in Thailand and converted to the Protestant faith. Almost all of these refugees took up residence primarily in the United States, France, Australia, and New Zealand.[204]

In 1979, the Vietnamese invaded and occupied Cambodia, after which only one thousand Christians and three Cambodian church leaders remained in the country, meeting for worship in secret because of persecution. By 1990, Cambodia's evangelical population had dwindled to no more than six hundred believers, the Vietnamese ceded control to the Cambodians, and a free election was held in 1993.[205]

In 1991, mission organizations reentered Cambodia and reestablished their work. In the aftermath of the war and oppression, the Cambodians were open to the gospel; however, the infant Cambodian church lacked biblical training, and their leaders were young and inexperienced. From 1996 onwards, Protestant Christianity was reported to have doubled in size every two years. By 1999, the number of Protestant believers had risen from six hundred (in 1990) to more than sixty thou-

---

203 Frankcois Ponchaud and Jean Clavaud, "Cambodia," in *A Dictionary of Asian Christianity*, ed. Scott W. Sunquist (Grand Rapids, MI: Eerdmans, 2001), 111.

204 Brian M. Maher, "Cambodian Church History," July 2007. http://www.cambodianchristian.com/printer_friendly_folder/church_histor_printer_friendly.htm.

205 Peter C. Phan and Violet James, "Vietnam," in *A Dictionary of Asian Christianity*, ed. Scott W. Sunquist (Grand Rapids, MI: Eerdmans, 2001), 878.

sand. The greatest growth was among the Baptists with ten thousand members in two hundred churches, followed by an indigenous Campus Crusade denomination, then the Christian and Missionary Alliance. In 2004, the Evangelical Fellowship of Cambodia, a member of World Evangelical Fellowship, estimated as high as 200,000 Christians in more than two thousand churches in Cambodia.

Cross-cultural Missions of the Cambodian Churches within National Borders

The history of cross-cultural mission of the Cambodian churches can be traced back to the beginning of the C&MA in 1928 when eight Cambodian Christians were working under its auspice as both evangelists (within one's own culture and people) and missionaries (cross-culturally with another ethnic group). These Cambodian evangelists and missionaries labored among the ethnic Khmer, as well as Cham of central Cambodia who were traditional Muslims. This resulted in Christian conversion in both of these groups. In addition, the Cambodian missionaries of the Cambodian Evangelical Church were reaching the Vietnamese, Jarai, Phnong, and several other minority groups, and churches were established among them.[206]

The Cambodian expatriates returning from other countries were also reaching out cross-culturally to minority groups in Cambodia's northwest and planting churches among them. An example of Cambodian expatriates is the Kampuchea for Christ, which began mission work in Cambodia in 2005. The Evangelical Fellowship of Cambodia's vision is to see a church in every village by the year 2020.

---

206 C&MA Mission, The C&MA—Cambodia. http://www.cmalliance.org/printView.jsp.

Missions of the Cambodian Churches beyond National Borders

Cambodian (Khmer) Christians now live in many parts of the world because of the atrocities of the Khmer Rouge regime, when thousands of Cambodians fled to other countries where they formed their own churches or joined existing churches. Cambodian churches now exist throughout the United States, Canada, Australia, France, New Zealand, and Japan.

In the United States' New England area, fifteen Cambodian churches have been started. The Living Fields Ministry and Cambodian New Life Ministries (CNLM) have been organized to evangelize the non-Christian Cambodian refugees in New England, and to conduct mission work back in Cambodia. Both the Living Fields Ministry and CNLM are involved in missions in Cambodia, including starting churches, Bible and leadership training, developing training curricula, and supporting Cambodian evangelists and missionaries. Also, the Living Fields Ministry mobilizes expatriate Cambodians to return to Cambodia to spread the gospel to the ethnic Khmer as well as other ethnic groups.[207]

An excellent example of a Cambodian church ministering to its own people and cross-culturally to other ethnic groups is the Cambodian Christian Reformed Church (CCRFC) in Salt Lake City, Utah. This church was planted in 1987 because of the First Christian Reformed Church's outreach to Cambodian refugees. Now, the CCRFC is not only reaching Cambodians, but also is working with other ethnic groups and has transformed itself into a multiethnic church.[208]

Finally, Cambodian churches ministering from the United States to the different ethnic groups in Cambodia can be no bet-

---

207 Emmanuel Gospel Center (Cambodian Ministries: Living Fields, 2009). http://www.egc.org/programs/intercultural_ministries/Cambodian_ministries.html.

208 Cambodian Christian Reformed Church, "Who We Are" (Cambodian Christian Reformed Church), 2008, http://www.cambodiancrc.org/present.

ter illustrated than by the work of Kampuchea for Christ (KfC) founded in 1995 by Pastor Setan Lee. Its first ministry back in Cambodia was the establishment of the Ministry Training Center for equipping evangelists, church planters, and pastors to reach out to all ethnic groups within Cambodia. Within two years after its initiation, KfC had trained thirty-eight Cambodian evangelists or missionaries who went out and successfully planted forty-eight churches among different ethnic groups throughout Cambodia.[209]

Thailand

A Brief Church History

Thailand (formerly Siam) is the only country in Indochina that was never colonized. Despite extensive efforts, Christianity was unsuccessful in penetrating Thailand. Christians account for 0.98 percent of the population (0.52 percent Protestants and 0.46 percent Catholics).

The Protestants first entered Thailand in 1828; however, permanent Protestant work did not begin until the later arrival of American Baptists and American Presbyterians. Early converts were among the Chinese and other ethnic minorities. Only thirty years later, after the Protestants' arrival in Thailand, did it succeed in gaining its first Thai convert (1859).

The Church of Christ in Thailand (CCT) became organized in 1934. The rapid increase in the number of missionary agencies, not affiliated with the CCT, entering Thailand after 1945, led to the formation of the Evangelical Fellowship of Thailand (EFT) in 1969. In 1978 and onwards, the Thai churches expe-

209 Setan A. Lee, Kampuchea for Reaching a Hurting Country for Christ Newsletter. September. http://www.intercedenow.ca/news.php?ID=61.

rienced rapid growth, following the arrival of Pentecostal and charismatic movements.

In 1988, all three main Protestant denominations, namely the CCT, EFT, and Thailand Baptist Churches Association, united to form an umbrella organization, Thailand Protestant Churches Coordinating Committee, for collaborating Protestant work. Its objective is to establish a church in every district throughout Thailand by 2010.

Cross-cultural Missions beyond National Borders

The initiative to work among the ethnic northern Thai (Lao) came from Bradley, who was working among the Siamese (Thai) in Bangkok. After the board rejected his request to start work among the ethnic northern Thai, Bradley convinced Daniel McGilvary of the American Presbyterians to begin the Laos Mission in northern Thailand.

The history of the church in northern Thailand began in 1869 when the first believer, Nan Inta, an ethnic northern Thai (Lao) received baptism. Subsequently, six other men of position and influence converted to Christianity. In just a little over two years later, the Laos Mission in Chiang Mai accomplished far more than the Siam Mission in Bangkok. However, soon after, the ruler of northern Thailand, Kawilorot, moved against the young ethnic northern church and killed some of its best leaders.

Nevertheless, the church in the North subsequently revived (after 1875). By 1880, the church in the North had eighty-three baptized members. From the main church in Chiang Mai, it planted three other churches: Bethlehem Church, Lampang Church, and Mae Dok Daeng Church. However, it was not until 1885 that the northern Thai church experienced its first cross-cultural mission by planting its first ethnic Karen church at Long Koom village, just south of Chiang Mai. Nevertheless, the northern Thai church still did not have a missions program as it was still in its young stage. The work among ethnic Karen remained small until after 1914.

The cross-cultural missions program of the Thai church did not begin until the late 1890s and early 1900s because of its expansionist doctrine. In 1886, through the leadership of McGilvary, an American Presbyterian missionary, the northern Thai church made contact with an Akha, a northern tribal group. By 1892, it had converted and baptized thirteen Lahu. By 1899, a strong Christian Lahu community and church in Chiang Rai resulted from the northern Thai church's cross-cultural mission effort. However, it should be noted that the initiation of the northern Thai church to reach out cross-culturally came through contacts of its Thai members, but the missionaries were the ones who exercised the authority to incorporate the believers into a church. The mission of the northern Thai church also extended the Lahu in Laos in 1904. The work among other tribal groups such as the Yao tribal group in the Chiang Rai area resulted in very few results due to the lack of personnel and funds.

After 1914, seven Karen Christians came to study with the Christians in a church in the Lamphun province. A year later, six young Karens spent half a year with the northern Thai church of Wang Mun. Later, one whole village of Karens was baptized, and northern Thai evangelists were sent to work with them and to evangelize other Karen villages. While starting cross-cultural church planting among the Karens in north Thailand, the northern Thai churches under American Presbyterians found three Karen Baptist churches started by American Baptists in Lampang, one of the northern provinces of Thailand. Surprisingly, these churches demonstrated active Christian life without any outside support, while the northern Thai churches started by the American Presbyterians were dependent upon support from the missionaries.

Although the northern Thai church's earliest reported work of cross-cultural ministry among the Chinese began in Lampang in 1893, significant mission work with the Chinese did not start until 1913, when seven young Chinese men were converted in the church in Lampang. In the following year, the church reported forty-three Chinese members. While the northern Thai church under the Presbyterian's Lao Mission continued the expansionist doctrine in which the church was viewed as an agency for mission, the central Thai church under the Siam Mission in Bangkok also reached out cross-culturally to various ethnic groups. In 1899, the central Thai church expanded its cross-cultural work among the Muslims of Nakon Srithamarat, a southern province of Thailand. Ten years later, in 1910, it spread further to Trang province to begin mission work among the Malays.

Church Missions beyond National Borders

The northern Thai church's cross-border mission work among the Khmu, a northern tribal group, began after a few years following its work with the Lahu. The cross-border mission work that involved the northern Thai church came from the mission trips of American Baptist missionary, Daniel McGilvary, into northern Laos (Luang Prabang) and resulted in the conversion of the Khmu tribe as well as the establishment of the Khmu church. During one of the trips, ten villages became interested in Christianity, and in one of those villages, a chieftain was converted, while in others, chieftains were near conversion.

Subsequently, the ruler of Luang Prabang complained to the French, since Laos was a French protectorate, and McGilvary was forced to cease his missionary work among the Khmu of northern Laos. To make the Khmu into a major mission project for the northern Thai churches, local Thai churches became involved. Northern Thai churches sent missionaries as well as funds into northern Laos to nurture the growth and expansion of the Khmu work. Later, after 1929, the Khmu church in northern Laos was handed over to the C&MA after 1929.

Through the Baptist missionaries, the northern Thai church began mission work in the Kengtung area in Burma in 1904. In 1913, it opened mission work in Chiang Rung, Yunnan province, China, to start work among the Thai Lu, ethnic cousins of the northern Thai. The northern Thai church provided financial assistance for the cross-border mission work in Chiang Rung. In addition, three northern Thai churches sent nine northern Thai missionaries for varying periods to establish the work in Chiang Rung. Through its missionary leadership, the northern Thai church was positioning itself as a missionary church.

Apart from the cross-cultural and cross-border mission work in conjunction with the Baptist missionaries who founded the CCT, the CCT as a corporate body in itself has done very little to promote missions. It was not until 1999 that the CCT created a committee for missions in a neighboring country (Thai-Lao). Yet, throughout the history of the national church, individual Thai churches and Thai Christian groups have taken responsibility upon themselves for missions.

During 1956 through 1958, the Thai Maranatha Church sent two Thai missionaries into Laos for two years. In 1957, Mitrichit Chinese Baptist Church (MCBC) in central Thailand (Bangkok) commissioned its missionaries to spread the gospel among the ethnic Chinese (Haw) in northern Thailand (Chiang Mai). Afterwards, MCBC also sent missionaries to Burma. From 1963 to 1964, students from a seminary in Chiang Mai started Thailand Overseas Missionary Society and sent their first three missionaries to spread the gospel in Sarawak, Malaysia.

In 1977, alumni of Payao Bible College in northern Thailand founded Thai Church Development, an organization with the purpose of doing cross-cultural ministry among various ethnic groups. In 1978, Emmanuel Church sent its own missionaries to work with Cambodian immigrants along the Thai-Cambodian borders in eastern Thailand. In 1988, Mitrichit Charoen Krung Church sent Suree Anderson as a missionary with Wycliffe Bible Translators to Indonesia and New Vision Church sent Pastor Pongsak Angsatarathon to be a missionary in China and another missionary in Russia. In 1994, MCBC commissioned Pastor Vicha and Susan Chanwittakoun as missionaries in Hong Kong in cooperation with the Chinese churches in Hong Kong.

In addition to the Thai churches being involved in missions, Thai Christian individuals also have taken on responsibility to spread the gospel across the globe as they go overseas for reasons of education or business. While there, they become involved in spreading the gospel and planting churches among the Thais or other ethnic groups that are kin to the Thais. Some become involved in missions overseas with existing organizations and churches to reach out cross-culturally to the Thais in the area.

Examples of individual involvement in missions are Pastor Supot and Dr. Savang Rojratanakiat Lin. Pastor Supot migrated from Thailand to the US, began outreach to the thirty-thousand Thai diaspora in Washington, D.C. and planted a church among them.[210] Savang Rojratanakiat Lin went to study in the US and started Thai/Lao Baptist Church in the San Francisco area after God called him into the ministry. Most members of his church come from Thailand and Laos as well as dozens of other ethnic minorities, including the Chinese.

Laos

A Brief Church History

In 1950, when a C&MA missionary, Ted Andrianoff, converted a Hmong shaman, Mua Yia, a movement of the Hmong tribe to

210 OMF, Outreach to Thai Diaspora in Washington, D.C. May 6, 2008, http://www.omf.org/omf/thailand/god_at_work/stories_from_thailand/outreach_to_thai_diaspora_in_washington_d_c.

Christ then began. Afterwards, through the ministry of Mua Yia (Hmong) and Nai Khen (Khmu), Laos' first recorded missionaries, over one thousand Hmong people turned to Christ. Three years later (1953), the mission work among the Hmong resulted in five thousand converts in northern Laos and, thus, a strong Hmong church was organized.

The Lao church affiliated with the Swiss Brethren sent a Lao missionary, Saly Kounthapanya, to work in northern Laos under the auspice of the C&MA to evangelize different ethnic groups.[211] The church, which developed in Luang Prabang, also included lowland Lao, in addition to the Khmu and Hmong. The C&MA and Swiss Brethren were the only two mission societies working with the three ethnic churches.

While foreign missionaries labored closely with the national church, always the initiative to reach ethnic minorities came from missionaries rather than the national church. The national church—particularly the LEC—would incorporate churches from the ethnic minorities into the national church. After the change of government, in the late 1980s and early 1990s Christian development organizations, such as World Concern, Food for the Hungry, and CAMA Services, engaged in missions among the unreached minority groups of Laos. As a result, more churches have been started among them. David Andrianoff, a recognized researcher of Lao Christianity, explains in an email to the author:

> While the national church takes credit for new churches among previously unreached ethnic groups, it has not established a program to reach unreached ethnic minorities. The national church of Laos has a strong program of outreach and

211 Winburn T. Thomas and Rajah B. Manikam, "The Church in Indochina," in *The Church in Southeast Asia* (New York: Friendship Press, 1956), 125.

> evangelism, but it has not yet established its own mission program.[212]

The LEC as a corporate entity does not have a strong mission initiative. Lao churches, Lao organizations, or individual leaders, however, have taken on the responsibility to reach out cross-culturally to other tribal groups within their networks. A well-known organization working with the Lao is the Mekong Evangelical Mission (MEM). Originally, MEM registered in the US in the state of Tennessee in 1994 as Lao Foreign Outreach. Its purpose was to spread the gospel to Southeast Asian nations, with a particular emphasis on Thailand and Laos. Its founder, Chansamone Saiyasak, born to a Thai father and a Lao mother, resettled with his parents in Nashville, Tennessee, as Lao refugees. He was converted through an outreach of Lighthouse Baptist Church. Answering the Lord's call to spread the gospel back to his native countries as well as other countries of Southeast Asia, Saiyasak received his doctorates from the US as well as from Belgium. Saiyasak's ministry, headquartered in Northeast Thailand, reaches out to various parts of Thailand, Laos, and Burma. MEM is involved in church planting, Bible training, leadership development, education, relief work, radio, an orphanage, and advocacy for persecuted Christians.[213]

Working with the Lao evangelists and missionaries trained in the Mekong Bible Seminary in Northeast Thailand and its satellite training centers in Laos, MEM conducts ongoing missions among the minority groups in Laos. The most noticeable people among them who have experienced mass conversion are the Bru tribal groups, primarily located in Savannakhet province and part of Saravan province. Altogether, MEM is working

---

212 David Andrianoff, e-mail message to author, February 12, 2009.

213 Chansamone Saiyasak, "A Study of the Belief Systems and Decision Making of the Isan People of Northeast Thailand with a View Towards Making Use of These Insights in Christian Evangelism" (PhD diss., Evangelische Theologische Faculteit, Lueven, Belgium, 2007), 22.

crossculturally in planting churches among twenty-one ethnic groups in seven provinces in Laos.

Missions of the Lao Churches beyond National Borders

The mission of the Lao church in Laos beyond national borders started with the Lao church in diaspora. The Hmong in the United States have been most aggressive, sending missionaries to Thailand and China and short-term mission teams to Vietnam. The Lao in the US have also been involved in outreach in major US cities to other Lao and other Southeast Asian refugees. LSBF and LCC (1981), organized in the US, served the purpose of networking, fellowship, revival, and training, among the Lao churches in diaspora. Currently, Christians and churches within these two organizations are involved in supporting ministries of the local Lao churches and pastors as well as Lao evangelists and missionaries in Laos.

Initially, mission support from MEM, LSBF, and LCC was channeled through the LEC. Subsequently, however, individuals and churches in these two organizations work directly with Lao churches and individuals in Laos, thus causing some conflict with the leadership of LEC. Nevertheless, several Lao churches and Christians in the US are individually involved in supporting the work of local churches in Laos, as well as taking mission trips back to Laos. These organizations include MEM.

The primary strategy for both the Hmong and the Lao has been to reach Hmong and Lao in other countries. However, the Hmong now have one couple in Northeast Thailand reaching local Khmer. Hmong radio broadcast (from California) has been spectacularly successful. Because of radio broadcasting, currently there are more than 200,000 Hmong believers in northern Vietnam, whereas before the late 1980s there was not a single Hmong believer. The Hmong missionaries in Thailand have had considerable success adapting and developing training materials for developing church leaders.

Vietnam

A Brief Church History

Vietnam, a former French colony, achieved its independence in 1975. Protestants through the C&MA first entered Vietnam in 1911. Sixteen years later in 1927, they had gained four thousand members with the formation of the Evangelical Church of Vietnam (ECVN), a national church of Vietnam, and a Bible training center. Solely working in Vietnam, the C&MA enforced self-support policies from the onset of the work, leading the ECVN churches to self-support by the end of World War II.

In 1954, Christian refugees fleeing Communist North Vietnam were admitted into the ECVN in South Vietnam. While the C&MA and the ECVN, identifying and cooperating with the American-Vietnamese government of South Vietnam, created opportunities to expand their work, it would later result in negative repercussions.

As the war intensified, new evangelical groups started arriving in South Vietnam, and programs were implemented to respond to the people's social and physical needs. Even though the ECVN had focused only on the spiritual need, they also became involved in social and educational work. Amid the suffering, the Vietnam church nonetheless continued to flourish. One evangelical group in Vietnam reported 150,000 evangelical Christians in 1975. This number grew to an estimated 2.1 million by 2002.

In 1975, all missionaries and numerous Christians were forced to leave the country, leaving at least five hundred Vietnamese and tribal church leaders to face execution and reeducation camps. Ninety percent of the tribal churches and one hundred Vietnamese churches were closed down. Notwithstanding the suffering, the Vietnamese church experienced revival and rapid growth.

With the government today remaining practically in full control of all religious activities, persecution continues to be severe for unregistered and ethnic minority churches. Nevertheless, the growing trend of Christianity, particularly among tribal groups, is evident; and churches are vibrant and thriving, with 1.7 percent of the population being evangelical Christians.

Cross-cultural Missions of the Vietnamese Churches

WITHIN NATIONAL BORDERS

Soon after the C&MA entered central Vietnam (Danang) in 1911, they began mission work among the Kin (ethnic Vietnamese). By 1929 their work resulted in the establishment of a strong, self-supporting national church (ECVN).[214] Later, the mission work was turned to the tribal groups. Working with the ECVN, the C&MA began sending out Vietnamese missionaries to evangelize the mountainous tribal groups. By the 1930s, some of the fifty-four tribal groups in the mountains of the North and the mountains of the Central Highlands began to respond to the gospel brought by the Vietnamese missionaries.[215]

In 1942, the Vietnamese missionaries of the ECVN began to discuss the need for an autonomous missionary agency within the ECVN to handle cross-cultural missions among the tribal groups. The plan was put into action. However, although they called themselves a missionary "society," they functioned like a mission committee with the church structure of the ECVN. In 1970, under its revised constitution, the ECVN restructured its

---

214 Overseas Missionary Fellowship, Vietnam. http://www.omf.org/omf/buddhism/people_and_places/countries/vietnam.

215 James F. Lewis, "Christianity and Human Rights in Vietnam: The Case of the Ethnic Minorities (1975–2004)," paper presented at the Christianity and Human Rights Conference (Fourth Annual Lilly Fellows Program, Sanford University, 2004).

missionary operation as a minor committee under the direction of a general secretary of evangelism.[216]

By 1975, the Vietnamese church claimed up to 200,000 converts, one-third of whom were mountainous minorities, primarily located in the Central Highlands. The number continued to increase, even after foreign missionaries were not allowed to continue their work in the country. By 2000, the number of evangelical Christians in Vietnam grew to an estimated 1.2 million, about one-third of whom belonged to the government-registered ECVN of both North and South Vietnam.[217] The other two-thirds came from the evangelical Christians of (1) the house-church movements, (2) the Montagnards of the Central Highlands, and (3) the Hmong of Northern provinces. The mobilization of Vietnamese missionaries, who ministered cross-culturally, initially alongside the foreign missionaries, and, afterwards, totally under the national church, was foundational to achieving such a large number of converts in the ECVN, Montagnards, and Hmong.

Interestingly, all Vietnamese missionaries were financially supported by the C&MA, but setbacks were experienced due to the wars that forced foreign missionaries out of the country. Other difficulties faced by the Vietnamese missionaries working with the tribal groups stemmed from resentments because of the ethnic Vietnamese's prior oppression and mistreatment of the tribal groups.

Another fast-growing national church in Vietnam is the Grace Baptist Church of the Southern Baptists who entered Vietnam in 1950s, but left Vietnam in 1975. Under its present leader, Le Quoc Chanh, the Baptists have grown to five thousand members

---

216 Reginald E. Reimer, "The Protestant Movement in Vietnam: Church Growth in Peace and War Among the Ethnic Vietnamese," M.A. Thesis, Faculty of the School of World Mission and the Institute of Church Growth, Fuller Theological Seminary, 1972).

217 Jeff Taylor, "Yearning to Be Free in Vietnam," December 31, 2001, http://www.charismamag.com/index.php/covers/304-asia/1567-yearning-to-be-free-in-vietnam.

in ninety churches in a dozen cities and provinces across the country. The Baptist church, now recognized by the government, has fifteen Vietnamese missionaries working cross-culturally to reach different ethnic groups in Vietnam.[218]

Missions of the Vietnamese Churches beyond National Borders

The mission of the national church of Vietnam beyond its national borders resembles many other countries in Indochina, with the exception of Thailand. It is a mission born out of the Indochina's diaspora caused by political conflicts, wars, and persecution. Presently, Vietnamese diaspora are scattered in sixty-eight countries, with two million of them residing in Cambodia.[219] Almost one million Vietnamese refugees resettled in to the US, most of whom have called southern California, particularly Los Angeles and Orange County, their home. The Vietnamese diaspora have either started their own Vietnamese church or joined an existing church in the city of their settlement. These churches not only minister to ethnic Vietnamese Christians or Christians from other tribal groups from Vietnam, but they are also reaching out to other non-Christian Vietnamese refugees. In addition, they send support and are involved directly with outreach back in Vietnam and in other Vietnamese communities throughout the world.[220]

The Vietnamese Baptist Church (North Carolina) and Vietnamese Hope Baptist Church (Louisiana) are examples of Vietnamese diaspora reaching out to other Vietnamese in the US, reaching back to Vietnam with the gospel, and being involved in missions in other parts of the world. Hoa Duc Vo, pastor of Vietnamese Baptist Church (VBC), was sponsored by Southside Baptist Church in Greensboro, North Carolina. With the assis-

218 "Vietnam Church Gains Legal Status, Leads National Outreach," released by Baptist Press January 17, 2008, http://nuoctroi.com/?q=node/1449.

219 Vietnam Ministries, Inc., http://www.vpns.org/print.php?sid=21.

220 Operation World Detailed Information—Vietnam (2008) http://www.operationworld.org/country/viet/owtext.html.

tance of Southside Baptist, he reached out to the first nine families of Vietnamese refugees in Greensboro and started a Vietnamese church. Subsequently, other Vietnamese have moved into the community and VBC is there to welcome them to the Christian faith. In addition to spreading the gospel to Vietnamese in the US, VBC is making several mission trips every year, reaching back to Vietnam with revival meetings, training, and leadership and discipleship conferences.[221]

Vietnamese Hope Baptist Church (VHBC) in Louisiana was started with a missionary mindset. In its purpose statements, VHBC proposes to send and support missionaries and workers as well as to help medical teams doing outreach in Vietnam and Cambodia. Mission teams from VHBC travel to Vietnam and Cambodia to work every year to provide general healthcare, distribute medicines, teach, build water wells, and create the opportunities to spread the gospel to different ethnic groups in Vietnam. In addition, VHBC sends its mission teams to Mexico and started Harvest Campus Ministry at Louisiana State University.

Conclusions

The primary foreign missionary societies who founded the national churches in Indochina were the American Baptists, C&MA, and American Presbyterians. The mission histories of the national churches—Burmese, Thai, Cambodian, Lao, and Vietnamese—are deep-rooted in the mission work of these three societies. Much of the way the national churches carried out their mission work resembled the patterns of their predecessors.

Strategies and philosophies adopted by foreign missionaries in the implementation of their work still have tremendous

221 Dianna Cagle, "N.C. Pastor Returns to Vietnam to Evangelize His Homeland," Associated Baptist Press, February 16, 2007: Archives, 1. http://www.abpnews.com/index.php?option=com_content&task=view&id=1840&Itemid=120.

impact on the national churches' mission policies and programs, which later either hindered or furthered the mission of the national churches. Some of the strategies, however, arose from the national churches themselves as they began to discover their own mission and develop their own history, while realizing their missionary responsibility in their own context.

Receptivity

Many pioneer missionaries based many of their strategies on receptivity. Receptivity indicators drove the mission policies of the early missionary societies as well as the national churches that resulted from their work. All three missionary societies typically began their outreach among the dominant group or groups in their targeted countries or areas. Then they measured receptivity for further improvement or modification of the missionary outreach plan.

In Burma, when receptivity was not found among the Burmese Buddhist population, the American Baptists turned to the tribal groups in the British-ruled territory. Thus, one of the greatest movements of people to Christ started: first among the Karen, followed by Chin and Kachin. In Vietnam, the C&MA encountered low receptivity among the Kin (ethnic Vietnamese) so they turned to the mountainous tribal minorities, where great movements to Christ took place among the Montagnard and the Hmong people.

In Laos, the C&MA started out with the Buddhist Lowland Lao of Luang Prabang in northern Laos. However, when minimal progress was made among them, the C&MA turned to the Khmu and then the Hmong, where people movements were experienced. In Thailand, the American Presbyterians attempted work among the central Thai with very little success until they turned to the Lana people (northern Thai) in Chiang Mai and tribal groups in other northern provinces.

This strategy can turn a large number of people groups to Christ in a short period; however, it is not without some weaknesses. One weakness is that Christianity is viewed primary as a religion of the minorities, who are without rights and privileges and have very little role in the national life.

Subsidy System

Secondly, the systems of subsidy and self-support implemented by early missions still have an effect on the national churches. Early national missionary forces in Indochina were mostly tied to the support of the missions that started them, not the national churches. The national missionaries were paid and directed by the missions.

Later, after the national churches received leadership of their church bodies, church and individuals within national churches in these nations began to reach out cross-culturally. Tensions often arose between paid evangelists or national missionaries paid by the missions and pastors paid by local churches.

While the subsidy policy initially accelerated the spread of the gospel leading to the development of the national churches, the changeover from the subsidy system of national pastors, national evangelists, and national missionaries to a self-support system created negative effects on many national churches. Although the changeover has some advantages, it negatively affected the relationships between the national churches and foreign missions. The impact came mostly from the way the changeover was handled than any other factors.

A View of the Church as a Missionary Agency

In all countries in Indochina, foreign missionaries full of missionary vision became the primary organizers or founders of the national churches. The national churches, therefore, came to be viewed as agencies for expanding mission work into the unreached territories. In early missions, new converts of the national church were quickly employed by the missions in order to carry out expansionist philosophy. Churches were primarily viewed not as communities of believers but as agencies for expanding into new territories. This applied to the northern Thai church of the American Presbyterians as well as other national churches of the C&MA and American Baptists in their respective countries. Newly planted churches were neither given sufficient time to grow nor developed to be part of the community, and their personnel and material resources were pulled in all directions to achieve the expansionistic purposes, resulting in weak national churches. Nevertheless, more unreached territories have been reached with the gospel because of the expansionist ideology.

The Use of National Workers to Reach Their Own People Group

Finally, both foreign missionary societies and the national churches favored the strategy of utilizing nationals to reach their own people without crossing wide cultural and linguistic gaps. This approach allowed the gospel to disseminate rapidly among the nationals' own tribe or among tribes with cultural and linguistic similarities. Expatriate national Christians from various countries of Indochina who resettled into the US and developed countries are following this approach to reach back to their countries with the gospel.

According to David Andrianoff, the strengths for both the Hmong and the Lao are that they are reaching their own people of the same language and culture. However, these strengths can also be weaknesses. Andrianoff further stated, having been sent out from the US, many of the national expatriate missionaries go assuming they know their own culture; but only after arriving, do they begin to experience how much the US culture affects their perspective. They often find the cultural adjustment much more difficult than they had anticipated. However, the success outweighs the disadvantages, especially when considering the success of the Hmong radio broadcast (from California), resulting in more than 200,000 Hmong believers in northern Vietnam, whereas prior to the late 1980s there was not a single Hmong believer.[222]

Bibliography

Albrecht, Mark. WEF Religious Liberty Conference, October 7, 1999. http://www.worldevangelical.org/noframes/2rlcintr.htm (accessed December 1, 2009).

Andaya, Barbara Watson. "Religious Developments in Southeast Asia, c. 1500–1800." In *The Cambridge History of Southeast Asia*. Volume One, From Early Times to c. 1800, edited by Nicholas Tarling, 508–71. Cambridge: Cambridge University Press, 1992.

C&MA Mission. *The C&MA—Cambodia*. http://www.cmalliance.org/printView.jsp (accessed March 1, 2009).

Cagle, Dianna. "N.C. Pastor Returns to Vietnam to Evangelize His Homeland." Associated Baptist Press February 16, 2007: Archives. http://www.abpnews.com/index.php?option=com_content&task=view&id=1840&Itemid=120 (accessed March 1, 2009).

Cambodian Christian Reformed Church. "Who We Are (Cambodian Christian Reformed Church)." http://www.cambodiancrc.org/present (accessed March 3, 2008).

Chain, Tun Aung. "Myanmar." In *A Dictionary of Asian Christianity*, edited by Scott W. Sunquist, 574-57. Grand Rapids, Michigan: Eerdmans, 2001.

Compass Direct. "Authorities Destroy "Church" in Vietnam." *Christianity Today*, July 27, 2000. http://www.christianitytoday.com/ct/2000/julyweb-only/44.0c.html (accessed March 1, 2009).

Emmanuel Gospel Center. *Cambodian Ministries: Living Fields*. 2009. http://www.egc.org/programs/intercultural_ministries/Cambodian_ministries.html (accessed February 23, 2009).

Johnstone, Patrick J. and Jason Mandryk. "Operation World—Detailed Information—Thailand." 2005. http://www.operationworld.org/country/thai/owtext.html (accessed September 30, 2008).

222 David Andrianoff, "Lao Mission History," e-mail message to the author, February 12, 2009.

———. "Operation World—Detailed Information—Vietnam." http://www.operationworld.org/country/viet/owtext.html (accessed February 20, 2009).

———. "Operation World—Kingdom of Cambodia." http://www.operationworld.org/country/camb/owtext.html (accessed September 30, 2008).

Kham, Cin Do. "The Untold Story: The Impact of Revival Among the Chin People in Myanmar (Burma)." *Journal of Asian Mission* 1, No. 2 (1999): 205–22.

Lee, Setan A. *Kampuchea for Reaching a Hurting Country For Christ Newsletter.* September. http://www.intercedenow.ca/news.php?ID=61 (accessed January 3, 2009).

Lewis, James F. "Christianity and Human Rights in Vietnam: The Case of the Ethnic Minorities (1975–2004)." Paper presented at the Christianity and Human Rights Conference. Fourth Annual Lilly Fellows Program, Sanford University, 2004.

Lin, Savang Rojratanakiat. "Thai Lao Baptist Church—Our Pastor." http://www.thai-laobaptistchurch.com/about/pastor/myexp.html (accessed March 1, 2009).

Maher, Brian M. "Cambodian Church History." http://www.cambodianchristian.com/church_history.htm (accessed February 21, 2009).

OMF. *Outreach to Thai Diaspora in Washington, D.C.* May 6, 2008. http://www.omf.org/omf/thailand/god_at_work/stories_from_thailand/outreach_to_thai_diaspora_in_washington_d_c (accessed March 1, 2009).

———. "Vietnam." http://www.omf.org/omf/buddhism/people_and_places/countries/vietnam (accessed January 2, 2009).

Phan, Peter C., and Violet James. "Vietnam." In *A Dictionary of Asian Christianity*, edited by Scott W. Sunquist, 876–80. Grand Rapids, MI: Eerdmans, 2001.

Ponchaud, Francois, and Jean Clavaud. "Cambodia." In *A Dictionary of Asian Christianity*, edited by Scott W. Sunquist, 110–13. Grand Rapids, MI: Eerdmans, 2001.

Pongudom, Prasit, and Herbert R. Swanson. "Thailand." In *A Dictionary of Asian Christianity*, edited by Scott W. Sunquist, 831–34. Grand Rapids, MI: Eerdmans, 2001.

Reilly, Sarah. "Missions, the Message, and the Means." PRISM (2008).

Reimer, Reginald E. "The Protestant Movement in Vietnam: Church Growth in Peace and War Among the Ethnic Vietnamese." Master's thesis, Fuller Theological Seminary, Pasadena, California, 1972.

Saiyasak, Chansamone. "A Study of the Belief Systems and Decision Making of the Isan People of Northeast Thailand with a View Towards Making Use of These Insights in Christian Evangelism." Doctoral dissertation, Evangelische Theologische Faculteit, Lueven, Belgium, 2007.

Thomas, Winburn T., and Rajah B. Manikam. "The Church in Indochina." In *The Church in Southeast Asia*, 120–26. New York, NY: Friendship Press, 1956.

Vietnam Ministries, Inc. http://www.vpns.org/print.php?sid=21 (accessed January 2, 2009).

"Vietnam Church Gains Legal Status, Leads National Outreach." Released by Baptist Press January 17, 2008. http://nuoctroi.com/?q=node/1449 (accessed March 1, 2009).

About Dr. Chansamone Saiyasak

Chansamone Saiyasak was born in Pakse, Laos. He earned his BA in Religion with a concentration in Cross-Cultural Studies from Liberty University in Lynchburg, Virginia in 1990. He also attended Mid-America Baptist Theological Seminary in Tennessee and graduated with a MDiv in 1994 and a DMin in Missiology in 2000. Saiyasak served as the Minister of Missions at Lighthouse Baptist Church and founded and directed the Mekong Evangelical Mission (MEM) in Nashville, Tennessee. He helped established the Mekong Bible Institute and Seminary (MBIS), the Mercy Christian School (MCS), the Mercy Home for Children (MHC), the Mekong Radio Station (MRS), the Mercy Church Association (MCS), and a number of the Mekong/Mercy churches throughout the country. He currently serves as president at Mekong Bible Seminary in Ubonratchatani, Thailand.

5

A Mission History of Indonesian Church

PURNAWAN TENIBEMAS, PHD

Introduction

Indonesia is a big nation located between the two continents of Asia and Australia. It is the fourth largest nation in the world. The total population of Indonesia is presently around 240 million people. Indonesia is the world's largest archipelago with 17,000 islands covering an area wider than the continental United States, three thousand of which are inhabited. Seven hundred and twenty-six people groups inhabit Indonesia. It is one of the most diversely peopled nations of the world. Since each of these people groups has its own language and culture, from a mission viewpoint, Indonesia is a huge challenge for cross-cultural mission.

Christians of all kind of groups comprise 10–12 percent of the total Indonesian population. Patrick Johnstone and Jason Mandryk (*Operation World, 21st century edition*) report that Christians in Indonesia have now reached 16 percent of the total population. They also report that Muslims represent now only 80.3 percent of the population. However, many Muslim leaders believe that Christians in Indonesia form less than 10 percent of the population. I myself have some doubt regarding the reliability of both these extreme views and tentatively suggest 10–12 percent to be a more probable estimate.

Christians in Indonesia are found in over 230 Protestant denominations, twenty independent churches, as well as in the Roman Catholic Church. The total number of Indonesian Christians today is more than 24 million people. It makes Indonesian Christians one of the largest Christian communities in Asia. The Indonesian churches represent a great resource of people for doing mission. In addition, according to cultural background, Indonesian churches have a good potency for doing cross-cultural mission.

However, the Republic of Indonesia has one of the lower income-to-person ratios among Asian countries. It is also tragic that three of the four poorest provinces in Indonesia are Christian enclaves: Papua, Maluku, and the eastern part of southeast islands. Economic conditions are a big obstacle to the Indonesian church doing mission, especially to sending missionaries to distant regions.

According to history, Christianity was first introduced in Indonesia through the Portuguese in the early sixteenth century. The Dutch East India Company (VOC) then followed this in the early seventeenth century and established themselves in the area known as Jakarta today. Most of the Christian churches in that time were for the Dutch people. Only in Maluku Islands was there a church for local people. The Portuguese, on the other hand, came not only to colonize the islands, but also to Christianize them. Java was closed to evangelism until 1850.[223] Moreover, Banten, an area in the westernmost part of Java Island,

223 Muller Kruger, *Sedjarah Gereja di Indonesia* [Church History in Indonesia] (Djakarta: Badan Penerbit Kristen, 1966), 156.

where Islam was more rigid and legalistic, was closed until the end of the colonial time.[224]

Most of the data for the following review of Christian mission are based on that of Muller Kruger (*Sedjarah Gereja di Indonesia*). Christian missions in Indonesia depend on the political and economic conditions, and can be divided into four major periods according to the political conditions and the major performers:

1. Christian Mission under Portuguese Suzerainty (1520–1615)
2. Christian Mission under the Dutch East India Company (1615–1815)
3. Christian Mission during the era of Foreign Missionary Societies (1815–1945)
4. Christian Mission in the Contemporary Period (1945–2009)

Christian Mission under Portuguese Suzerainty

Christianity came to the peoples of Indonesia when the Europeans came to the Indonesian archipelago to get spices directly from the farmers. The Portuguese were the first Europeans who came to Indonesia, followed by the Spanish. These nations' adventurers were Roman Catholic, and they came with a mandate from the Pope in Rome to colonize and to Christianize called *Padroado*. The mandate of Padroado was to build and maintain church buildings, prayer meeting houses, and monasteries; to supply the need of these facilities; to take care of the church members and priests; to support priests in their duties including the practice of active mission. According to the letter of King Joao III, written

224 Van den End, *Harta Dalam Bejana* [Treasures in Jar] (Jakarta: BPK Gunung Mulia, 1980), 155.

on March 8, 1546, the primary duty of these colonizers was to enhance and to spread Christian faith.[225]

The Portuguese first arrived to the original Spice Islands of Maluku as early as 1512. Systematically, they colonized this region and some of the local people converted to the Roman Catholic Church following the principle of *cuius regio eius religio*, meaning, "Those who possess the region also make its religion." However, it is fair to say that the local people changed their original belief systems into the Roman Catholic religion of the new rulers without much understanding of this religion.

At this time, the Jesuit order was the leading mission organization among the Roman Catholic orders in Maluku, and many local kings invited them to Christianize their regions. Many probably invited the Roman Catholic priests because they were worried about the expansion of Islam from Ternate, North Maluku. As a result, thousands of people were baptized; however, through a lack of understanding or through Muslim persecution, thousands also returned to their tribal religions or converted to Islam.

Therefore, Christianity came to Indonesia. In 1588, it was reported that the Christians among the Maluku people numbered 150,000 souls. The report also mentioned that up to sixty thousand new Christians were martyred during a very difficult period between 1560 and 1570. It is thought that up to two hundred priests from three orders (Jesuit, Franciscan, and Dominican) worked among the Maluku people during the Portuguese suzerainty period, which lasted nearly one century.

In addition to their Maluku mission, the Dominican order also worked in the Southeast Islands of Solor and Flores, but their work had suffered much reversal after the Dutch attacked the area. The Franciscans also worked among the Javanese in Blambangan and Panarukan from 1585 until 1598. This was the

---

225 Muller Kruger, *Sedjarah Gereja di Indonesia* [Church History in Indonesia] (Djakarta: Badan Penerbit Kristen, 1966), 21.

very first time that Javanese people heard the gospel and hundreds of Javanese Hindu background had been baptized. However, this movement was halted when the Muslims from Pasuruan and Surabaya attacked them.

In 1605, the Dutch colonizers ousted the Portuguese from Ambon, and then the Spanish from Halmahera, North Maluku in 1613. At this time, the religion of the local people of Maluku was changed to the Protestant Christian faith. The Roman Catholic mission in Maluku came to an effective end.

Christian Mission under the Dutch East India Company

The Dutch East India Company (VOC) came to Indonesia and succeeded the Portuguese. This political change brought a new period of mission to Indonesia. The pastors and evangelists were ordained by VOC and financial support came from VOC. While the central organization of all the churches in Indonesia was run by the VOC in Jakarta, the model of the church was the church in Netherlands. Indeed, the Netherland Church practically became a mother church for the churches in Indonesia.

The focus of VOC was commerce, so they restricted Christian mission wherever it might threaten commercial interests of the VOC. For example, the VOC made an agreement with the Sultan of Ternate called the "Ternate Charter," which stated the nonintervention of the VOC regarding local religion and belief systems. Because most of their counterparts in commerce were Muslims, the VOC tried hard to keep peaceful and safe relations with the Muslim communities. In their minds, since Christian evangelism would harm their commercial interests, Christian evangelism was forbidden, and so for two hundred years, the VOC churches kept the light of the gospel safely under a bushel (Matt 5:15, NKJV).

Besides the Maluku churches, there were other churches in Indonesia in VOC times. These churches were in Jakarta,

Semarang, Surabaya, Padang, and Makassar. Most of the members of these churches were Europeans, and any Indonesian members in these churches were largely passive. They were considered as an additional group attached to the European true members. In fact, during this whole period there was no single Indonesian elder in any of these churches. The architecture, the organization, the theological belief, and other aspects of church life were all based on the mother churches of the Netherlands. These conditions led to the common understanding among the Indonesian people that Christianity was the religion of Dutch people.

Christian Mission in the Era of Foreign Missionary Societies

The VOC became bankrupt on 1799 and was dissolved. This economic condition brought a new period to mission and politics in Indonesia as the country now came directly under the Dutch government. In the same period, war in Europe brought instability to the Dutch government as France intermittently occupied the Netherlands. The VOC economic monopoly was broken, as well as the spiritual monopoly of Dutch Calvinism. The Roman Catholic Church was permitted to enter Indonesia again, and the government supported its missionaries in the same way as the Protestant Church.

In the chaos of European politics, the British formally took over the governing of the Indonesian colony from 1811 to 1816. It was during this governorship that Sir Thomas Stamford Raffles first allowed missionaries and evangelists to enter among Muslim communities. At the same time in Europe, the churches of Europe had become aware of the command to preach the gospel and many evangelistic and mission societies were being formed. Some of these now opened branches in Jakarta among the colonial churches.

From 1813–1816, the London Missionary Society sent ten missionaries to Indonesia. Among these were the Nederlands

Zendeling Genootschap (NZG) missionaries: Joseph Kam, who was sent to revive Maluku churches; Supper, who ministered in the Malay-speaking congregation in Jakarta; and Bruckner, who was sent to Semarang. The evangelists brought a new spirit to awaken the existing churches in Indonesia. Previously forgotten churches, such as those in East Indonesia were revitalized under the inspiration of men like Joseph Kam in Maluku. Today, he is still remembered as the apostle of Maluku, although, according to Kruger, perhaps the reformer of Maluku is a more appropriate title for this remarkably influential missionary.

Joseph Kam worked in the Maluku Islands, in North Sulawesi and in the southeast islands for seventeen years. He revitalized the dying churches that had been left untended in VOC times. He published catechisms, distributed books of Psalms, and founded a school for Christian teachers. From this work, four large Protestant synods would eventually form Minahasa Evangelical Christian Church (1934), Protestant Church of Maluku (1935), Timor Evangelical Christian Church (1947), and the Protestant Church of Western Indonesia.

The spirit of evangelism continued to be influential after the Dutch government returned to Indonesia in 1816. In the second half of the nineteenth century, the new spirit of evangelism reached out to new regions in Indonesia. Even though the Dutch government hindered evangelistic mission in new regions among Muslim communities, the churches continued to grow.

Mission in the Maluku Islands

After the days of Joseph Kam, NZG missionaries continued to build up the church and reach out to other Maluku Islands. The Indonesian Christians, especially Ambonese believers, became involved in a mission movement to reach unreached people groups. Ambonese teachers went to Buru Island in 1879 to reach the Ambonese immigrants who resided in the North part of the island. From 1885, the Utrechtse Zendingsvereeniging (UZV) supported the mission in Northern Buru.

In 1865, the UZV also entered the Halmahera Islands of North Maluku. It was a difficult ministry because of two strong Islamic sultanates in this region, Ternate and Tidore. Indeed, the Dutch regent in charge of this region asked the central Dutch colonial government in Jakarta to order the UZV evangelists to leave the Halmahera Islands as their presence endangered the peaceful and safe condition of the islands. However, God opened a door for the UZV missionaries to stay. One of the kings of Jailolo of the Tobelo tribe had rebelled against the Sultan Ternate. He was calmed by a UZV evangelist and became the first king of the Tobelo tribe to be baptized in 1898. This was followed by mass conversion among Tobelo people. In 1901, 3,200 Tobelo people were baptized, and a door was opened wide for evangelism to move forward in the Halmahera Islands. In 1947, the Halmahera Evangelical Christian Church was formed.

Mission in Papua

The UZV began work in Papua in 1862. While today we know that there are at least 247 people groups in Indonesian Papua, in the nineteenth-century missionaries had minimal information regarding the tribes and their cultures. The challenges were many: first, there were no roads; second, many of the Papuan tribes practiced cannibalism; third, in the coastal areas and on many of the smaller islands, Islam was already a growing presence. Concerning this third challenge, the Sultan of Tidore had a plan to Islamize all the coastal areas of Papua. He built up strong influence among the coastal peoples through commerce.

Mission in Papua did not prosper until the twentieth century, but through the persistence of American and Dutch mission organizations, the numbers of Christians steadily increased to over twenty-five thousand in 1931. However, evangelism among unreached Papua tribes was still considered a very high-risk activity even after 1960. Don Richardson's famous book, *The Peace Child*, tells one such mission story of how the Sawi people came to Christ. Today, the majority of the Papua people are considered Christians.

Mission in Sulawesi

Since 1563 the area of Minahasa, North Sulawesi was protected by the Spanish from Islamization by the Ternate Sultan. The Roman Catholic Church continued to take care of Roman Catholic congregations among the Minahasa people until 1663, when the VOC replaced the Spanish. Under the VOC, the Minahasa church became Protestant. Initially, this church was well looked after, but this care later became weak.

In 1817, Joseph Kam visited this region and in 1822, two NZG evangelists (Muller and Lammers) were sent to Minahasa. At that time, there were five churches with three thousand members, but this was only 2 percent of the total population of Minahasa, which numbered 150,000 people. However, other NZG evangelists came to spread the gospel among the Minahasa people, and in just forty years, the majority of Minahasa people had been reached. In 1876 when the churches of Minahasa were formally joined with the Protestant Church, their total registered membership numbered eighty thousand. Indeed, the story of the Minahasa people is the first example of mass conversion through Protestant mission in Indonesia.

Education and schooling had a vital contribution in this success story. Teachers taught Christian faith to children in schools, whilst local evangelists used their own houses to train adults. The church of Minahasa is also considered the first church in Indonesia to have ordained local people as pastors, these being Adrianus Angkuw and Silvanus Item who were ordained in 1859.

In 1886, a Roman Catholic mission reentered Minahasa. At first, they ministered to the European Roman Catholic believers in the region, but later they formed a congregation for locals and built churches, schools, and a hospital. Today, there is a large Roman Catholic Church in this region.

Although the neighboring region of Bolaang Mongondow had seen many local people become Christians, they returned to their tribal religion due to neglect. In the second part of the nineteenth century, Gorontalo Muslims Islamized this region so the Dutch colonial government forbade missionaries to enter this region until the early twentieth century. When the NZG did finally enter this region, they found progress very slow and, until today, only a few thousand people have come to Christ.

Since the region of Gorontalo had already been firmly Islamized, the NZG was forced to look beyond this region to Central Sulawesi. In 1893, the NZG sent Dr. Albert C. Kruyt to Central Sulawesi to work alongside Dr. N. Adriani of the Dutch Bible Society. Kruyt spent seventeen years studying the local language and culture and translating the scriptures. With Adriani, they endeavored to offer the gospel in a way that the local people could understand. In particular, Kruyt and Adriani perceived that the people of this region approached life as a community rather than individuals. They believed the gospel should be presented to whole communities, not just individuals in these communities. God blessed their understanding and culturally sensitive approach, and the gospel spread from clan to clan through "mass conversion." Teachers and evangelists from Minahasa, who in turn started courses to prepare local teachers, supported this community approach. The missionaries also started courses for local evangelists and pastors.

From 1912 onwards, the gospel was taken to Luwuk and Banggai, where tens of thousands of people came to Christ and mass baptism became common. By 1938, Christianity was rooted among whole tribes in Central Sulawesi. By the end of the colonial era (1945), the synod of the Central Sulawesi Christian Church covered twenty-one Christian community clusters scattered across Central Sulawesi.

Next, the gospel was taken to the regions of South Sulawesi. In 1913, Gereformeerde Zendingsbond (GZB) sent the first missionary to reach the Toraja people, A. A. Van Loosdrecht. When Van Loosdrecht was killed in a rebellion against the Dutch government, more evangelists were sent with a language expert from Bible Society, Dr. Van der Veen. They all worked tirelessly, building a school, then a hospital, and translating the scriptures. Their work was not in vain, and mass conversion among the Toraja people followed quickly. Today, the majority of Indonesia's 2 million Torajanese people claim to be Christian.

Mission in the Southeast Islands

Mission in this region began in 1612 at Kupang, Timor under the supervision of the Protestant Church in Jakarta. By 1758, the church in Kupang had thirteen thousand members; by 1760, there were 5,870 Christians on the island of Roti in fifteen congregations, whilst on the island of Sawu there were 825 Christians in five congregations.

However, the congregations in these three islands almost vanished through ten years of total neglect. In 1820, the Dutch government restarted Christian mission to these islands under van Troostenburg De Bruyn. Several NZG evangelists, who succeeded in reviving the church, accompanied De Bruyn. Since 1947, the churches in this region have been organized as the Timor Evangelical Christian Church.

Between 1870 and 1875, a Dutch regent named Esser operated a transmigration program to help the Sawu people of Timor settle on land that is more fertile. He chose for them the island of Sumba, west of Timor. Since some of the Sawu transmigrants were now Christians, Esser urged Nederlands Gereformeerde Zendingsvereeniging (NGZV) to send missionaries to Sumba Island. In 1881, two NGZV missionaries entered Sumba. However, they had to wait for more than thirty years before any local Sumba people received baptism. Since then, the growth of the Sumba church has been steady. The independent Sumba Christian Church was formed in 1947.

Bali is the only remaining majority Hindu island in Indonesia. This island has been considered a difficult region for mission work. In 1866, the UZV entered Bali and worked in Bali for seven years before the first Balinese person received baptism. However, this man became very frustrated by the opposition and rejection he experienced from the Balinese community. In his frustration in 1881 he, with two accomplices, tricked and murdered the evangelist who brought him to faith. Because of this incident, the Dutch government closed Bali to mission work until 1929, when a Chinese CMA evangelist, Tiang Kam Foek, was allowed to minister there to other ethnic Chinese. Through the ministry of this remarkable man, 113 Balinese people were baptized in November 1932. After this, the Dutch government withdrew its permission and Foek was forced to leave Bali. Instead, the East Java Church was encouraged to send Javanese evangelists to work in Bali. Today, Christians in Bali are still a minority among the Hindu majority. Although these believers frequently suffer persecution, the Balinese Protestant Church is one of the most progressive churches in Indonesia concerning contextual ministry.

Roman Catholic mission has also long been very active in the southeast islands. Almost the entire population of Flores is Catholic, and we can find many Roman Catholic churches in the north and east parts of Timor, as well as the western parts of Sumba.

Mission in Kalimantan

Although Kalimantan or Borneo is the largest island in the Indonesian archipelago, no Christian missionaries came to the people of Kalimantan people until the nineteenth century. By then, Islam had already become established in the coastal areas, and Muslim communities controlled most of the trade and commerce of Kalimantan. Because of these economic conditions, the Dayak people, who reside in the hinterlands of Kalimantan, were very dependent upon the Muslim traders.

The German Rheinische Missionsgesellschaft (RMG) came to South Kalimantan for the first time in 1836. They faced many difficulties in reaching Dayak people. After twenty years of hard work, only 261 people had been baptized. After a rebellion broke out against Dutch colonialism in 1859, the Dutch colonial government withdrew all permission to missionaries to continue their mission. During this time, the embryonic church almost vanished.

In 1866, mission activity was resumed using river transportation to reach the Dayak people in the inaccessible hinterlands of Kalimantan. Progress, though, was still slow. In 1925, after ninety years, Basle Missiongesellschaft (BMG) replaced the RMG and there were only 5,400 Christians in fifty congregations.

The Christian and Missionary Alliance (C&MA) began work in East Kalimantan in 1930. This region proved more fruitful than southern Kalimantan; in ten years, five thousand people were baptized as believers. Today, there are many more Christians in East Kalimantan than in South Kalimantan, including a large number of ethnic Chinese who have been converted to Christ.

The Board of Foreign Missions of the Methodist Episcopal Church began work among ethnic Chinese in West Kalimantan in 1906. This work has been very fruitful and has gone on to include outreach to the Dayak people of West Kalimantan, and to involve the Gereformeerd Church, C&MA, and other mission agencies.

Mission in Java

During the VOC mission period (1615–1815), there were churches in several cities in Java, but most of the members of these churches were European. Generally, these congregations had no vision to share the gospel with their local neighbors, as the VOC opposed such a vision. Java had been largely Islamized by the early sixteenth century, and the VOC desired above all to keep peaceful relations with the Javanese Muslim community. Even though in reality Islam had not really rooted itself in the heart of the peoples of Java, the island of Java was closed by the Christian VOC for Christian mission throughout the VOC period.

When LMS and NZG sent their missionaries to Java, the Protestant Church in Jakarta typically sent them on to East Indonesia or away from Java. Bruckner, for example, was sent to become the pastor of the European church in Semarang. Here, he worked long and hard translating the New Testament into the Javanese language, as well as writing many Christian tracts in the Javanese language. Although these tracts and Bible portions were highly valued by Javanese people (who were often willing to pay a high price to own one), the colonial government confiscated all his printed literature in 1831 and forbade their distribution. This decision was reversed in 1848, when it was discovered that most of the Bibles that had been printed had been eaten by termites.

However, through God, Bruckner's labors were not in vain. Individual Christians still shared the gospel and the Javanese were typically very open to hearing these personal witnesses. When a Madurese person from Wiung, East Java was given the Javanese Gospel of Mark while attending an exhibition of animal husbandry in Surabaya, he brought this Bible portion home and began to study it with his friends. When a member of this group was invited to a wedding ceremony, he was amazed to hear a prayer that reminded him of the message in the Gospel of

Mark. Through this incident, the Wiung group met Coolen, the son of a Dutch army officer and his Javanese wife. At that time Coolen lived in Ngoro, East Java and was known as a good landlord who had a heart to share about Christianity to the Javanese people around him. Through Coolen, the Wiung group of seekers learned about Christianity, especially about the possibility of being a "Javanese Christian."

The Wiung group was then introduced to a German Pietist called Emde. Emde was an ex-sailor who now worked as a clocksmith in Surabaya. Joseph Kam, the first NZG missionary, had inspired Emde when Kam had passed through Surabaya. From this visit, the Surabaya Fellowship for Supporting Evangelism had been formed and this group had begun to distribute Javanese translations of the Gospel of Mark, one of which was being read by the Wiung group of seekers. Emde now taught the Wiung group according to "Western Christian" norms and in 1843, thirty-five of them were baptized. In the following years, there was a steady flow of groups of people coming forward to receive baptism. By 1845, 220 Javanese had been registered in the baptism book of Surabaya Protestant Church. These Javanese Christians used the Javanese *wayang* puppet shows as a media of communication in sharing the gospel of Jesus. Later, they founded a center for Javanese Christians in Majowarno. This was the beginning and the seed for the East Java Christian Church.

Christian mission in Java took a different pattern to mission on other islands. In Java, God frequently used individual Christians to sow the first seeds, rather than evangelists from mission organizations. The mission organizations were most effective doing follow-up and building on these individual ministries. The first NZG evangelist, J. E. Jellesma arrived in East Java in 1849, after a change in the colonial government policy. Not only did Jellesma receive permission to work among the Javanese, but he also obtained permission to distribute the Bruckner Javanese

New Testament translation, which was previously banned for seventeen years.

What could be Jellesma's most valuable contribution to Javanese Christianity was his work on harmonizing the dichotomy of "Javanese Christians" and "Western Christians" into one believing fellowship in Majowarno, East Java. After Jellesma had worked hard to form a vibrant Christian Javanese community in Majowarno, Majowarno became a base out of which many evangelists were sent throughout Java. Christianity grew in East Java, until in 1931 when the churches in East Java became an independent church.

In Central Java, as with East Java, God used particular lay individuals to sow the first seeds of the gospel. In southern Central Java, Mrs. Oostrom-Philips of Banyumas and her sister-in-law, Mrs. Philips-Stevens of Purworejo, gathered the local people who worked for their families to hear the gospel. While Oostrom-Philips focused primarily on her employees, Philips-Stevens also visited villages to share the gospel with the local Javanese people. After their work had been well received, Philips-Stevens requested some Javanese evangelists be sent to help her share the gospel more fully her region. Three evangelists were sent. Among those trained by F. L. Anthing together with a Chinese evangelist was Paulus Khow Tek San.

Later, the Nederlands Gereformeerde Zendingsvereeniging (NGZV) sent Vermeer, the pastor of the European Church in Tegal, to support Mrs. Oostrom-Philips in her ministry. He moved from Tegal to Purworejo and by 1873, after fifteen years of ministry, he had baptized over two thousand Javanese believers.

One of the evangelists who worked alongside Philips-Stevens became so successful, that he is remembered as the greatest evangelist of the Javanese Church. His name was Sadrach and God used him amazingly in bringing many thousands of Javanese Muslim people to Christ. Eventually, Sadrach was to break away from the Dutch-led churches and become the sole leader of about sixty-three congregations of new believers with 6,374 registered church members. He became a champion of Javanese Christianity. His successor, Tunggul Wulung, continued this ministry in the northern regions of Central Java.

Mission in the north region of Central Java followed a similar pattern to that in the south. Although the Dutch regent of Tegal (the north region of Central Java) had earlier invited two local evangelists to start evangelism in his region, there was little progress until a European laywoman started to witness. In 1853 in Simo plantation in Salatiga, a city in Central Java, Mrs. Le Jolle began to fill her empty hours with outreach to the inhabitants and workers. She requested and was sent an Indonesian evangelist (Petrus Sadoyo). In 1855, she was able to ask W. Hoezoo, a foreign missionary based in Semarang, to review the first ten candidates for baptism before this rite was given. Through this modest beginning, the first Javanese church of north Java became established.[226]

After Le Jolle had returned to her home country, the Netherlands, in 1857, she became the key person behind the foundation of the Salatiga Mission in 1889. Based in Utrecht, this mission built schools and hospitals in and around Salatiga and provided vital support to the growing congregations of local Javanese.

In Central Java, the influence of Islam was very strong in the far north of the province, and was expected to be the most difficult region in Java. However, when the Mennonite Mission began work in this region, they were blessed by about two thousand baptized people (Cooley 1968, 93).

Instead, West Java proved to be the most difficult region for Christian mission in Java. The people of West Java were (and are) Sundanese and speak Sundanese, not Javanese.

---

226 Th. Sumartana, *Mission at the Crossroads* (Jakarta: Badan Penerbit Kristen, 1984), 19.

Furthermore, the Dutch started their colonization of Indonesia from this region. Dutch colonialism may well have been the major factor in the Sundanese resistance to the Christian religion, which they considered the religion of the colonialist. Kraemer catches the difficulties facing the missionaries when he reports,

> No wonder, that in 1876, 1879 and 1881 the board of NZV, also at the instigation of several missionaries, seriously considered withdrawal, and that the Memorial Volume, commemorating the 25th anniversary of NZV invokes a dreary sky of questioning despair. Everything seemed to break down in their hands. [227]

In West Java, God used individual lay believers as his effective tool in bringing Sundanese people to Christ. When F. L. Anthing retired from his senior position in the Jakarta legal courts in 1865, he set his energy to reaching the Sundanese. Deeply aware of economic, social, and political differences between European and Sundanese people in West Java, he invited Javanese evangelists to come and present the gospel, not as the religion of the Dutch, but as the highest truth of Javanese spirituality. By 1877, his group had baptized and registered 750 Sundanese believers, among whom there were fifty trained evangelists. This compares favorably with the results of the Dutch NZV missionaries who, after fifty years of ministry, had only baptized 130 Sundanese people.

Mission among Chinese in Indonesia

A large number of Chinese came to Indonesia in the colonial period in search of a better life. Mission outreach to the Chinese communities in Indonesia began about the same time that mission began to the native peoples of Java Island. While mission among

---

227 Hendrik Kraemer, *From Mission Field to Independent Church* (The Hague: Boekencentrum, 1958), 98.

the Chinese was started by European evangelists, soon Chinese Christians from China were leading this outreach. For example, evangelist Gan Kwee, originally from Amoy, China, traveled throughout Java preaching the gospel to his fellow citizens.

Initially, the Chinese who became Christians joined congregations of local believers that were led by the local evangelists. The first Chinese church began in Indramayu, West Java after Ang Boen Swie came to faith and reached out to her Chinese compatriots through meetings in her home. Although normally the Chinese believers were not separated from native believers, in the north region of Central Java under the Mennonite Mission, the Javanese Christians were organized under the Javanese Evangelical Church while the Chinese Christians were organized under Indonesia Muria Christian Church (Muria is the name of a mountain in the region).

Mission in Sumatra

The British governor, Sir Stamford Raffles, gave the first permission for missionaries to enter Sumatra in 1811. Therefore, in 1820, a small group of British Baptist missionaries came to Bengkulu, Padang, and Sibolga. Because of the strong influence of Islam among these coastal tribes, two of this group—Ward and Burton—moved into the Sumatran hinterland to work among the Batak Toba people in 1824. However, this first mission among the Batak Toba people was without any result as the British mission was withdrawn in 1826. Eight years later, in 1834, two American Baptist missionaries, Munson and Lyman, tried to enter the region where Ward and Burton had preached years before, but they were killed and eaten.

In 1861, the Rheinische Missiongesellschaft (RMG) responded to the challenge of reaching the Batak People of North Sumatra by sending a number of missionaries. Among them, L. J. Nommensen was the only RMG missionary who initiated to go to the north region without the Dutch protection. The Lord, though, was very much with him and the Batak people turned to Christ in a remarkable way. In 1918, when Nommensen, the apostle to the Bataks died, almost the entire of the Batak Toba people had been evangelized. Nommensen was buried at his request in Batak land. In 1930, the Batak Church was organized under the name Batak Protestant Christian Church. Today, the Huria Kristen Protestant Batak Church is the largest Protestant church in Indonesia with over 4.3 million members.

The remarkable mission story of Sumatera, an island in western Indonesia, was continued with similar success among the Simalungun people, the Batak Karo people (from 1890 onwards), and then spread to the western islands of Nias (from 1874 onwards), Batu (from 1889 onwards), Mentawai (from 1901 onwards), and Enggano (1903 onwards). In 1905, the American Methodist entered Sumatera focusing on the Chinese in Medan (North Sumatera) and Palembang (South Sumatera), then the Batak Toba people in Asahan. A Batak Christian alumnus of Methodist Gospel School in Singapore led this later evangelism.

A Brief Overview of Christian Mission under Foreign Mission Societies

During the period 1815–1945, new churches were planted in new regions. Outside Java, whole tribes were reached and most of the tribal churches in Indonesia were started in this period. In general, the peoples reached were largely following tribal religions, and those who were already Islamicized were largely left untouched by the gospel.

Mission on the island of Java, which had already been largely Islamicized, followed quite a different pattern. There, God used individual Christians to open opportunities for the gospel among

Muslim people. In this context, the foreign mission societies typically followed and supported, rather than led and created.

Christian Mission in the Contemporary Period

After Indonesia became an independent nation on August 17, 1945, the churches in Indonesia entered a new era. While many synods had been founded before Indonesia became an independent nation, many other Protestant churches relied on the financial support of the Dutch colonial government. After the country's independence, all the churches of Indonesia needed to become self-supporting organizations.

Moreover, through the circumstances of World War II and the revolutionary struggle for independence, practically all foreign missionaries had been removed from the Indonesian churches. The Indonesian churches needed to become self-supporting, self-governing, and self-propagating for the first time. According to Soejana, a Sundanese church leader, the Christians had already done much, through their involvement in the nationalist struggle, to remove the stigma of "foreignness" or "Dutchness" that was associated to Christianity.[228] Although there were many challenges, this may have been a time of church growth both in maturity and in numbers. Cooley suggests that at this time the Indonesian churches were the most vigorous and fastest growing in the world.[229]

Since Indonesia became an independent nation, millions of people moved from one region to another for many reasons: studies, business, work, duties, and marriage. Many Christians also moved to new regions. Because of this new mobility, we can find Batak Protestant Christian churches everywhere in Indonesia

228 Koernia Atje Soejana. *Benih Yang Tumbuh II* [The Growing Seed II] (Bandung-Jakarta: GKP & LPS-DGI, 1974), 49.

229 Frank L. Cooley, *Indonesia Church and Society* (New York: Friendship Press, 1968), 42.

today. Not all of these Batak migrants followed their Batak denominations. Many joined other churches and some became active in evangelism.

Similarly, Christians from Maluku, Minahasa, and Timor who moved did not necessarily join their tribal denomination. In fact, they usually joined the Gereja Protestan di Indonesia bagian Barat (GPIB) or Protestant Church in West Indonesia—an ecumenical church composed of the Minahasa Evangelical Christian Church, the Maluku Protestant Church, and the Timor Evangelical Christian Church, who found themselves away from their homelands.

Both cases are examples of the dissemination of church members throughout Indonesia in this, but dissemination is not a positive form of church growth in itself. According to Church Growth Studies, there are three forms of church growth: (1) biological; (2) transfer; and (3) conversion. The dissemination of churches is a transfer growth. While this means that some churches grow, they only do so as the sender churches are deflated.

While biological growth has been a significant factor in Indonesian church growth, Muslim biological growth is slightly faster than Christian; the increase in population in Indonesia can explain the increase in total numbers of Christians, but not the percentage of Christians in Indonesia. Since this has grown in the contemporary period this growth must be explained through conversion.

One explanation of conversion growth has been foreign mission partnership with the Indonesian church, particularly North American mission societies. For example, the Southern Baptist Church entered Indonesia in 1951. Starting in Bandung, they focused their work on the large conurbations of Bandung, Jakarta, Semarang, Jogjakarta, Surabaya, Kediri, and Palembang. Because of their mission, the Southern Baptist Church has been one of the fastest growing churches in Java in the contemporary period. While most of their members in larger cities are Chinese, a large number of the Baptist Church in east Java is Javanese.

Another North American foreign mission success story has been the Christian and Missionary Alliance (C&MA), who founded the Gereja Kemah Injil in Indonesia. While there are still many foreign C&MA missionaries in Indonesia, there are also many C&MA Indonesian missionaries working in West Kalimantan, East Kalimantan, East Indonesia, Papua, southeast islands, and Java. These were the cross-cultural missions within the Indonesian people groups.

In the contemporary period, evangelization and discipleship among the tribes of Papua has become more thorough and intensive. Some local tribes were very active in reaching the unreached tribes of Papua. However, there are also evangelists from outside Papua island who work among the Papua. Although the majority of tribes in Papua today are Christian, discipleship ministries are still needed. Many tribes are still living in very simple conditions, and a large number are still illiterate.

Besides the foreign mission societies that have come to Indonesia, many Indonesian evangelistic societies have been founded in the twentieth century. According to Johnstone, this has been a global phenomenon in the twentieth century.[230] God has used these societies mostly to boost church-planting churches within Indonesia, the fourth most populous nation in the world. These societies have undoubtedly accelerated church growth in Indonesia. Some of them work in cross-cultural settings. A lot of missions and church organizations from Java work among the Dayak people group of Kalimantan. A Chinese-background church sent their evangelists to plant churches among the Dayak

---

230 Patrick Johnstone, *The Church is Bigger than You Think,* (Great Britain: Christian Focus Publications, 1998), 153.

people, especially in West Kalimantan. In East Kalimantan, a Chinese church supported mission among the Dayak people.

In the nineteenth century, foreign mission societies from Europe were most significant in Indonesian church planting and growth. In the twentieth century, the contribution of foreign missions from the United States, alongside the Indonesian mission foundations, has been significant. Perhaps in the twenty-first century, the contribution of Indonesian mission societies will prove to be the most significant in Indonesian church planting and growth. However, the challenge of mission in the Indonesian archipelago remains huge. There are twenty-three clusters or 127 unreached people groups[231] in Indonesia,[232] and the Indonesian church still needs the partnership of the international mission community in facing this huge challenge. Many mission and church organizations take a part in doing mission among these unreached people groups. The result of this mission activity is still insignificant. I hope that one day in the future the patient evangelists will see the harvest time of these fields.

The Javanese Phenomenon

The Indonesian government succeeded in suppressing a potential Islamic rebellion in 1962 and a potential Communist revolution in 1965. The Communist Party managed to assassinate six top Army generals, but ultimately failed to take over the government. Following this abortive Communist coup, hundreds of thousands of Communists and their sympathizers were massacred, especially in Central and East Java.

---

231 The unreached people groups could be a tribe or subtribe who the number of this group is no less than ten thousand and among them the Christians less than one percent. This group of people need outsider Christians to share the gospel with them. This phenomenon is a challenge for cross-cultural mission within Indonesia.

232 Persekutuan Jaringan Riset Nasional (Indonesian National Research Network). Indonesian People Profiles Unreached People Groups (n.c: PJRN, 2001).

After this political chaos, Indonesia entered into an economic crisis. During these hard times, Christian compassionate witness shone brightly, especially within the Javanese community. In some places, this led to remarkable conversion movement to Christ. According to some observers, this may have resulted in over two million Javanese Christians in Central and Eastern Java. This may have been the first time in the history of Christian mission that millions of Muslims had come to Christ. Unfortunately, the churches in Java were not ready to welcome so many Javanese truth seekers at that time, and so the flood of seekers became a trickle. Though growing at a slower rate today, the Javanese church is still growing.

Java Island, populated by around 120 million people, is the most populous island in the world. Because of overcrowding in Java, the Indonesian government has run various transmigration programs. Through these programs, hundreds of thousands of Javanese resettled in Sumatra, Kalimantan, Sulawesi, and Papua islands. Away from their close-knit communities, Javanese are often very open to consider Christianity, and some thousands of Javanese transmigrants have became Christians. In Sumatra, we could find many Javanese congregations. Some others joined with the local churches. A similar phenomenon has happened among the Balinese transmigrants who reside in the Central Sulawesi resettlement area. It is estimated that around five thousand Balinese transmigrants have become Christians. They are members of the local churches there.

Among the Sundanese of West Java, the abortive Islamic rebellion and Communist coup did have an impact, but not so large. After these events, many Sundanese were also ready to consider Christianity. Evangelism among Sundanese in that time moved into a new hope. However, only some hundreds of Sundanese received baptism, perhaps from fear of persecution from within their communities. The Sundanese also have been reluctant to follow the transmigration programs, so evangelism and migration did not have great impact among them.

Pentecostal Mission

Since the 1920s, the Pentecostal church has grown in Indonesia. Today there are many synods of Pentecostal churches in Indonesia. Pentecostal churches are very aggressive in their mission strategies and preaching. They have attracted many ethnic Chinese, who make up a significant percentage of their membership. There are many huge congregations among the Pentecostal churches. Today, the second largest Protestant church in Indonesia (after the Huria Christian Batak Protestant) is the Indonesia Bethel Church (GBI). At present, the GBI members number around 2.5 million. The majority of them are of Chinese background but do not speak Chinese.

The Pentecostal churches continue to grow in both number and variety. They tend to attract people from Christian backgrounds (ethnic Chinese, Batak, and Minahasa people). Some Pentecostal churches are also effective in reaching out to non-Christian peoples.

The Chinese Phenomenon

The majority of the ethnic Chinese Christians attend ethnic Chinese churches. Ethnic Chinese congregations can be found in many denominations (Protestant, Roman Catholic, Baptist, Bethel, Pentecostal, and more), and there are Chinese-speaking denominations as well. After the abortive Communist coup, the ethnic Chinese in Indonesia found themselves in a critical situation, because the People's Republic of China had supported the Indonesia Communist Party. The Chinese in Indonesia at that time felt very vulnerable, and many turned to Christ in this crisis.

Today, Chinese churches are found almost everywhere in Indonesia. Usually these churches are financially well off.

Although the Chinese churches tend mostly to reach out to other ethnic Chinese, Chinese churches are increasingly considering how they can help meet the wider mission challenge of reaching the unreached peoples of Indonesia. Fortunately, some Chinese churches have a heart to reach the unreached people groups in Indonesia. Right now, we could find some evangelistic activities among Dayak people in Kalimantan run by Chinese churches. Some other Chinese churches support or contribute in some other evangelistic mission among unreached people groups. There are five churches in Bandung, Java that support Christian mission among the original people of Papua.

Missions Overseas

One of the characteristics of the modern times is the function of transportation. Varieties of transportation help people move easily from one place to another. Indonesia as a big nation contributes to a huge number of economic migrants on the world. We could find Indonesian migrants and students in every continent in the world. This phenomenon challenges Indonesian churches to reach them in their work countries.

Some Indonesian churches and evangelistic organizations participate in sending evangelists to reach the Indonesian communities and planting churches abroad. Some Indonesian students and immigrants have also been involved in evangelistic missions among their fellow students and immigrants.

God blesses the missions abroad of Indonesian churches; the fruits of the missions abroad are Indonesian churches in every continent. A big number of Indonesian churches are in California and New York. Nevertheless, we also could find Indonesian churches in other states in the US, Canada, northern part of Brazil, and other South American countries. Indonesian churches also exist in many countries in Europe. In some African countries, Australia, New Zealand, and in many countries in

Asia, there are Indonesian churches. In these countries, most of the members of Indonesian churches are Indonesian women workers. For example, most of the Indonesian churches in Hong Kong are women churches.

The majority of the Indonesian missionaries abroad are working among the Indonesian students and immigrants. But there are some Indonesian missionaries who work among the local people abroad. For example, there is an Indonesian family and a single person who works among the local people in the southern part of the Philippines, and another family and a single person in the northern Philippines. There are also Indonesian missionaries who work among the local tribes in India, Nepal, and Tibet. In Africa, there are Indonesian missionaries in South Africa, Ivory Cost, and Guinea Bissau. Some Indonesian missionaries work among some local tribes in China. There is a single man in Brazil and six Indonesian families working in Kyrgyzstan.

Contextual Mission

Sensitive missionaries have long practiced context-sensitive mission. In the contemporary period, more and more mission societies and churches have come to appreciate the importance of contextual mission: that is, being aware and respectful of local cultural norms. The main motives behind this have been so: (1) the gospel can be easily understood, and (2) the stigma of foreignness of Christianity can be removed.

I would like to end this review of the history of mission in Indonesia with two Indonesian examples of contextual mission. The first example comes from Bali. Bali has long been considered one of our toughest mission regions, and the Balinese church has remained small and weak. However in 1972, a breakthrough occurred. Dr. I Wayan Mastra introduced cultural contextualization as part of the theology of God's blessing. In this program, he worked to equip the church pastors with work skills, so they could become self-supporting. Then, he emphasized various social activities, so that each church member would also support his or her neighbor. Third, all the aspects of Balinese culture (architecture, music, musical instruments, dress, and so on) that were not against biblical values were actively adopted into the life of the church community. Today, the Balinese church has been accepted as a positive and meaningful aspect of Balinese community life and culture.

My second example comes from the Sundanese context. In our third mission period, F. L. Anthing pioneered a contextualization approach that brought many Sundanese people to Christ. The stigma that Christianity is the religion of foreigners has not disappeared from the Sundanese consciousness. Since the 1980s, new attempts have been made to encourage and train evangelists and pastors to respect and use Sundanese culture in their ministries. Elements of Sundanese culture have been accepted as an enriching factor in the Christian life of Sundanese people. Since then, several thousand Sundanese people have come to Christ. While problems of persecution and other pastoral issues are still common, the Sundanese church is growing.

Closing Statement

Indonesia is a big country with big challenges. Indonesia has the largest Muslim-population in the world. Nevertheless, its constitution maintains that Indonesia is not an Islamic nation. The government of the Republic of Indonesia recognizes Islam, Protestantism, Roman Catholicism, Hinduism, and Buddhism equally, and strives to give each full freedom before the law. Pancasila, the five principles underlying the constitution of the Republic of Indonesia, ensures this freedom. God has blessed the Indonesian church with freedom to bring God's blessing to Indonesia.

In the past centuries, millions of Indonesians have joined the worldwide church, and the churches in Indonesia are still growing. Many of these people have come to Christ from Muslim backgrounds, and they are still coming.

Cultural sensitivity and contextual mission have borne much fruit in the more difficult mission regions of Indonesia. Today, Indonesian missionaries are increasingly being used by God to lead their Indonesian brothers and sisters to Christ. Many foreign missionaries are also walking alongside their fellow Indonesian missionaries. Under the sovereignty of God, we hope these mission activities continue until the second coming of Christ.

Bibliography

Cooley, Frank L. *Indonesia Church and Society*. New York: Friendship Press, 1968.

End, van den. *Harta Dalam Bejana* [Treasures in Jar]. Jakarta: BPK Gunung Mulia, 1980.

Johnstone, Patrick. *The Church is Bigger than You Think*. Great Britain: Christian Focus Publications, 1998.

Johnstone, Patrick and Jason Mandryk. *Operation World*, 21st Century Edition. Carlisle, Cumbria: Paternoster Lifestyle, 2001.

Kraemer, Hendrik. *From Mission Field to Independent Church*. The Hague: Boekencentrum, 1958.

Kruger, Muller. *Sejarah Gereja di Indonesia* [Church History in Indonesia]. Jakarta: Badan, 1966.

Penerbit Kristen. *Indonesian People Profiles Unreached People Groups*. n.c: PJRN Persekutuan Jaringan Riset Nasional [Indonesian National Research Network], 2001.

Richardson, Don. *Anak Perdamaian* [Peace Child]. Bandung: Kalam Hidup, 1977.

Soejana, Koernia. *Atje Benih Yang Tumbuh II* [The Growing Seed II]. Bandung-Jakarta: GKP & LPS-DGI, 1974.

Sumartana, Th. *Mission at the Crossroads*. Jakarta: Badan Penerbit Kristen, 1994.

About Dr. Purnawan Tenibemas

Purnawan Tenibemas was born to a non-Christian family. At a young age, he accepted Christ and became actively involved in evangelism. Right after high school, he studied theology at Tyrannus Bible Seminary in 1976 and earned his ThM in 1984 from Jakarta Theological Seminary. He earned his PhD in 1996 from Fuller Theological Seminary, in Pasadena, California. He serves as the principal of Tyrannus Bible Seminary (TBS) and is the academic dean of Consortium for Graduate Program in Christian Studies (CCS).

6

Missionary Movement of the Korean Church

TIMOTHY K. PARK, PHD

Introduction

The Korean church has been a missionary church from the beginning. In the 1980s, the church shifted from being a "missionary-receiving" to a "missionary-sending" church. Today, thousands of Korean missionaries are going into the corners of the world, risking their lives for Christ.

The *New York Times* wrote,

> South Korea has rapidly become the world's second largest source of Christian missionaries . . . it is second only to the United States and ahead of Britain. The Koreans have joined their Western counterparts in more than 160 countries, from the Middle East to Africa, from Central to East Asia. Imbued with the fervor of the born again, they have become known for aggressively going

to—and sometimes being expelled from—the hardest-to-evangelize corners of the world.[233]

Christianity Today predicted that the Korean church would soon become the "number one" missionary-sending church: "South Korea sends more missionaries than any country but the US. And it won't be long before it's number one."[234] The Korea World Missions Association (KWMA) also recently released statistics on the Korean mission. The number of Korean missionaries at the end of 2008 was 19,413 in 168 countries. In 2008, leaders of Korean churches and mission organizations made a resolution to send one million tentmaking missionaries by 2020 and 100,000 missionaries by 2030.[235] It is a bold faith projection, but not an impossible task.

Many churches around the world have begun to recognize the dynamic emergence of the Korean church as a missionary church. It is expected that the Korean church will play an important and unique role in the missionary movement of the twenty-first century.

In this analysis, I will present a brief overview of the missionary movement of the Korean church from its origin to the present, describe the current situation of the Korean mission, examine the contributing factors to the growth of the Korean mission, assess its strengths and weaknesses, and make suggestions for more effective missionary work.

A Brief History of the Korean Mission

The story of church growth in Korea has become widely known throughout the world for several decades now. However, the missionary movement of the Korean church did not garner much attention until the beginning of the third millennium, though

233 Norimitsu Onishe, "Korean Missionaries Carrying Word to Hard-to-Sway Places," *New York Times*, November 1, 2004.

234 Rob Moll, "Missions Incredible," *Christianity Today*, February 24, 2006.

235 http://www.kwma.org.

the Korean church had been a missionary church from the time of its conception.

Mission history of the Korean church can be divided into three periods: 1) mission during Japanese colonial rule (1907–1957); 2) mission after the independence of Korea (1955–1991); and 3) current mission (1980–present). Each period is unique in terms of its characteristics, so I will examine each period separately.

Mission during Japanese Colonial Period (1907–1957):

The Korean church's missionary work outside of the Korean peninsula began as early as 1907, when the self-supporting, self-governing Presbytery of the Presbyterian Church in Korea was formed. As the first native Presbytery was constituted, seven men, the first graduates of the Theological Seminary of Korea (Pyongyang), were ordained to the ministry. Yi Ki-Poong, one of the seven, was commissioned to Jeju Island as a missionary.

George L. Paik wrote:

> Yi Ki Poong, one of the seven ordained ministers, volunteered to go to the Island of Quelpart [Jeju], about sixty miles off the southern coast of the mainland, as the first Protestant missionary of the Korean church. The Presbytery accepted his offer and appointed a missionary committee to administer the undertaking and ordered the whole church to make a special offering to carry on the propagation of the faith.[236]

"So, from its very organization," William D. Reynolds said, "the Presbytery of Korea unfurls its blue banner to the world as a missionary church."[237] The movement gradually won the support

236 George Lak-Geoon Paik, *The History of Protestant Missions in Korean 1832–1910* (Seoul, Korea: Yunsei University Press, 1929).

237 W. D. Reynolds, "The Presbytery of Korea," *Korea Mission Field*, 3, no. 11, eds. C. C. Vinton and W. G. Cram (Seoul: Evangelical Missions in Korea), 1907.

of the believers as the church sent missionaries to other parts of the world.

In 1909, the church ordained a second group of ministers. There were nine. The church sent one of them, Reverend Choi Kwan-Heul, as missionary to Vladivostock, Siberia. In the same year, the Presbytery of the church also sent Reverend Han Suk-Jin to Korean students in Tokyo, and Pang Hwa-Chung to Korean emigrants in California and Mexico.[238]

In 1912, the Presbyterian Church in Korea made a resolution to send three ministers to Shantung, China—the birthplace of Confucius and Mencius—to mark the organization of the General Assembly. The three missionaries went into the field the following year in 1913. Korean Mission Field reports: "Again, as an expression of the joy of the Church in the great event, a 'thank offering' was taken throughout Korea and the three pastors and their families were sent to open a real Foreign Mission work in the Chinese language for the Chinese in Shantung, China."[239]

The Korean church sent about eighty missionaries outside the Korean peninsula during the Japanese colonial regime. Missionaries were sent to Jeju Island, Siberia, Japan, California, Mexico, Manchuria, Shantung, Shanghai, Nanking, Peking, and Mongolia, among others. Most of the missionaries ministered to Korean immigrants in other countries, but also engaged in ministries to evangelize natives and second-generation Koreans, whose languages and cultures were vastly different from people in Korea.

The most significant of the Korean church's missions was its mission to Shantung, China because it was the first to be solely geared toward natives. In fact, it was the first Asian mission carried out by Asian people to other Asian people since the days of the apostles. Though Korea was a destitute, powerless nation, the

238 Paik, *History*, 390; Northern Presbyterian Report for 1910, 281.
239 C. A. Clark, "The Missionary Work of the Korean Presbyterian Church," *Korean Mission Field* ed. Ellasue Wagner, 30, no. 8, August 1934.

Korean church sent a message to the world that even a young, poor, and powerless non-Western church could carry on hefty missionary responsibilities.

Unlike Western churches and today's Korean churches, the Presbyterian Church in Korea dispatched her missionaries to Shantung, China in consultation with and approval of the Chinese church and the American Presbyterian mission that began work there already. They worked in the areas both the Chinese church and American Presbyterian Missions assigned to them. They did not transplant their home church in the field, but transferred their membership to the Chinese church to work as member of the Chinese church. They worked as a team among fellow Korean missionaries and in good partnership with the Chinese church and foreign missions in the field. Because of their country's loss of sovereignty to Japan, Korean missionaries carried on their missionary responsibilities from the position of weakness. Denominations played a major role in the missionary movement of the church during Japanese colonial rule.

Mission after the Independence of Korea (1955–1991)

After World War II, the missionary movement of the Korean church was greatly hindered because of political strife in the Far East. The Communist Revolution in mainland China and the Korean War compelled the church to suspend temporarily its missionary work. Although Korea restored its sovereignty in 1945, the country still suffered from the consequences of war. Nevertheless, before long the Korean church resumed its missionary work:

> After the Korean War, the Churches in Korea were looking for new mission fields besides the Red China area. In 1956, the Korean Church began to send two missionary couples to Thailand and [others] to other parts of the world. It was the signal for the missionary advance of the Korean

> Church for new fields and new era. The burning missionary zeal was rising from the dedicated Christians amid the ruined streets of the war. Even before they were restored from the destruction of the war and from the poverty, they sent many full-time missionaries to various places such as Thailand, Taiwan, Japan, Vietnam, Hong Kong, Indonesia, Pakistan, Nepal, Ethiopia, Okinawa, Brazil, Mexico, Argentina, Brunei, USA, and so forth. The total number of Korean missionaries overseas are 234 (M2 and M3).[240]

Though Korea regained sovereignty in 1945, the nation underwent civil war from 1950 to 1953. Thus, missionaries during the three decades after Korea's independence carried out their responsibilities without any strong political, ecclesiastical, or financial support. They also carried their missionary responsibilities from a position of weakness. During this period, most missionaries worked under or in partnership with Western missions, as well as with churches within their mission fields.

Mission in Affluence (1980–Present)

Though the Korean church has been a missionary church since its founding, it was in the 1980s that the aggressive missionary-sending movement began. This period can be characterized as "mission from affluence." Multiple factors contributed to the phenomenon, including explosive church growth, economic growth, increase in immigration, improved diplomacy, higher education, and accumulated missionary experience. These factors, among others, have enhanced the missionary movement of the Korean church in recent years. Abundant resources of Korea, however,

240 Samuel I. Kim, "Korea," *New Forces in Missions*, ed. David J. Cho (Seoul: East-West Center for Missions Research and Development, 1976), 124.

were not always beneficial. A rise in wealth also brought negative consequences, such as an increased dependence on material resources rather than on the Holy Spirit and the Word. In doing so, receiving natives were inadvertently taught to depend on missionaries and their material resources.

The Current Situation of the Korean Mission

The Korean church has emerged as a new missionary force in the twentieth century and has aggressively launched its missionary enterprise to the world. There is a strong sense among church leaders that the Lord is using the Korean church to usher his kingdom.

Current Status of the Korean Mission

According to a survey recently conducted by the Korea World Missions Association, 19,413 Korean missionaries are working

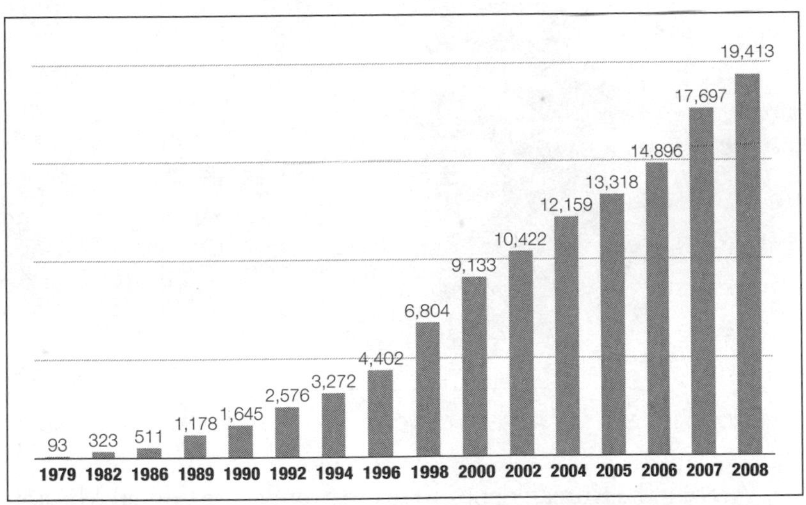

INCREASE OF KOREAN MISSIONARIES[241]

241 In Sook Chung, "A Report on the Status of Korean Missionaries," *Korea Missions Quarterly* 9, No. 3 (Spring 2010), 78–79.

in 168 countries as of 2008. This means that there has been an average increase of 1,317 missionaries every year since 1998. That number increased sharply in 2008, with an additional 1,716 more missionaries.

In 2008, there were 8,723 missionaries (42.5% of the total missionaries) sent by Korean church denominations, and 11,780 (57.5% of the total missionaries) sent by Korean mission organizations around the world. This includes 493 additions in 2008 by denominations and 1,385 new missionaries by mission organizations. Of the total, 2,180 missionaries have dual membership. Those who have dual membership are counted only once in the total number of Korean missionaries.

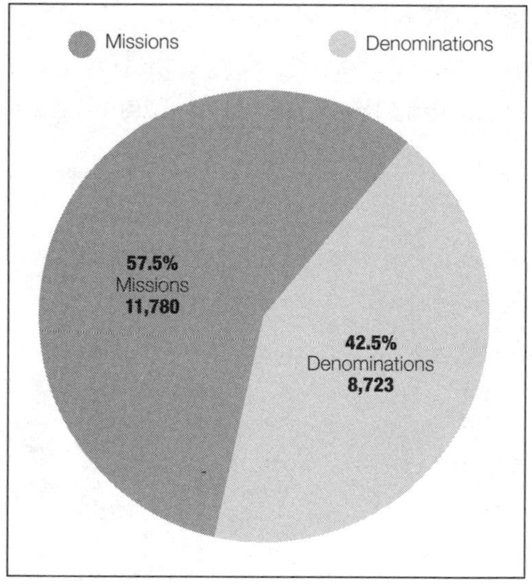

MISSIONARIES SENT BY KOREAN DENOMINATIONS VS. KOREAN MISSIONS[242]

Among the Korean denomination groups, the Global Mission Society (GMS) of the Presbyterian Church in Korea-Hapdong has the largest number of missionaries (2,005) in the field. The Presbyterian Church of Korea-Tonghap is the second largest with

242 Ibid., 82–83.

1,102, then Korea Methodist Church (907), Korean Assembly of God (834), Korea Baptist Church (612), Presbyterian Church in Korea-Daeshin (394); Presbyterian Church in Korea-Hapjung (370), Presbyterian Church in Korea-Hapshin (369), Korea Evangelical Holiness Church (307), and Presbyterian Church in Korea-Koshin (295).

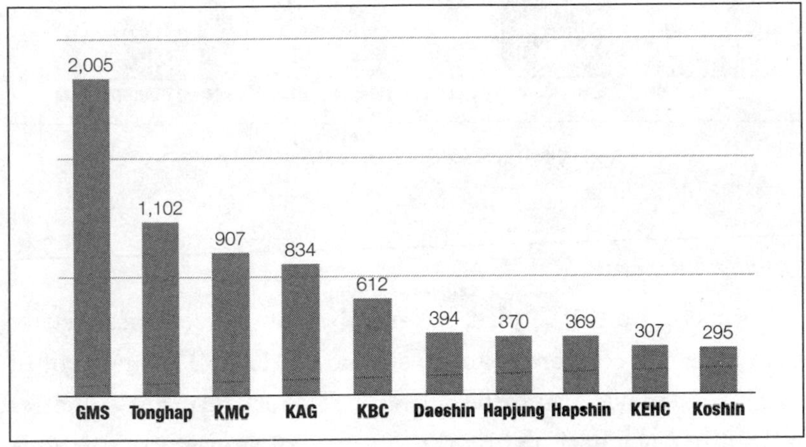

MISSIONARIES AMONG KOREAN DENOMINATIONS[243]

Among Denominations

Among the mission organizations, the University Bible Fellowship has the largest number of missionaries (1,567) in the field, followed by Campus Missions International (628), Full Gospel Mission (598), Korea Food for the Hungry International (508), InterCP (460), Youth With A Mission (454), WEC International Mission Korea Center (418), Korea Campus Crusade for Christ (417), Tyrannus Overseas Mission (304), and Paul Mission (298).

243 Ibid.

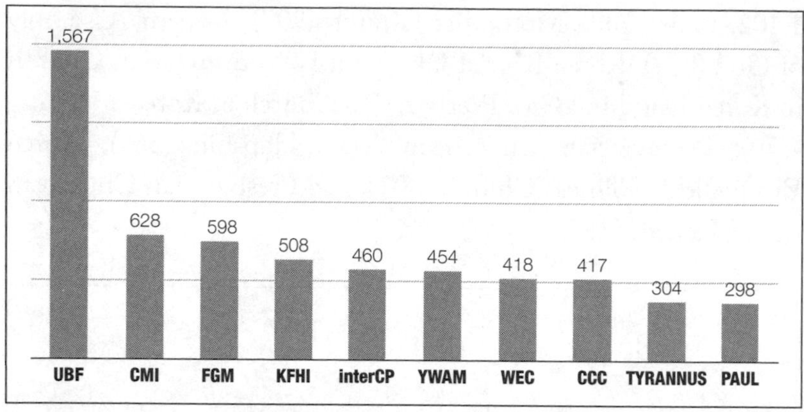

MISSIONARIES AMONG DENOMINATIONS[244]

Among Missions

In terms of years of service, the number of a career missionaries who have served more than three years is 19,050 (93 percent of total missionaries), and the number of short-term missionaries is 1,444 (7 percent). While the number of short-term missionaries is increasing gradually, the number of career missionaries increases at a greater rate.

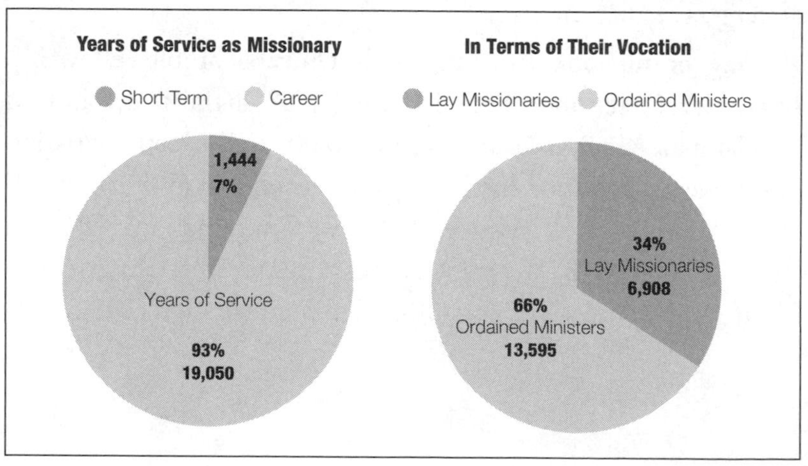

244 Ibid.

In terms of vocation, the number of ordained ministers—including spouses—is 13,595 (66 percent of total number of missionaries), while the number of lay missionaries is 6,908 (or 34 percent of the total). The proportion of ordained to nonordained missionaries is significant.

Geographical data of Korean missionaries shows that 5,353 (26.1% of total number of missionaries) are working in Northeast Asia (seven countries) including China and Japan. Three thousand three hundred seventy-seven missionaries (16.5%) are in Southeast Asia (eleven countries). The figure below provides the breakdown.

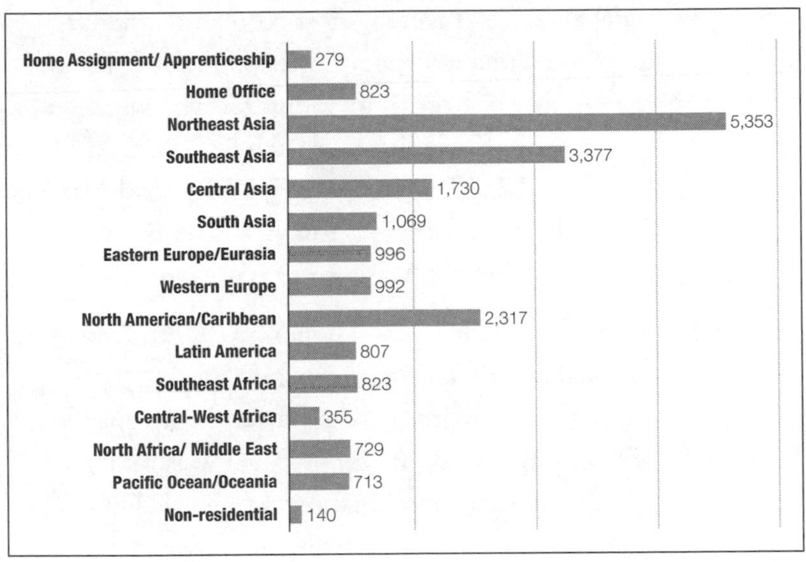

GEOGRAPHICAL DATA OF KOREAN MISSIONARIES[245]

Some Major Changes of the Korean Mission

Major changes in the Korean missionary movement have occurred in the last three decades.

245 Ibid.

1. From "Mission toward Korean Immigrants" to "Mission toward Unreached Peoples": Korean missionary work in the 1970s was mainly targeted toward Korean immigrants in other countries. Today, however, the majority of Korean missionaries are involved in cross-cultural missions, particularly among unreached people groups.
2. From "Western Missions" to "Korean Native Missions": Another change is the emergence of native Korean mission organizations. After the independence of Korea, most Korean missionaries worked under Western mission groups. Today, the number of Korean missionaries who work under native Korean groups such as Global Mission Society, Global Partners, UBF, GMF, Paul Mission, INTERCP, and others is much greater than the number of those in Western organizations.
3. From "Denominational Mission" to "Both Denominational and Parachurch Mission": During Japan's colonial rule and immediately after the independence of Korea, the missionary movement was carried on mainly through denominations and local churches, with the exception of a few mission organizations. Today, however, the movement has been carried on both by denominational missions and mission organizations. The number of Korean missionaries sent by mission organizations is slightly greater today than that sent by denominations. Unlike in the past, both denominations and mission organizations are able to maintain a symbiotic relationship.
4. From "Mission from a Position of Weakness" to "Mission from a Position of Strength": During

> Japan's colonial rule and after the Korean War, missionaries performed their responsibilities from a position of weakness. During the last three decades, however, they performed their responsibilities from a position of strength. Instead of relying on the life-changing power of the Holy Spirit and the word of God, Korean missionaries today have tendencies to rely on the material resources of the Korean church.

Contributing Factors to the Growth of the Korean Mission

Various factors have contributed to the missionary movement of the Korean church. They include divine, human, organizational, and contextual factors.

Divine Factors

Manifestations of the power of God, including revival movements, kept missions growing. Revival movements, particularly the Great Revival Movement in Pyongyang in 1907, contributed to the growth of missions. Because of the fire of spiritual movements, the Korean church experienced a dynamic vigor in sending missionaries out to surrounding nations. It was customary for the Korean church to have two revival meetings every year in the spring and fall. This tradition helped keep the Korean church spiritually strong.

Manifestations of the power of God and of the Holy Spirit also contributed to the widespread growth of missions. Healings of the sick were often seen in the missionary works on the island of Jeju.

Human Factors

Human factors, such as a spirit of gratitude and capable leaders are notable contributions to the missionary movement of the Korean church. Koreans by nature are a people who pay a debt of gratitude when they are shown grace. When the Presbyterian Church in Korea dedicated one out of seven of its first ordained ministers as a missionary to the Island of Jeju, they were expressing their joy and gratitude to God for founding the Presbytery in 1907. Sending three missionary families to Shantung, China was also an expression of gratitude to God for the General Assembly of the Presbyterian Church of Korea, and to China, where they learned the ethical standards of Confucius and Mencius. On both occasions, the church collected a "thank offering" throughout the nation to support these missionaries.

There were many capable leaders in the Korean church who made great impacts on the Korean missionary movement. Among those who made significant contributions to the growth of the Korean mission are: Reverend Kil Sun-Choo, one of the Presbyterian Church in Korea's first ordained pastors; Helen Kim of Ewha Woman's University; David J. Cho of Korea International Mission; John E. Kim of Chongshin University; Joon Gon Kim of the Korea Campus Crusade for Christ; and Tai-Woong Lee of Global Missionary Fellowship.

Organizational Factors

From the outset, the Korean church created a mission committee to organize and coordinate missionary work. The church also collaborated with Western mission groups. Korean student groups also played a significant role in contributing to the movement.

Much of the success of today's mission growth in the Korean church is due to the organization of missions committees. By creating structures, missionary works were simultaneously conducted according to the church's structure (modality) and mission's structure (sodality). When one group was in need of support, the other undertook those responsibilities. In recent years, hundreds of native missions have emerged. Some examples are the Korea World Mission Council (KWMC), Korea World

Mission Association (KWMA), World Korean Missionary Fellowship (WKMF), and Mission Korea (MK). These groups have facilitated much of the missionary movement in the past three decades.

The missions committee of the early Korean church comprised both Korean and Western missionaries. Western missionaries mentored Korean missionaries and helped them to enter new mission fields. Unlike today's missionaries, the early missionaries often worked in partnership with Western mission organizations and national churches, especially in China.

Students have played a crucial role in the widespread growth of the Korean mission. During the Japanese colonial rule, students organized missionary societies and sent or supported missionaries. After Korea's independence from Japan, students at Ewha Woman's University, Chongshin University, and Daejon University among others started their own student missionary movement. Since 1990, Mission Korea (Chul Ho Han) has held biannual mission conferences for students and young Koreans. About 45,000 total students have attended the conferences held by Mission Korea and among them, 29,000 have made commitments to serve as missionaries.

Contextual Factors

Contextual factors that have contributed to the spread of the Korean mission movement are: increased Korean immigration, growing influence of the international missionary movements, spread of information, Korea's burgeoning economy, and improved diplomatic ties with foreign nations.

1. Immigration Growth: Political, social, and economic conditions in Korea have led to a rise in immigration to countries all over the world. Through immigration, Korean emigrants have become a great missionary force:

> Wherever Korean Christians have gone, their churches have accompanied or followed them for the quickening of the peoples among whom they have come to live. This is true to the North in Manchuria and Siberia, to the south on the island of Quelpart [Jeju], to the West in Shantung, China, and to the East in Hawaii, Mexico, on the west coast of America, and among the Korean students in the city of Tokyo.[246]

Korean emigrants and residents have served as missionary forces for the evangelization of the world.

2. International Conferences: The success of Korea's missionary movement is largely connected to international conferences. For example, the first mission to China was tied to International Missionary Council held in Edinburgh in 1910 and the mission to Thailand was a result of the work of the World Council of Churches.

3. Information Distribution: The spread of information through newspapers and magazines has stimulated Christians to be aware of their missionary responsibility and has served as a call to action. The *Korea Mission Field*, a monthly publication by the Evangelical Missions in Korea, was distributed to foreign missionaries in Korea and to their sending and supporting bodies. The *Christian Messenger*, a weekly joint publication by Methodists and Presbyterians in Korea, was also used as a great informational source.

---

246 C. A. Clark, "Korean Student Work in Tokyo," *Korea Mission Field* 11, No. 7 (July 1915).

These newspapers shared news about missionaries and their works with the public. The *Christian Messenger* stirred up the missionary spirit within the Korean church by printing an article about missionary David Livingstone in forty-four consecutive issues. This newspaper also published news about Korean missionaries in other countries. Today, many Christian newspapers and mission journals distribute information about Korean missionary works in many nations.

4. Burgeoning Economic Growth: With the dynamic growth of the church, Korea's economy has also achieved incredible growth during the last decade. Abundant material resources of Korea have had both positive and negative effects on Korean mission.
5. Diplomatic Ties with Foreign Nations: Korea's economic growth and successful hosting of the Seoul Olympic Games in 1988 created opportunities for Korea to establish diplomatic ties with almost all nations in the world. Doors were opened wide and today Koreans can travel almost anywhere with a Korean passport.

Strengths and Weaknesses of the Korean Mission

Like any organization, the Korean mission movement has its strengths and weaknesses.

Strengths include: (1) dynamic church growth; (2) ample financial resources; (3) widespread Korean diaspora; (4) strong diplomatic ties with foreign nations; (5) high levels of education; (6) long mission history; and (7) deep passion, courage, and commitment for the cause of the Great Commission.

Weaknesses include: (1) an unbalanced mission theology; (2) monocultural perspective; (3) lack of field research;

(4) inappropriate missionary deployment; (5) improper selection and training of missionaries; (6) competitive individualism; (7) weak administration of mission organizations; and (8) lack of cooperation among the sending, receiving, and supporting bodies.

While remaining faithful to the preaching and teaching of God's word, the Korean church has in some aspects neglected its social responsibilities. More leaders have become church-oriented instead of kingdom-oriented. It is imperative that leaders preach the gospel in both word and deed. Theology produces methodology. The Korean church must practice a mission theology that incorporates all spheres of society including politics, business, media, culture, and education.

The Korean culture is, in essence, monocultural. This creates a tendency to impart the missionaries' culture to the people and churches they serve. It is important to respect the host cultures and communicate the gospel in a way locals can accept. Unfortunately, some Korean missions and missionaries work without accurate information or a workable strategy for their fields.

Many missionaries have also been inappropriately selected, trained, and deployed. This results in a lack of cooperation, creating problems of competition among missionaries in the field. Local church pastors who may not have proper knowledge and experience are often in a position of control over their missionaries and their ministries.

Summary and Conclusion

The Korean church has been a missionary church almost from the beginning. The Korean missionaries are willing to go to any place of the world risking their lives for Christ even to the hardest-to-evangelize corners of the world.

The Korean church's bold faith projection to send one million tentmaking missionaries by 2020 and 100,000 career missionaries by 2030 continues to challenge Korean believers around the world. Despite setbacks, most notably the 2007 kidnapping incident in Afghanistan, the Korean church is expected to play an important and unique role in the missionary movement in the twenty-first century.

In light of this overview of the missionary movement of the Korean church, here are several suggestions for the Korean church and Asian churches to consider as we look to missions in the twenty-first century:

1. Establish a mission theology that is biblically sound and culturally relevant. The focus must be on the kingdom of God, not on transplanting denominational teaching. Missions should include both bringing people to Christ and enhancing God's rule on earth.

2. Pray for revivals and renewals of the church that the church may continue to become dynamic and missional.

3. Promote dependence on the Holy Spirit and the word of God, instead of material resources or funding.

4. Build effective partnerships with local churches and other mission organizations at home and abroad.

5. Recognize the importance of laypeople and challenge them to become short-term missionaries, professional missionaries, nonresidential missionaries, and business missionaries.

6. Avoid paternalism over local people. This only hinders the indigenization of the gospel and the independent spirit of local churches. Instead, missionaries should develop methods that promote self-sustenance in local churches, as the early

foreign missionaries did to Korea, according to the Nevius principles.

7. Continue to hold mission conferences for students and other believers.
8. Develop viable methods through in-depth field studies, discerning each missionary's unique gifts to ensure strategic deployment and effective ministry.
9. Learn from past successes and failures to better adapt to changing trends as we move into the twenty-first century.
10. Develop mission leaders who will lead the missionary movement of the church.

Bibliography

Clark, C. A. "Korean Student Work in Tokyo." *Korea Mission Field* 11. No. 7, July 1915.

———. "The Missionary Work of the Korean Presbyterian Church," *Korean Mission Field* 30, No. 8 (August 1934).

Kang, Sung Sam. "The Statistics of the Korean Church Mission and Future Ministry." Kidok Shinmoon, February 15, 2006.

Kim, Samuel I. "Korea: New Forces in Missions," edited by David J. Cho. Seoul: East-West Center for Missions Research and Development, 1976.

Moll, Rob. "Missions Incredible." *Christianity Today*, February 24, 2006.

Onishe, Norimitsu. "Korean Missionaries Carrying Word to Hard-to-Sway Places." *New York Times*, November 1, 2004.

Paik, George Lak-Geoon. *The History of Protestant Mission in Korea 1832–1910*. Seoul, Korea: Yonsei University Press. 1929.

Reynolds, W. D. "The Presbytery of Korea," *Korea Mission Field* 3, No. 11, edited by C. C. Vinton and W. G. Cram. Seoul: Evangelical Missions in Korea, 1907.

About Dr. Timothy K. Park

Timothy Kiho Park is the director of Korean Studies and associate professor of Asian Mission at Fuller Theological Seminary School of Intercultural Studies in Pasadena, California. He is the founding director of Institute for Asian Mission and president emeritus of Asian Society of Missiology. He received his MDiv at Chongshin University and ThM in Missiology Asian Center for Theological Studies and Mission (ACTS), in Seoul, Korea. He received his MA in Missiology and PhD in Intercultural Studies in 1988 and 1991 respectively from Fuller Theological Seminary. Park was a missionary to the Philippines where he coestablished and served as president of Presbyterian Theological Seminary (PTS). He also helped establish several local churches in Metro Manila, Bulacan, and Laguna.

7

The Church and the Missionary Movement in Singapore

VIOLET JAMES, PHD

Introduction

The coming of the Roman Catholic and Protestant missions coincided with the arrival of Sir Stanford Raffles and the beginning of British colonialism in 1819. Singapore was only a fishing village then, and the Malay people, who were indigenous to the island, had some loose control over it. Chinese and Indian migrants started coming to Singapore with the hope of finding their fortune and then returning to their homelands. It turned out that these people remained on the island and became a vital part of the political, economic, and social structure of the up-and-coming nation. The Chinese, who make up seventy-eight percent of the total population of Singapore today, are the main economic backbone of the country. How did this small obscure fishing village became a major hub of Christianity and even come to be regarded by some as the "Antioch of Asia"?

As we trace the history of the birth of Christianity through the labors and sacrifices of the Western missionaries from

Britain, Europe, and America, we see the hand of God guiding, shaping, and orchestrating men and women to impact this land with the word of God through creative methods and strategies such as education, medicine, and other social means to facilitate the gospel. The national church eventually came of age and started replicating what they experienced and saw in colonial missions. This paper will trace the impact of colonial missions in the nineteenth and twentieth centuries, the beginning of mission involvement by the national church in the last quarter of the twentieth century, the significant breakthroughs in the missionary movement; also it will make some observations about the challenges for the twenty-first century church and critique the church's mission involvement.

Colonialism and Missions in the Nineteenth and Twentieth Centuries

When the British arrived in Singapore in 1819, one of the first things they did was to provide chaplains for their own people who had come to reside in Singapore. They did not immediately see the need to evangelize the local people. The London Missionary Society (LMS), an interdenominational mission body from Britain, came to Singapore through Malaya (the earlier name for Malaysia), and it was through these missionaries that work was first done among the local people. These missionaries were focused on China for the long haul but because the doors were temporarily closed, they decided to relocate to Malaya and Singapore as a stepping-stone while waiting for the doors in China to open. They made good use of their time and expertise to prepare themselves for China by producing and printing Chinese literature and training Chinese men so they could enter their homeland as effective evangelists and pastors to serve among their own people. One such person was Liang Ah Fa, who was converted and trained by LMS missionary

William Milne. Ah Fa was used by God mightily to reach not only his own people in Malaya and Singapore, but eventually in his native land as well.[247]

One of the most outstanding missionaries from LMS was Benjamin Keasberry. Like all the other LMS missionaries, he viewed his stay in Singapore as temporary, his long-term goal being China. However when the doors in China opened, all the missionaries left Singapore, but Keasberry and his wife decided to remain because of the great need, especially among the Malay people. He resigned from the mission and devoted the rest of his life to mission work in Singapore independently. While he was not successful in sustaining a Malay congregation or a school for Malay boys, both of which he pioneered, God used him to start a church for the "Straits-born" Chinese Christians (Peranakan). This church, Prinsep Street Presbyterian, is a testimony to this man's vision and effort and is vitally involved in missions today. Keasberry also collaborated with a Chinese Christian, Tan See Boo, to plant the first Chinese church, Glory Presbyterian.[248] This church currently has a few missionaries serving in different parts of Asia as well as a few ministries to migrants at her doorstep.

One very interesting observation about Keasberry and Milne was their partnership with the local people in doing mission, evangelism, and church planting. This, as evidenced in the study of other missionaries like William Carey, is essential to mission work. Teamwork among different groups of people is imperative: missionaries with their special expertise and the local people with their ability to connect with their own people. Together, they make an excellent partnership in God's kingdom work.

---

247 Bobby Sng, *In His Good Time: The Story of the Church in Singapore, 1819–2002* (Singapore: Bible Society of Singapore, 2003), 30.
248 Ibid., 72.

The Roman Catholic mission was established in 1821. Unlike the Anglican Church, this mission immediately involved itself with the local people through various social works, especially in education. They started schools to equip the local people that became the means to propagate the Roman Catholic faith. Some of their schools, such as St. Joseph's Institution (1864) and the Convent of the Holy Infant Jesus, or CHIJ, (1862), continue to reflect outstanding scholarship and academic excellence. The Roman Catholic missionaries did not incarnate the word of God by giving to the people the Bible in their own languages, something that the Protestant missionaries excelled wherever they went. Soon after Vatican Council II in 1965, the Roman Catholic Church decided to translate its Latin Bible into the vernacular of the people.

Three other groups entered Singapore in the nineteenth century: the American Board of Commissioners for Foreign Missions (ABCFM) in 1834, the Church Mission Society (CMS) in 1837, and the Brethren Assemblies in 1864. Of the three, the Brethren assemblies had the greatest impact in terms of church planting and evangelism especially in the twentieth century. The Brethren who are noted for their Bible teaching and Sunday schools, used these strengths to facilitate outreach and church planting.

The American Methodists entered Singapore in 1885. Their greatest contribution was in education. They established schools of high quality and trained young men and women, many of whom eventually took up significant places in the society, therefore contributing to nation building. The coming of the Methodists to Singapore is in itself an amazing story![249]

Charles Phillips was sent to Singapore in 1864 to serve in the British Army. He was influenced by the work of the Methodists in his homeland and longed for the gospel to impact the needy society. He invited Bishop Thoburn, who was serving in India, to

249 Sng, *In His Good Time*, 105–7.

come to Singapore and start a Methodist work. One day, Phillips had a dream that Thoburn and a team were coming to Singapore, so he went to the port to receive them. Thoburn had made no contact with Phillips and told no one of the exact date and time of their arrival. When Thoburn and his team saw Phillips, they were amazed! Indeed, God had prepared Phillips for their arrival. In that team was a young man, William Oldham, who later became one of the most effective pioneer missionaries in the Methodist Church. He was the founder of the Anglo-Chinese School (ACS) and instrumental in bringing Sophia Blackmore from Australia to be involved in female education. Blackmore started two Methodist Girls' Schools in 1887 and 1888, and worked tirelessly in this ministry for forty-one years. Girls and women who had been marginalized for centuries were sought out and given an education. Like her predecessor Sophia Cooke from the LMS, she educated and trained the young girls in the Christian faith and for life duties such as marriage and ministry. Some returned to China and were used by God as wives of pastors and evangelists. Others remained in Singapore and impacted other girls and women. The mission schools for girls and boys were noted for their excellent education. Thousands of children were given a solid education in English and in Christian education. Many became Christians and contributed to the expansion of the faith, while many others were influenced by the faith, even if they did not give total adherence to it. In 1957, when Singapore gained her independence from Britain, and in 1965, when she broke from her merger with Malaysia, the mission schools became part of the Ministry of Education (MOE) and received financial help from the government. This meant that the government was free to send any trained teacher, Christian or otherwise, to teach in the mission schools where once the missionaries and Christian teachers had enjoyed complete monopoly. This also meant that the chapel attendance, which once was mandatory, was now optional for students who embraced other religions. Today there are more than sixty mission schools, thirty-five of which were started by the Roman Catholic Church.[250] Despite the restrictions from the government and parents, these schools continue to make significant impact on the children, even if conversions are not so apparent.

In the twentieth century, the following denominations came to Singapore: Seventh-day Adventists (SDA) in 1908, Assemblies of God (AOG) in 1928, and Salvation Army in 1935. In the 1950s, the Southern Baptists, the Lutherans, the Church of Christ, the Bible Presbyterians (BP), the Evangelical Free, and the Finnish Pentecostal churches were established. These churches were involved in direct evangelism, while the SDA established churches, schools, and a hospital.

The BP Church was established as a reaction to their perception that liberal theology had crept into many of the mainline denominations. Although the BP churches grew because of direct outreach through evangelism and church planting in the 1960s, they did so at the expense of isolating themselves from the existing churches.

The National Church and Missions from Mid-twentieth Century to the beginning of the Twenty-first Century

The mission churches were forced to stand on their own feet suddenly when the whole island fell into the hands of the Japanese between 1941 and 1945. During this time, all the missionaries were either imprisoned or repatriated. The Japanese persecuted the missionaries and all local Chinese and Indian Christians who were associated with the missionaries. Indirectly, the Japanese aided the national church and forced her maturity. The Singapore

---

250 Robbie Goh, *Christianity in Southeast Asia* (Singapore: ISEAS Publications, 2005), 40–41.

church was forced to stand on her own feet as she was thrust into positions of leadership. Through trial and error, the local leaders extended leadership to the struggling and suffering church. The churches were filled with thousands of people, and the local leaders were forced to meet these challenges. The church grew into maturity and handled the crisis as best she could. The spirit of nationalism was ripe. The nationals clamored for freedom from colonial and oppressive powers that were also evident in the church. The local Christians, who had risen to the challenge of taking on leadership under the Japanese rule, became bold and confident as they recognized their ability to teach and govern the church. In 1945 when the Japanese were forced to surrender, the British powers and the missionaries returned only to find that their positions were ambivalent. The missionaries were amazed that the church was still standing and in certain cases, even thriving! Soon they also realized that the local leaders, especially in the older denominations, were not going to easily give up their positions or allow themselves to be ruled by the missionaries. The younger and newer churches, such as the Southern Baptist, Lutherans, and EFC, continued to be led by foreign missionaries for several decades before they too were emancipated.

The church in Singapore, having gone through deep tragedies and trials, was ready to consolidate its structure and policy. In the midst of busyness to organize the church and have the right structure in place, it neglected its primary calling to evangelism and mission.

Most of the churches had their children and youth programs and their regular worship services, but the Great Commission of Jesus Christ was somehow lost in the maze of activities. The Brethren Assemblies continued to actively conduct evangelistic services every Sunday evening regardless of whether there were non-Christians present. The basic assumption of the church was for non-Christians to "come" into the church and integrate into the life of the church, rather than for the church to "go" into the world and impact society, which is what the early Christians did.

By the providence of God, during the 1950s and the 1960s, parachurch organizations were established in Singapore. The Youth for Christ (YFC), the Scripture Union (SU), and especially the Inter-School Christian Fellowship (ISCF), had a unique ministry to reach out to the primary and secondary schools. The Navigators and the Campus Crusade for Christ (CCC) worked primarily among the tertiary students. All these organizations were foreign-based organizations, but they shared one common goal—to evangelize students of different levels through their areas of specialization.

In the 1960s and 1970s, God prospered these organizations and thousands of children and youth were brought to Christ. As evangelism thrived, the vitality from these organizations spilled into the church as many young people were challenged to serve God in some concrete way. But the church was not ready and the mission organizations that were in Singapore, such as OMF, were not ready to recruit non-white missionaries. It was in this context that God called a Singaporean-Indian Christian to become a catalyst in establishing a local mission organization. That would enable young Singaporean Christians, who had heard God's call clearly, to find an avenue of service and even to go to the regions beyond.

GD James, a convert from Hinduism, was called by God to serve his own people, the Indians. Later, he widened his involvement and served as an itinerant evangelist for twenty-two years in India, Malaysia, and Singapore. In 1960, while James was recovering from a heart attack, God called him to start an organization that could train many young people in Asia who in turn could empower other people in the region. This resulted in the birth of the Asia Evangelistic Fellowship (AEF).[251] The AEF is an indigenous and interdenominational faith organization that is dedicated to the task of evangelism and pioneer missions. The AEF focuses on mobilizing and equipping Asian nationals to train their own people. Currently AEF Malaysia, Nepal, and Myanmar have a theological training program through the Asia College of Ministry (ACOM). This has enabled the nationals to reproduce themselves within their own countries and to continue to engage in the work of equipping and training for evangelism and missions. Today, the AEF is one of the largest indigenous missions in Asia, with its international office in Perth, Australia. Currently, there are over two hundred workers and associates serving in Singapore, Malaysia, Indonesia, Myanmar, Philippines, India, Nepal, Cambodia, and Vietnam. The mission continues to identify new ministries with the purpose of reaching out to the unreached.[252]

The Overseas Missionary Fellowship or OMF (formerly the China Inland Mission or CIM), worked exclusively in China until 1949, when the country became Communist. All the foreign-based missions had to leave China, and so in 1950 the CIM relocated to Singapore, changed its name to OMF, and focused on ministries primarily in Southeast Asia. Today OMF Singapore is the center for orientation training of recruits before they are sent forth to the mission fields.

Other international organizations also chose Singapore as their headquarters, and by 1992, there were more than twelve organizations in Singapore, with distinct ministries. Today, there are more than two hundred and fifty parachurch organizations. Of these, over fifty are directly involved in evangelism and mis-

---

251 This story is found in GD James, *Amazed by Love*, 1977.

252 The writer wrote chapter 1 of this book, *That Asia May Know,* entitled, "G D James: The Man, the Vision and the Mission," edited by Jonathan James & Malcolm Tan.

sions. Because of their presence, the Singapore church has been greatly exposed to missions.

In 1980, the Singapore Center for Evangelism and Missions (SCEM) was organized to stimulate mission interest among the local churches by organizing conferences and workshops and providing resources for the churches. In 1990 and 1992, Overseas Crusade Asia, under the direction of SCEM, did some research on the Singaporean church and missions. The results indicated that in 1988, 140 Singaporeans became career missionaries. The number grew to 177 in 1990. In 1992, there were 321 missionaries from 167 churches, serving in forty-three different countries, primarily in Asia![253]

The foreign-based organizations such as OMF, SIM, WEC, and Wycliffe began to open their doors to Asians who had a real passion to serve God in cross-cultural settings in Asia. Andrew Ng, was challenged while studying in the Medical College to give his life to missions. In 1977, Andrew and his wife Belinda went to Niger, Africa, with SIM because of the latter's long-standing ministry in Africa. The Ngs were one of the very first Asian missionary couples to become career missionaries with SIM.

From the 1980s to 1990s, hundreds of missionaries were engaged in cross-cultural ministries, serving for at least a period of three years or more. Of the 321 missionaries, most were involved in teaching and equipping (114), church planting (83), and evangelism (50). A good number of them (26) were also involved in administrative responsibilities. Another interesting finding was that the majority of the Singaporean missionaries, 200 of the 321, were single women.

Another project about the position of missions in Singapore, undertaken and completed by SCEM in 2001, revealed that of

---

253 Overseas Crusade Asia Research Department, "The Status of Mission Programs in English-speaking Protestant Churches," April 1992.

the 454 missionaries, 69 percent were serving in Asia, and about 39 percent were working in unevangelized areas.[254] This research also showed that the majority of the missionaries were involved in the three main ministries of equipping/teaching, church planting, and evangelism. There seemed to be a significant increase in mission involvement sometime between 1990 and the turn of the twenty-first century.

The Significant Breakthrough in the Missionary Movements in the Twenty-first Century

By the beginning of the twenty-first century, there were breakthroughs in missions. What were some factors for such an involvement? Did the church in Singapore come of age where missions is concerned? Were there other factors that forced the church to go in this direction?

Certainly, there was greater interest in missions in an unprecedented manner in the 1990s. With the presence of numerous mission organizations, mission conferences, seminars, and special focus groups such as "Adopt-A-People Group," "AD 2000," and "Joshua Project" all these contributed to a wave of excitement especially among youth and young adults who volunteered in some form of mission, be it short term or long term. The registration of the Operation Mobilization (OM) *Logos I*, and later the *Doulos*, which has the world's largest floating bookshop, became very popular as young Singaporean Christians were able to channel their passion for Christ by embarking on these ships, traveling around the world, and doing mission in the various countries.

Some churches were also very involved in missions because their pastors were particularly touched by God in special ways. This caused them to challenge the church members who then responded readily to go forth as missionaries directly under the

254 SCEM, Power Point Presentation, sent to the writer, February 2009.

auspices of the local church. Two churches need special mention. One is the Glad Tidings Church, an Assemblies of God denomination, whose pastor, Reverend William Lee, first caught the vision of training nationals when he visited countries like Indonesia. He started a training program to equip the nationals by starting Bible schools. Through this training, many local people were empowered to plant churches and to shepherd them. Through this method, hundreds of churches were planted in the various places.[255]

Another is Grace Singapore Chinese Christian Church. The pastor, Reverend Chan Fong, a graduate of Fuller Theological Seminary, chose to "do" missions in an intentional manner and so this became the priority of Grace Church. Chan Fong was first challenged when he made a trip to Thailand. There he saw the plight of the people and their lost state. In 1974, the church intentionally earmarked a mission budget, which has grown significantly over the years. In 1992, she had a budget of almost 500,000 Singapore dollars (S$), which supported more than thirty-four missionaries. Currently, the church is supporting sixty-five missionaries, with a budget of almost S$1.1 million.[256] Some of the mega churches (with congregations of several thousands) were part of "Antioch 21" which was organized almost like business corporations, encouraging entire cell churches to go on short mission trips, spending thousands of dollars each time to send their members to the needy fields, without adequate preparation. While this is a wonderful way to expose the Singaporean Christians to missions, the lack of preparation, intentionality, and sensitivity to the local religions and cultures can have repercussions. This has happened in some cases, setting back even further the years of bridge building with some hostile nations such as Acheh in North Sumatra.

---

255 Sng, *In His Good Time*, 317.

256 Interview with one of the pastors from Grace Chinese Christian Church, March 2009.

The idea of tentmaking has become very popular among the Singaporean Christians. The Singapore government has been encouraging Singaporean businessmen to undertake business ventures overseas especially in China, India, Vietnam, and Cambodia. Many Christians see this as an excellent opportunity to enter some of the countries that have been closed to the gospel. Singaporean professionals can now enter countries that were inaccessible to them before, and at the same time be available to do God's work. Hence, the term "tentmaking," patterned after St. Paul, came into vogue.

In the last decade, several Singaporeans were able to enter countries that were inaccessible to the gospel due to government restrictions. These countries are referred to as Creative Access Nations, or CAN for short. Reginald Tsang and James Hudson Taylor III established the MSI Professional Services, formerly known as the Medical Services International, in 1994. This is actually an arm of the OMF but since the latter is well known as a foreign-based western organization, the MSI was an ideal outfit to enter these nations without any suspicion. The MSI saw the tremendous opportunities that were made available to professionals who could be trained and sent to places that would otherwise have no means of hearing the gospel. Since its inception, more than thirty Singaporean missionaries have served in CAN, through MSI, in medical, community health, English language instruction, and in business and management positions.[257] However in order for greater effectiveness, there is a critical need to clarify what tentmaking really is: for proper understanding of cross-cultural involvement, sound biblical training and the church's responsibility to screen, select, encourage, and send tentmakers who will impact and influence the people for Christ and his kingdom.

In the last few decades, one phenomenal feature in Singapore has been a shift in the social demography of the society. As the

---

257 Sng, *In His Good Time*, 346 and interview with MSI missionaries, March 2009.

nation has opened its doors to foreign professional talent and blue-collared migrant workers, the island has been overwhelmed with a colorful spectrum of people from Southeast Asia, South Asia, the Far East, Europe, Australia, and North America. Some of the churches have begun to see the potential mission at their doorstep and are making small, but intentional ways to reach out to both professional and blue-collared workers. Among the domestic foreign workers from Indonesia and the Philippines alone, there are more than 180,000 working in Singapore.[258] The total number of foreign workers has probably exceeded more than 500,000! What an excellent opportunity to have missions at one's doorstep! Several churches have made small steps to minister to some of these migrants, such as the Indian, Indonesian, Thai, Chinese, and Myanmar migrants and professionals but only a few churches are intentional in their outreach ministries.

More recently, some churches have begun to experiment with creative ways to empower the poor by teaching them to learn a trade, plant crops, or do animal husbandry. The missions program at the Singapore Bible College is unique in that it emphasizes courses to empower the poor, such as microfinance and microfarming, under the main curriculum of microenterprise. Students from Myanmar, Indonesia, Philippines, Thailand, and India are given a holistic approach to missions. This allows them to build bridges with the people, thereby enabling them to break the poverty cycle and create opportunities to share the good news.[259]

---

258 The writer's church is involved with "mission at our doorstep" and some of the information has come in that context and from other interactions.

259 Interview with Dr. Eric Tan, lecturer in the Missions program at the Singapore Bible College, March 2009.

Evaluating the Strengths and Weaknesses of the Missionary Movement in Singapore

In the past thirty or forty years of the missionary movement in Singapore, the church has certainly come of age with regard to its involvement in missions both locally and globally. It has moved from doing missions tentatively, by trial and error, to becoming intentional, bold, and confident. It has seen the need to be more holistic in its approach and has broken new ground and ventured into some creative areas to reach the unreached and the unevangelized. The Singaporean missionary has certainly come a long way in learning and doing missions. The church has come to recognize its responsibility to the Great Command and the Great Commission.

The church has also seen the need for training nationals who in turn can train others in a manner that the missionaries will never be able to. This is certainly the success story of Asia Evangelistic Fellowship (AEF), Glad Tidings Church, and Grace Chinese Church.

From the AEF model, we learn how the leaders were willing to adapt with the times by developing new ministries that reaped a great harvest. In its initial stage, the methodology used was mass evangelistic rallies and crusades in the different countries in Asia. Thousands of people were converted through this method. The converts were channeled into the existing churches, but because of lack of follow-up and discipleship, many fell through the cracks. Later, the leadership saw the need to empower the nationals by establishing training centers such as the School of Missions and Evangelism (SOME), which later was replaced by the Asia College of Ministry (ACOM). Today, training is conducted in different parts of Asia with the purpose of equipping the nationals to train their own people. This has turned out to be a very effective method that others are slowly learning to emulate.

However, there are some important warnings that the church must pay heed. God has truly blessed the church in Singapore: today, more than 15 percent in a population of four million is Christian. Most of the Christians are English-speaking, white-collared professionals who are making a significant impact in the marketplace. Despite this breakthrough, some striking features of the Singapore churches are that it is monocultural and typically from the upper and middle class. One rarely would find English-speaking Singaporean Indians in these churches, which are predominantly Chinese in ethnicity, and vice versa. Among the Singaporean Chinese Christians who are professionals, rarely would one find blue-collared workers of the same ethnicity, worshipping side by side. Many of the local churches are distinctly Chinese, Indian, Indonesian, Korean, or representatives of other migrant communities. The church in Singapore must move cross-culturally and across the social strata within her own communities. The church must address some of these concerns in the context of evangelism and missions. The Church of Jesus Christ is called by God to represent every people group, tongue, nationality, and culture, as reflected in Revelation 7:9. Antioch is here in Singapore, but the church in Singapore is not a true reflection of the church in Antioch.

Vinod Ramachandra, from Inter-Fellowship of Evangelical Students (IFES), also made some astute observations about the Singapore church and missions. He believed that the churches are "still trapped in their heritage of western colonial mission." He explained this as mission from "top-down," that like the colonial missionaries, the Singaporean missionaries are doing mission from a position of wealth and power to people who have neither wealth nor power. Moreover, like the colonial mission, the Singapore church has failed to see that "the visible unity of the Church is part of the gospel."[260] Ramachandra also observed

260 Vinod Ramachandra, "Integral Mission and the Kingdom of God," 1.

that the local churches are very independent in the way they do missions and have isolated themselves from the larger body of Christ. The writer agrees with these observations. She is aware of some mainline denominations that have not only transplanted their denominations in other parts of Asia, but continue to govern these national churches. The right to control seems to be related to their financial support of these churches. These leaders continue to conduct baptisms and other important acts of governance, rather than allowing the national congregations to take leadership. Even similar denominations such as the Methodist, Brethren, and Baptist, are independent in their mission activities. This certainly goes against the very nature of Christ. In his high priestly prayer, Jesus prayed, "that all of them may be one, Father, just as you are in me and I am in you" (John 17:21). The world we live in is fragmented. The values and worldviews are pluralistic and secular. For the church to obey Christ's Great Command and Great Commission, it is imperative for the believers to rethink their position in the body of Christ and to make every effort to portray a visible unity. The Holy Trinity is one and Christ's Body must likewise be one. As Christ prayed, so must the church echo its Master's prayer, "May they be brought to complete unity to let the world know that you sent me and have loved then even as you have loved me" (John 17:23).

Conclusion

Is Singapore the Antioch of Asia? There are some external similarities with Antioch. Singapore is a cosmopolitan city with multicultural, multilingual, multireligious, multiethnic communities that are constantly evolving. The landscape of the church is generally monocultural which in itself makes her different from the church in Antioch. Singapore has become a hub for all kinds of Christian activity, serving as headquarters of several mission organizations is challenging the church to be more concerted and intentional in doing mission. However, the church in Singapore must also reflect the values and the worldview of God's kingdom, which were evident in the church in Antioch. The entire church in Antioch was involved in mission and the entire church sent forth Saul and Barnabas, their very best members, to the mission fields, because they were sensitive to the voice of God (Acts 13:1–3). Mission is not about programs and projects, although when we do missions, there will be some measure of those elements. Mission is not restricted to a handful of people from the church who cross borders to become career missionaries, although this is a vital part of missions. We need hundreds, if not thousands of career missionaries, who can reach out to the hundreds of people groups that have not heard the gospel or do not have access to Christians or the Bible in their own vernacular. Mission is about being the disciples of Jesus Christ, called to a life of obedience. This obedience is not restricted to a few areas but is all-pervasive—it embraces every facet of the disciple's life and activity. When we live out our faith in such a manner, others will be attracted to this faith. This is what Jesus meant when he said, "let your light so shine before men that they may see your good good deeds and praise your Father in heaven" (Matt 5:16). When we intentionally live our lives as the disciples of Jesus, obeying him in everything that he has called us to obey, this will happen! People will begin to take note of us and "see our good works." Then, they will glorify God! This is God's blueprint for doing missions in the twenty-first century, and when the church does missions in God's way, it will bear much fruit. One day, standing before the throne of God, we will see people from every nation, every tribe, every people group, every tongue, and they will sing with one voice, "Hallelujah to the Lamb!"

Bibliography

Athyal, Saphir, ed. *Church in Asia Today.* Asia Lausanne Committee for World Evangelization, 1996.

Darr, Darrell. "Centers for World Mission from Singapore 1988," *International Journal of Frontier Missions* Winter (2002): 28–30.

De Winne, Andre. "An Overview of Missions Movement in Singapore," February, 1996.

Goh, Robbie. *Christianity in Southeast Asia.* Singapore: ISEAS Publications, 2005.

Hoke, Donald, ed. *The Church in Asia.* Chicago, IL: Moody Press, 1975.

Horn, Tom. "The Singapore Missionary and Training, Sending and Supervision." OC Asia Research Department, January 1996.

James, G D. *Amazed By Love.* Singapore: Asian Action Press, 1977.

James, Jonathan and Malcolm Tan. *That Asia May Know.* Asia Evangelistic Fellowship International, 2000.

Johnstone, Patrick. *Operation World.* Grand Rapids, MI: Zondervan Publishing House, 1993.

Mays, David. *More Stuff You Need to Know About Doing Missions in Your Church, A Handbook of Lists.* Atlanta, GA: ACMC, 2002.

Overseas Crusade Asia Research Department. "The Status of Mission Programs in English-Speaking Protestant Churches." *Toward an Understanding of the Missions Movement in Singapore Churches,* April 1992.

———."The Status of Career, Cross-cultural Missionaries from Protestant Churches." *Toward an Understanding of the Singaporean Missionary Force.* October 1992.

Ramachandra, Vinoth. "Integral Mission and the Kingdom of God." *Perspective.* Singapore: IFES, 2008.

Sng, Bobby. *In His Good Time: The Story of the Church in Singapore, 1819–2002.* Bible Society of Singapore, 2003.

Sunquist, Scott, ed. *A Dictionary of Asian Christianity.* Grand Rapids, MI: Eerdmans, 2001.

Tucker, Ruth. *From Jerusalem to Irian Jaya.* Grand Rapids, MI: Zondervan, 2004.

Wall, A. F. *The Missionary Movement in Christian History: Studies in the Transmission of Faith.* Maryknoll, NY: Orbis, 1996

Winter, Ralph and Steve Hawthorne, eds. *Perspectives on the World Christian Movement, A Reader.* Pasadena, CA: William Carey Library, 1999.

About Dr. Violet James

Dr. Violet James received her PhD in 1990 from Aberdeen University, Scotland. She lectures at the Singapore Bible College (SBC) on Church History and Religions. She is the adviser to the Student Mission Fellowship at SBC and newly appointed as the dean of students at SBC. She is also an adjunct lecturer at the Biblical Graduate School of Theology in Singapore, where she teaches Religions in Asia. She also lectures at Asia Cross-Cultural Training Institute (ACTI) in Singapore to prospective missionaries before they go into the field. She is also an associate pastoral staff at the Yio Chu Kang Chapel, where she heads the children's ministry.

8

The Rise of the Filipino Missionary Movement: A Preliminary Historical Assessment

TERESO C. CASIÑO, THD, PHD

Introduction

The history of the missionary movement in the Philippines is as old as the "discovery" of the archipelago by European navigators, who were ordered to search for new lands to conquer and rule. Missionary movements do not develop overnight, and the one in the Philippines is no exception. Raising a nation for global missions has its own twists and turns; many times, the task seems almost impossible. Almost five hundred years have passed since the Roman Catholic version of Christianity arrived in the Philippines. Nevertheless, it is only during the past two decades that the Philippines has risen to become an emerging missionary force in its own peculiar ways. Canadian missionary to Kenya, Howard Brant, identifies the Philippines as one of the seven epicenters of the emerging mission movements. Brant observes, "Many thousands are Christian. Mission leaders in the Philippines recognize that if only some of these could be trained to share their faith effectively they could have the same effect as the little slave girl who advised Naaman the leper where to go for healing."[261]

This paper seeks to highlight the significance of particular events and circumstances that led to the rise and expansion of the Filipino missionary movement in and beyond the Philippine archipelago. It also provides a preliminary assessment of the expanding Filipino missionary movement, highlighting its promise and assessing its weaknesses in the face of the church's global missionary task.

A Roman Catholic Foundation

The current Filipino Protestant missionary movement did not come out of a historical vacuum, but was rather prepared by its religious predecessor, that is, the pioneering efforts of the Filipino Roman Catholic Church. The Filipino Catholic missionary movement began as early as the 1600s, less than one hundred years after the arrival of Christianity in the archipelago. The first Catholic Filipino missionary to serve overseas was a woman. A nun, Martha de San Bernardino, was sent to Macau in 1634. The first batch of nonclergy Catholic missionaries to serve overseas was appointed in 1668. Pedro Calungsod and sixteen others went to the Marianas after their missionary appointment. In 1701, the first Filipino priest sent out to China was Don Ignacio Manesay. Don Alfonzo Baluio y Garcia (ca.1679–1722) was the first Filipino priest-appointed missionary among his own people in northern Philippines.[262]

---

261 See http://www.sim.org/index.php/content/seven-epicenters-of-emerging-mission-movements. On top of Howard Brant's list is Korea followed by China, Nigeria, Ethiopia, Latin America, Northeast India, and the Philippines.

262 Luciano P. R. Santiago, *To Love and to Suffer: The Development of the Religious Congregations for Women in the Spanish Philippines, 1565–1898* (Manila: Ateneo de Manila University Press, 2005), 173.

Major Factors behind the Rise of the Filipino Protestant Missionary Movement

A closer examination of the rise of the Filipino Protestant missionary movement will yield the following four major factors: historical, political, ecclesiastical, and socioeconomic. The first concerns historical elements that brought Christianity to the archipelago, which serves as the backdrop to all succeeding missionary efforts in the country and beyond the Philippine shores. The second involves the political events that provide the background to the formation of the missionary consciousness among Filipino Protestants. The third deals with the clamor for a redefinition of ministerial identity as Filipinos serve alongside foreign missionaries and church leaders. The fourth reveals the major factors that push Filipinos to migrate domestically and globally, and how these movements shape the direction of the international missionary movement in the country.

Historical Factors

Christianity was first "shipped" to the Philippines by a Portuguese navigator-explorer named Ferdinand Magellan on March 16, 1521. Magellan set sail from Spain on September 20, 1519 to find a "westward route to the Spice Islands (the Moluccas) but accidentally sighted Limasawa Island, near Leyte. On March 17, 1521, Magellan set foot on the soil of Homonhon, and fifteen days after, on Easter Sunday, celebrated a mass on the island administered by Friar Pedro de Valderrama."[263] It was on the same day that Magellan laid claim to his "discovery," naming it the "Archipelago of St. Lazaro."

Like other conquistadors, Magellan believed that the spread of Christianity was an effective means by which Spanish political

263 Arthur L. Tuggy, *The Philippine Church: Growth in a Changing Society* (Grand Rapids, MI: Eerdmans, 1971), 25.

control could be implemented in the newly found islands.[264] The navigator also acted as "missionary." John Leddy Phelan writes:

> Magellan's newly found religious enthusiasm was not solely the consequence of imperialist motives. Magellan, the navigator and merchant, threw himself fervently into his new role as an apostle of the gospel until he reached a state of spiritual intoxication, which undermined his sound judgment of things mundane.[265]

The formal introduction, however, of Christianity as a rational faith had to wait until the coming of Miguel Lopez de Legazpi. In Legazpi's expedition, five Augustinian missionaries were on board, led by Father Andres de Urdaneta. Urdaneta, as a young man, visited the islands in 1525. Under Legazpi, Urdaneta served as both navigator and spiritual leader.

Spain successfully colonized the Philippines without interference from other foreign powers, except for the coming of the Dutch in 1610 and the Spanish defeat in the hands of the Americans in 1898. Since the Las Islas Filipinas was Spain's only colony in the Far East, it was easy for the Spanish regime to concentrate military forces on the area, as well as introduce development across the archipelago. At the time of Spanish conquest, Muslim intrusion into the area was just beginning, and the majority of the lowland natives seemed to be ready for change.[266] Moreover, the use of force to subdue the natives, particularly along the coastal areas saw little resistance, and, as a trend, "acceptance of Spain meant acceptance of Spain's religion."

---

264 John Leddy Phelan, "Prebaptismal Instruction and the Administration of Baptism in the Philippines during the Sixteenth Century" in *Studies in Philippine Church History*, edited by Gerald H. Anderson (Ithaca/London: Cornell University Press, 1969), 23.

265 Ibid.

266 J. Herbert Kane claims that the Roman Catholic Church must be credited for stopping the spread of Islam from Indonesia through the Philippine islands, from *A Concise History of the Christian World Mission* (Grand Rapids, MI: Baker Book House, 1982), 131–32.

Political Events

Revolt by the Filipinos against Spain paved the way for the introduction of Protestant missions in the Philippines. In the early 1800s, many natives in the archipelago started to identify themselves as "Filipinos" with heavy emphases on "independence," "nationalism," and "sovereignty." Their quest for identity led to the outbreak of hostilities between them and their Spanish conquistadors. Jose S. Arcilla, a Filipino Jesuit historian, points out three groups considered instrumental in the revolt against Spain, which commenced in 1896, namely, the Masonic lodges, Jose Rizal's Liga Filipina, and Andres Bonifacio's Katipunan.[267] The nineteenth century witnessed three major forces working side by side to eventually open doors for a revolution against Spanish regime: (1) the political chaos in Spain, (2) the Spanish-Filipino division among the clergy in the autocratic church in the Philippines, and (3) the breakdown of civil administration on the town level plus a mounting national unrest.[268]

Spain declared war against the United States on April 25, 1898. On May 1, 1898, under the tactical leadership of Commodore Dewey, the United States Navy defeated the Spanish armada in Manila Bay. On December 10, 1898, Spain ceded the Philippines to United States with the signing of the Treaty of Paris; hence, a new era of Protestant missions began.

In the aftermath of Spain's ceding of the Philippines to the US government, the expanding Protestant missions to the Philippines found an ally in the White House in the person of President William McKinley. President McKinley believed that the Philippines was "a gift from the gods" to the Americans. He noted that "there was nothing left for us to do but to take

267 Jose S. Arcilla, *An Introduction to Philippine History* (Manila: Ateneo de Manila Press, 1973), 96–104. Revolts began as early as 1621 (Bohol region), 1660 (Pangasinan), and 1661 (Ilocos).

268 See Nicholas P. Cushner, *Spain in the Philippines: From Conquest to Revolution* (Quezon City: Ateneo de Manila University Press, 1971), 210–229.

them all, and to educate the Filipinos, and uplift and civilize and Christianize them, and by God's grace do the very best we could by them, as our fellow-men for whom Christ also died."[269]

Political and religious revolution almost came hand-in-hand in the nineteenth century Philippines. Spanish friars were very reluctant in handing over the reign of ecclesiastical control to the Filipinos. In fact, an indigenous priesthood began to take shape only in the eighteenth century. However, the "spirit of nationalism" motivated many Filipinos to dream of having an indigenized clergy.[270] Wanton abuse of power and corruption among the ranks of the friars brought dissatisfaction to the masses. To combat abuses and eradicate corruption, Filipino priests banded together at the expense of the lives of many, three of whom became famous martyrs, namely, Jose Burgoz, Mariano Gomez, and Jacinto Zamora. Richard L. Deats observes,

> The Roman church, so hopelessly allied with Spanish interests, simply did not comprehend the scope of Filipino dissatisfaction with the friars, nor did it sympathize with the legitimate desires of the native priests. Thus, the native priests found themselves step by step drawing closer to the efforts of their fellow countrymen for political freedom.[271]

---

269 James Rusling, "Interview with President William Mckinley," *The Christian Advocate*, January 22, 1903, 17, cited in *The Philippines Reader: A History of Colonialism, Dictatorship, and Resistance*, edited by Daniel B. Schirmer and Stephen Rosskamm Shalom (Quezon City: Ken Incorporated, 1987), 22–23.

270 For an excellent treatment on the relationship between nationalism and indigenous clergy, see Richard L. Deats, *Nationalism and Christianity in the Philippines* (Dallas, TX: Southern Methodist University Press, 1967), 13–90.

271 Ibid., 63. Deats explains further: "Although these priests remained loyal to Rome, they found it impossible to remain loyal to the Spanish hierarchy and the Spanish friars. Despite their training in ecclesiastical obedience, the Filipino priests hoped that they could be loyal to both their country and the Pope while working for the ouster of the Spanish missionaries" (Ibid., 63–64). For a "nationalist" analysis of the marriage of religion and nationalism in the Philippines, see Renato Constantino, *The Philippines: A Past Revisited* (Quezon City: Published by the Author, 1975), 252–55.

One of the proponents of reform and indigenization was Father Gregorio Aglipay, whose group, La Iglesia Filipina Independiente, broke away from Rome on August 3,1902. Aglipay was a leading inspiration of many priests and laypersons in their dream to have a kind of Christianity which was supposed to be Filipino in form, leadership, and practice. Aglipay's break away from Rome gave a severe blow to the already shaky powers of the Spanish friars. It helped many Filipinos to believe that natives could become Christians, even without the blessing of Rome. Severing ties with Rome created confusion among dissatisfied Catholics. This had a significant bearing on the later success of Protestant mission in the Philippines.[272]

Ecclesiastical Elements

By 1903, 92 percent of the Filipino natives were Christianized lowlanders, 3 percent were Muslims, and 5 percent were animistic tribal groups.[273] When Protestant missions entered the country after Dewey's victory over the Spanish armada, it was clear that the task was not only evangelization but also "re-evangelization" of the already "evangelized" people. In a word, the story of the expansion of Protestant missions in the Philippines is not a story of evangelization but rather a story of "the re-evangelization of the Catholic Filipinos." This conviction serves as the foundation of the birth and development of the Filipino Protestant missionary movement.

The formation of the Iglesia Evangelica was crucial to the formation of mission consciousness of Filipino Protestants. Mission societies in America took two years to dispatch career

---

272 Describing the situation during the turn of the twentieth century Philippines, Pedro S. de Achutegui and Miguel A. Bernard write, "It was a confused era, a time of political, social and religious upheaval. In such a time, motives are often mixed and actions are often equivocal," from *Religious Revolution in the Philippines*, vol. 1 (Manila: Ateneo de Manila University Press, 1961), v.

273 Arthur Tuggy, *The Philippine Church: Growth in a Changing Society* (Grand Rapids, MI: Eerdmans, 1971), 87.

missionaries to the Philippines (March 1901). Seeing that Filipinos were hungry of the word of God, missionaries rushed to the archipelago with the intent of reevangelizing the Filipinos.[274] The receptive attitudes of the Filipinos made many mission societies in America panic, and eventually, send missionaries to the archipelago. Thus, eight missionary societies entered the country in four years as the following data show:

DENOMINATION	YEAR ENTERED
Presbyterians	1899
Methodists	1900
Northern Baptists	1900
United Brethren	1901
Disciples of Christ	1901
Protestant Episcopal	1901
Congregationalists	1902
Christian and Missionary Alliance	1902
Seventh-day Adventists	1905

EARLY AMERICAN MISSION SOCIETIES[275]

In 1901 alone, three mainline denominations entered the colony, and in that same year, six major denominations from America had already begun work in the country. This was a significant step for an infant mission work in a country of Catholic Christians. It soon became evident that working in a predominantly Catholic colony necessitates cooperation among the six

274 The sentiments of many Christians in America after the Spanish defeat in Manila Bay can be summarized by George F. Pentecost's words: "We cannot ignore the fact that God has given into our hands, that is, into the hands of American Christians, the Philippine Islands, and there opened a wide door and effectual to their populations and has, by the very guns of our battleships, summoned to us to go up and possess the land," from Arthur Judson Brown, *The New Era in the Philippines* (Nashville, TN: Nashville Publishing House, 1903), 174, cited in Tuggy, 97.

275 A. Leonard Tuggy and Ralph Toliver, *Seeing the Church in the Philippines* (Manila: OMF Publishers, 1972), 18.

denominations; hence, the birth of the Iglesia Evangelica or the Evangelical Union. Protestants found it important to band together for (1) unity of work and to avoid confusion among the Filipinos, and (2) to work on geographical allotments for each mission's work.

Part of the commitment of the Evangelical Union in 1901 was to allocate areas on which each denomination could do mission work under a "Comity Agreement." The Comity Agreement stipulates that each mission society would work only within its specific jurisdictional areas. The agreement proved to be an important strategy in expanding missions to the thousands of islands across the archipelago.[276] The Evangelical Union (EU) dissolved in 1929 and was succeeded by the National Christian Council (NCC), which lasted from 1929 through 1938. The NCC survived only for almost ten years and was renamed the Philippine Federation of Evangelical Churches (PFEC), which in turn lasted only from 1928 through 1949. By 1949, the PFEC dissolved and reorganized as the Philippine Federation of Christian Churches (PFCC), thereby dropping the Evangelical nomenclature. Then again, in 1963, PFCC reorganized and became the National Council of Churches in the Philippines (NCCP).[277]

Another ecclesiastical body that became instrumental in the formation of the missionary consciousness of the Filipino Protestant mind was the Philippine Council of Evangelical Churches in the Philippines (PCEC). An "evangelical alternative" to the NCCP, the PCEC was formed in 1964 by a "group of Christian leaders seeking to form an organization that would express their oneness in Jesus Christ and to formalize into a

276 See Ibid., for specific allocated areas for each mission society.

277 See http://www.nccphilippines.org/index_files/Page759.htm. The NCCP homepage notes, "During the Japanese occupation in 1942 to 1944, churches were merged to form the Evangelical Church of the Philippines under the auspices of the Religious Sector of the Japanese Imperial Army. This formation was dissolved after the Second World War as the Churches reconstituted the pre-war Federation."

distinct council the growing force and influence of evangelism in the country."[278] Accordingly, the "defense of the fundamentals of faith, the need to evangelize the Philippines, and the need to have a clearly evangelical witness were the primary factors that prompted" the formation of PCEC.[279]

Of course, the NCCP and its early predecessors and the PCEC are not the only ones responsible for the rise and expansion of the missionary movement in the Philippines. There are other ecclesiastical bodies and missions-minded organizations (e.g., Pentecostal, independent churches) across the nation that have also become instrumental for forming a missionary consciousness in the minds and heart of Filipino Protestants. Apparently, though, membership in one of these organizations encourages cooperation among member churches in missions and evangelization as well as creates and preserves unity and fellowship among organizational members.

Socioeconomic Factors

Socioeconomic situations and conditions in Philippine society led to demographic changes in the archipelago. In fact, ancient Filipinos were known to be "people on the move" and that the Philippines was born out of waves of migration.[280] In modern times, domestic migration within the country stretches the missionary vision and consequently drains resources allocated for local evangelism, thanks to Filipino families and individuals moving from one place to another across the islands. Many of these movements were politically motivated; others were simply voluntary with a dream to look for a greener pasture in some other parts of the Philippines. Prior to the Second World War,

---

278 See http://www.pceconline.org/about/beginnings.htm.

279 Ibid.

280 See F. Landa Jocano, *Philippine Prehistory: An Anthropological Overview of the Beginnings of Filipino Society and Culture* (Manila: Philippine Center for Advanced Studies, 1975).

the government initiated a colonial program that sent thousands of citizens from northern and central Philippines to Mindanao, especially in areas where Muslims had either inhabited or roamed around for centuries. The migration wave increased in the 1960s. Now, claim Macapado A. Muslim and Rufa Cagoco-Guiam, the Muslim population reduced "to around 25% of Mindanao's population, from about 75% at the turn of the century."[281] Proponents of this colonial program trumpeted southern Philippines as the "Land of Promise" despite the displacements of thousands of Muslims.

This demographic change created tremendous challenges to the Filipino Protestant Church, yet it also opened up opportunities for evangelism and missionary work. Since most of the domestic migrants were Roman Catholics, local Protestant congregations took up the challenge to re-evangelize the new neighborhood. Domestic migration accounts for the presence of the denomination in many parts of the country—for example, Ilongos and Ilocanos in western Mindanao. In a particular part of the region in southern Philippines, mainly congregations under the Baptist Conventions and the Christian and Missionary Alliance in the Philippines (CAMACOP) carried out local missionary outreaches.

While the Filipino Protestant Church was busy handling domestic missionary needs, a greater challenge arose, when, under the supervision of the American colonial government in the early 1900s, Filipinos began migrating to American territories for employment. In the course of history, the Philippines has witnessed at least four major waves of international migration. The first wave occurred between 1900 and 1945 as thousands of Filipinos went to Hawaii to work in pineapple plantations. Filipinos also moved to California and Washington to become

---

281 Macapado A. Muslim and Rufa Cagoco-Guiam "Mindanao: Land of Promise," http://www.c-r.org/our-work/accord/philippines-mindanao/promised-land.php.

agricultural workers. Later, many headed for Alaska for employment in fish canneries. The second wave took place between 1946 and 1965, at least in the United States, where "war brides" or brides of servicemen moved to the United States to join their husbands. These brides petitioned their families back home to join them in their adopted country, America. In a matter of two decades, more than 36,000 Filipinos migrated to the United States.[282] The third wave happened in the 1960s, when hundreds of Filipino professionals left the Philippines to work as medical doctors, nurses, and medical technicians in North America and many parts of Europe. The fourth migration wave occurred in the 1970s. Under a government-sanctioned program, Filipino skilled workers—euphemistically labeled by the government as Overseas Contract Workers (OCW)—were "exported" to the Middle East and developing economies in Asia and other continents. Thousands of Filipino engineers, architects, caregivers (nannies), and construction laborers left the country to work overseas.[283]

The Current State of the Filipino Sending Church

One hundred years of the presence of Protestant Christianity in the Philippines witnessed the ups-and-downs of the country's missionary movement. For years, Filipino church leaders and their foreign missionary counterparts continued debating on whether the Filipino Protestant Church can train, send, and support missionaries domestically and internationally. Evidently, the growth of the Protestant Church in a predominantly Roman Catholic country was slow, especially during years of American colonial rule. Growth became steady after the commonwealth;

---

282 Amador Remigio Jr., "A Demographic Survey of the Filipino Diaspora," in *Scattered: The Filipino Global Presence*, eds. Luis Pantoja, Enoch Wan, and Joy Tira (Manila: LifeChange, 2004), 27–29.

283 http://pmscontario.tripod.com/id1.html.

by the 1960s, the Protestant Church was gaining more adherents compared to the first fifty years of existence in the country. However, at the turn of the twenty-first century, the Protestant Church registered unprecedented growth.

Ferdinand Marcos' declaration of martial law in the early 1970s had little effect on the growth of evangelical churches in the Philippines. In fact, the Protestant Church, especially the evangelical congregations, thrived during the Marcos' years and experienced tremendous growth beyond the martial law era. The last two decades witnessed the unprecedented growth of Protestant churches across the country. By 2010, the number of Evangelical/Full Gospel churches across the nation stands around 77,000.[284]

Apparently, congregations belonging to the Pentecostal movement (in particular, the Assemblies of God) have experienced tremendous growth in the last two decades. Next in line are CAMACOP churches, followed by the UCCP congregations and the Baptists.[285] Whether this growth in domestic arena spilled into other countries relative to overseas mission is something that remains to be seen in the coming years. The Philippines does not yet have available data on the impact that domestic church growth has made on a particular denomination's vision for and commitment to world missions.

A Filipino Missionary Turning Point: The Semarang Connection

Semarang, Indonesia was the gracious host to the first woman Baptist missionary from the Philippines. The first Baptist church in the Philippines was founded in 1900 in Jaro, Iloilo (central Philippines) by Braulio Manikan, a Filipino missionary and Eric

284 http://www.philchal.org/dawn/philchurchsummary.asp.

285 For a summary of the statistics on denominational growth in the Philippines, see http://philchal.org/dawn/nationalsum.asp.

Lund, a Swedish Baptist missionary supported by the American Baptist Missionary Union (later became American Baptist Foreign Mission Society in 1910). Out of this work, the Convention of the Philippine Baptist Churches (CPBC) was born in 1935. The relationship with CPBC and the American Baptist Foreign Mission Society solidified, especially when, in 1935, the Philippines became a commonwealth of the United States. In 1969, the turnover of properties to CPCB by ABFMS coincided with the appointment and sending of the first Baptist Filipino missionary to Indonesia, Sharon Ruiz-Duremdez, in cooperation with the Southern Baptist Convention in Semarang, Indonesia.[286]

The Philippine Missions Association

Although records are scarce regarding pioneering missionaries from the Philippines, it can be established that the plan to appoint and send out missionaries overseas began in the 1960s, particularly 1968–1969. However, on the national scene, the missionary movement began to take shape only when the Philippine Missions Association (PMA) was launched in 1983. Met Castillo founded the PMA and stayed on as its general secretary until 1995. PMA was born with a vision to "train, send, and receive missionaries." As the association expanded, it later emphasized missions mobilization by partnering missions-minded churches and mission agencies in the Philippines. The primary purpose of PMA was to (1) challenge, (2) equip, and (3) mobilize the Philippine Church in reaching the unreached peoples of the world with the gospel of Jesus Christ.[287] The Philippine Council of Evangelical Churches (PCEC) adopted PMA as its missions commission in 1983. Since then, local churches across the coun-

---

286 Carla Gay A. Romarate-Knipel, "One Mission, Different Voices: Overseas Missions of the Convention of the Philippine Baptist Churches," http://findarticles.com/p/articles/mi_m0NXG/is_2_41/ai_n16609034/?tag=content;col1.

287 http://philippinemissionsassociation.com/about-us/mission-a-vision.html.

try started to think about missions. The PMA conducted a series of missions awareness seminars for local churches and leaders in key areas across the country. As a national association, PMA has united denominations, mission agencies, mission commissions, local churches, and cross-cultural missions training institutions.

Under its second national director, Rey Corpuz, who served from 1995–2003, the PMA grew to a membership of over one hundred mission agencies and mission commissions at the grass-roots level across the nation. Emphases have been on local church mobilization, youth mobilization, M2M mobilization, and tent-making mobilization. After twenty years of existence, the PMA increases its effort in mobilizing "the GLOBAL Filipino Church to evangelize the unreached peoples of the world."[288]

The main feature then of the PMA is mobilization of the Filipino diaspora, thanks to the leadership of its third national director, Robert Lopez. Today, the PMA stresses on (1) partnership development to accelerate missions participation; (2) mentoring structures to advance mission paradigms; (3) and advocacy programs to address mission priorities.[289] In his 2007 National Director's Report, Lopez cites increasing collaboration between the PMA and partner members and networks that would aid the Philippine Missions Mobilization Movement (PM3). Notable of these partners are the Missionary Trainers Network, the Kairos Prayers Movers, the National Youth Missions Movement, the Ministry to Muslims (M2M) network, the Ummah Fellowship, Frontiers Movement International, the Ethne Movement, regional Unreached People Group organizations, and regional Filipino networks in Europe and the Middle East.[290]

---

288 For additional information on the ministries of the PMA, see http://philippinemissionsassociation.com./about-us/pma-history.html.

289 Ibid.

290 For a full report, see Robert Lopez, *From Missionary Field to Missions Force* (Manila: Philippine Missions Association, 2007), 24–25.

In its effort to fast track the mobilization and involvement of churches in the PM3, materials have been developed and produced specifically for a national mission mobilization. These include the *Worker to Witness* workbook, which was developed under the collaborative efforts of Glicerio Manzano and Jonathan Lewis; *Higher Purpose for Your Overseas Job* by Robert Clark; *Storying and the Acts Principle* by Johani Gauran; *Church Planting* by David Lim; "Sending with Care" by Meg Alag (video); *God's Foot Soldiers* by Joy Solina; and *Get Involved: Developing a Church Missions Program* by Met Castillo, the founder of the PMA.[291]

The Twin Thrusts of the PMA

In cooperation with the Philippine Council of Evangelical Churches (PCEC), the PMA views the equal importance of doing mission across the Philippine archipelago and beyond the shores. Lopez believes that local churches in the Philippines can fulfill the missionary mandate inside the country by mobilizing local churches; he also believes that the unreached people movements, the so-called religious block, can be reached with the gospel by mobilizing the millions of Filipinos in diaspora. "Without wanting to establish an 'elitist' category of missionaries/tentmakers," Lopez explains, "we at PMA feel that there is a great need to encourage and rally believers to bring an effective witness and plant churches among the least evangelized peoples. This has been the primary focus of PMA since its inception in 1983."[292]

The twenty-four sending bases that the PMA surveyed have deployed 649 long-term missionaries. This is approximately 21 percent of the total evangelical missionaries from the Philippines. Overall, there are 3,125 Filipino missionaries sent out by churches cross-culturally within the Philippines and overseas. In 2007

291 Ibid., 24, 33.

292 Robert Lopez, e-mail message to author, June 3, 2009.

alone, the PMA conducted seventy-five events in 180 domestic and overseas locations, reaching approximately over 140,000 individuals who attended PMA activities and programs.[293] By 2008, the PMA has reportedly trained 4,165 persons for missions, of which 2,781 received training locally and 1,384 obtained training overseas. In the missions mobilization area (PM3), the PMA scores very high with 8,924 people trained—5,004 in the Philippines and 3,920 overseas.[294]

Filipino Missionary Networks Overseas

While the PMA leads strongly in enlisting and training missionaries as well as mobilizing local church agencies on the Philippine shores, two major Filipino networks promote Filipino missionaries abroad, namely, the EURONET TRUST and the Filipino International Network. Other smaller Filipino networks for cooperative missionary tasks also exist in Hong Kong, Singapore, South Korea, Japan, North America, Taiwan, and some parts of Africa and South America.

EURONET TRUST

In 1994, diaspora Filipino leaders in Europe formed the EURONET TRUST (E-TRUST) with the primary aim to unite and mobilize Filipino Christian workers and Filipino-oriented ministries that operate in various parts of the European continent. The E-TRUST is "an inter-denominational networking whose purpose is to promote unity, provide fellowship and encouragement, to help equip the churches in Europe for the work of the ministry, to promote prayer and intercession, to be a prophetic voice for the Filipinos in Europe and to work together

293 Lopez, *From Missionary Field to Missions Force,* 24.

294 Roselyn Kuizon, the Trainers Network coordinator of the PMA, provided this information in an e-mail correspondence with the author on May 20, 2009.

for the evangelization and harvest of souls in Europe."[295] The current board of directors of E-TRUST include Ricardo Bolus Jr., senior pastor of Agape Christian Fellowship in London, UK, Antonio Ibarra, of the International Church in Frankfurt, Germany, and Francis Santos of ADI Missione Evangelica Filipina in Rome, Italy.

E-TRUST is essentially mission minded and considers the Great Commission (Matt 28:19–20; Mark 16:15) as one of the basic doctrines of the Bible. Once a year in November, E-TRUST holds a mission leadership conference dubbed as the "European Filipino Christian Workers Networking Conference" (EFCWNC), which is designed primarily to provide training to diaspora leaders across the continent. Between three to four hundred diaspora leaders attend this conference yearly.

PLACE OF CONFERENCE	YEAR HELD
Rome, Italy	2002
London, England	2003
Vienna, Austria	2004
Palma de Mallorca, Spain	2005
Florence, Italy	2006
Brussels, Belgium	2007
Palma de Mallorca, Spain	2008
Venice, Italy	2009 (November)

CONFERENCES BY E-TRUST

Filipino International Network (FIN)

The largest missionary network outside the Philippines is the Filipino International Network (FIN), with headquarters in

295 See http://www.euronettrust.com/index.html.

Canada. Joy Sadiri Tira, in consultation with leaders of CCC in Canada and the Christian and Missionary Alliance in Canada, convened a conference of mission-minded people in Larnaca, Cyprus on May 3–6, 1995. Thirty-one delegates from Europe, several Limited Access Nations, the Philippines, and North America participated in the conference, which produced the Larnaca Covenant. The Larnaca Covenant affirmed the "sovereignty of God in placing Filipino believers in the 10/40 window and the world."[296]

Since its inception, FIN has grown to become a global movement of Filipino believers who live and work outside their homeland, while fulfilling Great Commission tasks. The FIN website claims that it "is modern history's second ethnic mission movement to be global in scope, second to the Chinese diaspora mission movement, The Chinese Congress on World Evangelization (CCOWE) that started in 1976."[297] FIN organizes strategic consultations regularly. In the Middle East alone, FIN holds biannual consultations among diaspora leaders in the region. FIN does this by collaborating with other existing diaspora communities, such as Nepalese, Pakistanis, Chinese, Indians, and other Arab communities. FIN also publishes its books, runs a regular website,[298] operates the Institute of Diaspora Studies (in cooperation with Alliance Graduate School in Manila and Western Seminary in Portland),[299] and networks with various diaspora organizations and communities around the world.

---

296 Sadiri Joy Tira, "Filipino International Network: A Strategic Model for Filipino Diaspora Glocal Mission," in *Scattered: The Filipino Global Presence*, ed. Luis Pantoja, Enoch Wan, and Joy Tira (Manila: LifeChange, 2004), 157.

297 See http://fin-online.org/cms/content/view/34/39.

298 www.fin-online.org

299 A plan to establish an Institute of Diaspora Studies (IDS) in Korea is in the offing, which will be a collaboration between FIN and the Korea Diaspora Mission (KDM). The KDM is a missiological forum founded in 2008 in South Korea under the leadership of Dr. Gwi-Sam Cho, Professor of Missiology at Han Sei University. The organization focuses on conducting studies on global diaspora, strategy design, and missions networking.

A Preliminary Assessment

The modern Filipino missionary movement is still young but it does have its own strengths and weaknesses. Estimates may vary, but there are between 8 and 10 million Filipinos living and working abroad in 203 countries and territories. In 2001 alone, 13 percent of Filipinos lived and worked abroad.[300]

Areas of Strength

An overview of the rise and development of the Filipino missionary movement unfolds at least five major areas of strength. Each strong point reflects the Filipino believers' indigenous aspirations for and vision of global evangelization.

First, the Filipino missionary movement has access to vast human resources. The global presence of the Filipinos has been considered phenomenal. As of 2008, Filipinos scattered in almost two hundred countries in the world, an unprecedented feat by any Asian nation. Over 10 million Filipinos live and work overseas; 8 million are Overseas Filipino Workers (contractual workers). In fact, Filipino seafarers comprise 20 percent of the total 1.3 million, making the Philippines the number one supplier of nautical workers in the world.[301] The Philippine Overseas Employment Agency deploys one million OFWs every year. In terms of number, the Filipinos are third in rank as a diaspora community, next only to the Chinese (35 million) and the Indians (22 million). However, when the national population ratio is taken into consideration, the Filipinos would top the Chinese and the Indians. Thus, the potential for a global missionary work is tremendous. Millions of Filipinos work in Limited Access Nations (LAN), with over one million in Saudi Arabia alone.

---

300 Rosalinda Dimapilis-Baldoz, "The Overseas Filipino Workers (OFW) Phenomenon," in *Scattered: The Filipino Global Presence,* ed. Luis Pantoja, Enoch Wan, and Joy Tira (Manila: LifeChange, 2004), 41.

301 Ibid., 40. Accordingly, Filipino seamen staff ships registered in 116 countries around the world.

Second, the Philippine missionary movement is committed to partnership in mission, in both domestic and global scale. For example, the PMA collaborates with the National Youth Missions Movement, a network of campus ministries whose aim is to "inform, inspire and involve the larger evangelical youth sector in bringing their witness to the world."[302] This network pools together organizations like the Campus Crusade for Christ, Navigators, Inter-Varsity, among others. Sending bodies and churches in the Philippines have collaborated with mission-minded organizations in different parts of the world, such as in the United States, Canada, Korea, Japan, Hong Kong, Taiwan, Singapore, United Arab Emirates, Bahrain, Kuwait, Qatar, Indonesia, Denmark, Norway, the Netherlands, and the United Kingdom, among others. Even the Global Committee of the FIN has non-Filipino members, such as Enoch Wan (Chinese-Canadian), Doug Nichols (American), and T. V. Thomas (Malaysian-Canadian). Working closely with FIN is Ted Yamamori (Japanese-American), former international director of Lausanne Committee for World Evangelization (LCWE). In Korea, Filipino missionaries have established strong partnering relations with Korean church leaders, organizations, and a few theological institutions.

Third, the active involvement of lay leaders in key ministry functions in mission churches abroad is commendable. In the Middle East, for example, it is estimated that more than 90 percent of the Filipino church leaders or "pastors" do not have ordination. Most of them became believers while working in the region. Because of tremendous needs in the ministry, they became senior leaders of a local congregation or a mission-oriented diaspora community. It is common then to meet Filipino missionaries in the Middle East who work as engineers or nurses

302 Robert Lopez, "A New Wineskin: The Filipino Global Missions Movement," in *From Missionary Field to Missions Force* (Manila: Philippine Missions Association, 2007), 32.

at day, and then become a leader of a worship service among a Nepalese or Indian congregation at night.

Professional or regular missionaries have difficulty entering the homes of Muslims in the Middle East. Such is not case of Filipinas who serve as nannies, therapists, cooks, or nurses as they fulfill duties every day in places that are inaccessible to regular missionaries. In their daily work, these Filipino workers can pray inside homes, offices, bathrooms, dining rooms, living rooms, and other places that are not normally accessible to regular missionaries. Filipina caregivers, of course, can teach gospel songs—even just the music—to kids or pray for them daily. By 2010, notes David Lim, the tentmaker movement in the Philippines would have recruited, trained, and sent out 200,000 tentmakers to serve all over the world.[303] This seems to be a doable plan because already, 7 percent of the 8 million OFWs are evangelical Protestants living and working in different parts of the world. Lopez estimates that "50,000 Filipino believers in and outside the country . . . are intentionally witnessing to non-Filipinos."[304]

Fourth, there is an increasing interest among the Filipino youth and young professionals to get involved in short-term missions. Many of those who participated in past short-term services abroad returned to the Philippines with a stronger commitment to long-term missionary work. In the last decade, a growing number of mission organizations have been established to enlist, train, and mobilize short-term missionaries. In Manila, Cross-Train offers aspiring OFWs a missionary training program based on the book, *A Higher Purpose for Your Overseas Job*.[305] Up north, in Baguio City, young people and local leaders participate in short-term services under the auspices of the Asia Vision for Short

303 David S. Lim, "Vignettes of the Filipino Tentmaker." http://tentmakernet.com/articles/vignettes.htm.

304 Robert Lopez's e-mail correspondence with the author on June 3, 2009.

305 See Robert Claro, *A Higher Purpose for Your Overseas Job* (Makati: Crossover Books, 2003).

Term Missions (AVSTM), a program initiated by Philippine-educated missionaries from Korea. A team of former Filipino AVSTM participants, with a continuing supervision of a Korean missionary-teacher, now operates the program.

Fifth, there is an increasing cooperation between theological institutions and mission organizations and denominations for missionary training. A growing number of seminaries in the Philippines now offer programs in intercultural studies or missiology and regular- or short-term courses related to missionary care, mission strategies, missionary leadership, and world religions, among others. Major theological institutions in the country that offer these courses or full degree programs include Asian Theological Seminary (ATS), Asia Pacific Nazarene Theological Seminary (APNTS), Presbyterian Theological Seminary (PTS), Biblical Seminary of the Philippines (BSOP), Alliance Graduate School (AGS), International School of Leaders (formerly ISOT), and Philippine Baptist Theological Seminary (PBTS), among others. PBTS became the first theological institution in the country to establish a campus-based missions training center, namely, the Asia Pacific Institute of Missions (APIM). Since its inception in 1997, APIM has trained more than five hundred missionary aspirants, students, researchers, and lay leaders for global mission through the institute's major programs. Increasing partnership among denominational bodies in the country also exists. For example, in 2008, five Baptist Conventions in Luzon, Visayas, and Mindanao agreed to cooperate in the enlistment, training, screening, and commissioning of missionary aspirants. These conventions established the One Sending Body (OSB), and later the Philippine Partnership for Global Community (PPGC). On June 15, 2009, the PPGC entered into an official partnership with Cross-Train in Manila, the APIM, and AVSTM in Baguio City for the training of missionary aspirants and candidates.[306]

306 Precy Caronongan's e-mail correspondence with the author on June 13, 2009.

Areas of Weakness

While the Filipino missionary movement possesses a good number of strengths, it does have apparent weaknesses. This section will identify five major weaknesses.

First, the tendency to overemphasize tentmaking at the expense of "regular" missionary mobilization could weaken local church participation in terms of giving to and support for world missions. Apparently, the concept of raising tentmakers to implement God's missionary plan finds support in the Bible.[307] Any attempt to overrate tentmaking at the expense of other proven missionary methods may diminish support from local church or mission-minded believers who want to support God's missionary intentions the "old, traditional way" (e.g., pledges, faith promise, etc.).

Second, the funding base, with its mechanism and strategies for fundraising, is still relatively weak in the Philippines. The Filipino missionary movement is full of reports about missionaries pulling out of the field because of lack of funds or beccause the support never arrives. Not a few sending bodies in the Philippines still practice the almost mythical belief that all that a missionary family needs in the field is faith in God for daily provision. This kind of mentality or "mission theology" damages the image of the missionary identity, not to mention the psychological stress that missionary children experience because of the lack of good financial planning and mission stewardship of their parents' sending body.

Third, the absence of a biblically sound theology of mission could hinder the effectiveness and long-term growth of the Filipino missionary movement. Some mission leaders in the country, including foreign missionary counterparts, still view mission

307 Robert K. Lopez, "The Unfolding Story of the Filipino Tentmaking Movement." http://www.wea connections. com/images/uploads/CN_200601_pag15-16.pdf.

as primarily cross-cultural in nature.[308] Mission leaders in the Philippines are still divided on viewing missionary work from the standpoint of elitist culturology or anthropology rather than soteriology. The former argues that cross-cultural elements determine missionary activity; the latter affirms the biblical teaching that accessibility to the gospel and its proclamation to those who need it define the global missionary task.[309]

Fourth, many Filipino diaspora congregations overseas suffer from weak ecclesiology. One may visit a congregation of twenty members with six "pastors"—none of whom has theological training whatsoever.[310] Yet, they became pastors by self-appointment. I once tried visiting Filipino churches in the Netherlands, Denmark, and Norway and found it almost impossible to talk with their pastors because they still have to obtain permission from their bishop in Manila.

Fifth, the lack of theological education and intentional training among Filipino leaders in many diasporic congregations is increasingly alarming.[311] Attitudes toward theological education and training vary. Some refuse to undergo training because they think that the Holy Spirit is enough to lead and educate them; others skip training because they do not want to invest in it financially.[312] They would rather send hard-earned money home than spend it on a textbook on theology or ministry leadership training.

---

308 See, for example, Claro, *A Higher Purpose*, 23.

309 For an extensive discussion on these views, see Tereso C. Casiño, "Is Diaspora Missions Valid? Disciple Making among the Filipino *Kababayans*," in *Scattered: The Filipino Global Presence*, ed. Luis Pantoja, Enoch Wan, and Joy Tira (Manila: LifeChange, 2004), 123–45.

310 This has been documented in Tereso C. Casiño, "Theological Education of Diaspora Leaders in the Asian Region," *Torch Trinity Journal* 11, no. 1 (November 2008): 47; specifically footnote no. 10.

311 For an extensive treatment on this theme, see Ibid., 45–62.

312 A case study on this issue from a Chinese perspective is given in Lewis Chau, "Creative Missions—Lay Leadership Training in Asian Context," in *Asian Mission: Yesterday, Today and Tomorrow*, ed. Timothy K. Park (Pasadena, CA: Institute for Asian Mission, 2008), 149–62.

The rest simply dodge theological education because they are busy in their regular jobs.

Conclusion

The rise and development of the Filipino missionary movement was a product of historical, political, ecclesiastical, and socioeconomic factors. The Philippine Protestant Church has been the recipient of missionary aids and support for one hundred years. The time has come for Filipino believers to double its efforts in becoming a missionary force worldwide. While the Philippine Church may lack strong financial resources to mount simultaneous global missionary efforts, it does have great potential to mobilize the diaspora Filipinos who are scattered in almost two hundred countries around the world. In this preliminary assessment, the history of the Philippine missionary movement has shown that Filipino Christians can have a global impact on countries where they live and work. It had been predicted that by 2010, Filipino tentmaking missionaries would be serving in many parts of the world. The global presence of Filipino Christians as a strategic missionary force is unprecedented in the history of the Philippine missionary movement.

Bibliography

Achutegui, Pedro and Miguel A. Barnard. *Religious Revolution in the Philippines.* Vol. 1. Manila: Ateneo de Manila University Press, 1961.

Anderson, Gerald H. *Studies in the Philippine Church History.* Ithaca/London: Cornell University Press, 1969.

Arcilla, Jose S. *An Introduction to Philippine History.* Quezon City: Ateneo de Manila University Press, 1973.

Baldoz-Dimaplis, Rosalinda. "The Overseas Filipino Workers (OFW) Phenomenon." In *Scattered: The Filipino Global Presence*, edited by Luis Pantoja, Enoch Wan, and Joy Tira, 37–48. Manila: LifeChange Publishing Inc., 2004.

Bello, Walden F., et. al. "Brain Drain in the Philippines." In *Modernization: Its Impact in the Philippines*. Quezon City: Ateneo de Manila University Press, 1974.

Bello, Walden F., et. al., eds. *Modernization: Its Impact in the Philippines*. Quezon City: Ateneo de Manila University Press, 1974.

Blair, E. H., and J. A. Robertson. *The Philippine Islands 1493–1898*. Vol. 1. Cleveland, OH: Arthur H. Clark Company, 1903.

Brown, Arthur J. *The New Era in the Philippines*. Nashville, TN: Nashville Publishing House, 1903.

Casiño, Tereso C. "Is Diaspora Missions Valid? Disciple Making among the Filipino Kababayans." In *Scattered: The Filipino Global Presence*, edited by Luis Pantoja, Enoch Wan, and Joy Tira, 123–45. Manila: LifeChange Publishing Inc., 2004.

Casiño, Tereso C. "Theological Education of Diaspora Leaders in the Asian Region." *Torch Trinity Journal* 11, no. 1 (November 2008): 45–62.

Castillo, Metosalem. *The Church in Thy House: A Study of the House Church Concept As It Relates to Christian Mission*. Manila: The Alliance Publishers, 1982.

Chau, Lewis. "Creative Missions—Lay Leadership Training in Asian Context." In *Asian Mission: Yesterday, Today and Tomorrow*, edited by Timothy Kiho Park, 149–162. Pasadena, CA: Institute for Asian Mission, 2008.

Claro, Robert. *A Higher Purpose for Your Overseas Job*. Makati: Crossover Books, 2003.

Constantino, Renato. *The Philippines: A Past Revisited*. Quezon City: Published by the uthor, 1975.

Cushner, Nicholas P. *Spain in the Philippines*. Manila: Ateneo de Manila University Press, 1971.

Deats, Richard L. *Nationalism and Christianity in the Philippines*. Dallas, TX: Southern Methodist University Press, 1967.

Eggan, Fred. *Area Handbook on the Philippines*. Vol. 2. Chicago: University of Chicago Press, 1956.

Gowing, Peter G., and William H. Scott. *Acculturation in the Philippines: Essays on Changing Societies*. Quezon City: New Day Publishers, 1971.

Gowing, Peter G. *Islands Under the Cross: The Story of the Church in the Philippines*. Manila: National Council of Churches, 1967.

Hollnsteiner, Mary R. "The Urbanization of Metropolitan Manila." In *Modernization: Its Impact in the Philippines*. Quezon City: Ateneo de Manila University Press, 1974.

Jocano, F. Landa. *Philippine Prehistory: An Anthropological Overview of the Beginnings of Filipino Society and Culture*. Manila: Philippine Center for Advanced Studies, 1975.

Kane, Herbert J. *A Concise History of the Christian Mission*. Grand Rapids, MI: Baker Book House, 1982.

Lim, David S. "Vignettes of the Filipino Tentmaker." http://www.weaconnections.com/getattachment/5543b9b3-f26f-42f0-8a2a-065609cdc53d/Vignettes-of-Filipino-Tentmakers.aspx (accessed March 1, 2009).

Lopez, Robert K. "The Unfolding Story of the Filipino Tentmaking Movement." Available at http://www.wea-connections.com/Back-issues/Tentmaking-in-Today-s-Global-Environment/The-Unfolding-Story-of-the-Filipino-Tentmaking-Mov.aspx (accessed March 1, 2009).

———. "A New Wineskin: The Filipino Global Missions Movement." In *From Missionary Field to Missions Force*, 29–33. Manila: Philippine Missions Association, 2007.

Lopez, Robert. "National Director's 2007 Report." In *From Missionary Field to Missions Force*, 24–25. Manila: Philippine Missions Association, 2007.

Muslim, Macapado A., and Rufa Cagoco-Guiam. "Mindanao: Land of Promise." Available at http://www.c-r.org/our-work/accord/philippines-mindanao/promised-land.php.

Neill, Stephen. *A History of Christian Missions*. London, UK: Penguin Books, 1990.

Phelan, Leddy L. "Prebaptismal Instruction and the Administration of Baptism in the Philippines during the Sixteenth Century." In *Studies in Philippine Church History*, edited by Gerald H. Anderson, 22–43. Ithaca, NY: Cornell University Press, 1969.

Regan, Joseph W. *The Philippines: Christian Bulwark in Asia*. New York, NY: Maryknoll Publications, 1957.

Remigio, Amador Jr. "A Demographic Survey of the Filipino Diaspora." In *Scattered: The Filipino Global Presence*, edited by Luis Pantoja, et al., 5–35. Manila: LifeChange Publishing Inc., 2004.

Romarate-Knipel, Carla Gay A. One mission, different voices: overseas missions of the convention of the Philippine Baptist Churches." http://findarticles.com/p/articles/mi_m0NXG/is_2_41/ai_n16609034 (accessed March 1, 2009).

Schirmer, Daniel B., and Stephen R. Shalom, eds. *The Philippines Reader: A History of Colonialism, Neocolonialism, Dictatorship, and Resistance*. Quezon City: Ken Inc., 1987.

Schumacher, John, and Gerald H. Anderson. "A Bibliographical Survey of the Philippine Church History." In *Studies in Philippine Church History*, edited by Gerald H. Anderson, 389–412. Ithaca, NY: Cornell University Press, 1969.

Tira, Sadiri Joy. "Filipino International Network: A Strategic Model for Filipino Diaspora Glocal Mission." In *Scattered: The Filipino Global Presence*, edited by Luis Pantoja, Enoch Wan, and Joy Tira, 151–172. Manila: LifeChange Publishing Inc., 2004.

Tuggy, Arthur. *The Philippine Church: Growth in a Changing Society.* Grand Rapids, MI: Eerdmans, 1971.

Tuggy, A. Leonard, and Ralph Toliver. *Seeing the Church in the Philippines*. Manila: OMF Publishers, 1972.

Verora, L. P. *Unreached Peoples '81*. Manila: World Vision Philippines, 1981.

Websites

EuronetTrust — http://www.euronettrust.com/index.html

Filipino International Network — http://fin-online.org

National Council of Churches in the Philippines — http://www.nccphilippines.org

Philippine Challenge — http://www.philchal.org/

Philippine Council of Evangelical Churches — http://www.pceconline.org/

Philippine Migrants Society of Canada — http://pmscontario.tripod.com/id1.html

Philippine Missions Association — http://philippinemissionsassociation.com

About Dr. Tereso C. Casiño

Tereso C. Casiño is a professor of Systematic Theology and Intercultural Studies/Missiology at Torch Trinity Graduate School of Theology in Seoul, Korea. He is the founding president of the Theological Society of the Philippines and editor of the *Asia Pacific Journal of Intercultural Studies*. He was founding director of the Asia Pacific Institute of Missions at the Philippine Baptist Theological Seminary. Since 1988, he has been involved in theological education and is presently involved in global initiative programs related to theological education, mission, and organizational networks. He currently ministers at the International Baptist Church in Seoul and the English congregation of Saejungang Presbyterian Church in Anyang.

Index

A

A Grammar of Hindi Language, 51
Abraham, P. T., 62
Abubakker, John, 79
accountability, 63, 73, 83–84, 86
 of missionaries, 46
 Standards and Monitoring Cell, 83
 structure, 69
Acheh, 186
AD 2000, 66, 185
Adopt-A-People Group, 185
Adriani, N., 130
Advancing Native Missions (ANM), 66
advocacy, 107
 programs, 209
Afghanistan, 171
Africa, 1–3, 5–6, 10, 15, 148, 153, 184, 211
 African
  continent, 6
  countries, 6, 147
   diaspora, 6
Agape Christian Fellowship, 212
Aglipay, Gregorio, 201
Ah Fa, 177
Alag, Meg, 210
Alaska, 206
Ali, Hyder, 47–48
All India Association for Christian higher Education (AIACHE), 65
Allen, Horace, 13
Allen, John, 12
Alliance Graduate School (AGS), 213, 217
Ambedkar, Dr., 49
Ambon, 125
 Ambonese
  believers, 127
  immigrants, 127
  teacher, 127
America(n). *See* United States of America.
American Baptist, 92–94, 100, 102, 113–14, 116
 missionary, 103, 139
American Baptist Foreign Mission Society, 208
American Board of Commissioners for Foreign Missions (ABCFM), 178
American Methodist, 140, 178
 bishop, 48
Amoy, 139
anatomical, 8–9
Anderson, Suree, 105
Andrews, C.F., 48
Andrianoff, David, 106, 116
Andrianoff, Ted, 105
Angkuw, Adrianus, 129
Anglican, 178
Anglo-Burmese
 war, 93
Anglo-Chinese School (ACS), 179
Anglo-Indian, 52
Angsatarathon, Pongsak, 105
Anhui, 24, 34
Anthing, F. L., 136, 138, 149
anti-American. *See* United States of America.
Antioch, 175, 190–92
Antioch 21, 186
Anyomi, Seth, 84
Appenzeller, 13–14
Arcilla, Jose S., 199
Argentina, 158
Asahan, 140
Asia, 1–4, 7, 10, 15, 52, 121–22, 148, 175, 177, 182–85, 189, 191, 206
 Asian, 16–17, 60, 184

Christianity, 2–3
churches, 7, 171
national, 92
countries, 37, 122
identity, 92
leader, 16
mission, 1, 18, 156
leaders, 15–17
strategies, 17
missionary, 15–17, 57, 184
leader, 16
movement, 7
nationals, 183
nations, 7, 214
people, 156
selfhood, 3
strategies, 15
Asia College of Ministry (ACOM), 183, 189
Asia Evangelistic Fellowship (AEF), 183, 189
Asia Missions Association (AMA), 3, 7
Asia Pacific Nazarene Theological Seminary (APNTS), 217
Asia Vision for Short Term Mission (AVSTM), 216–17
Asian Society of Missiology (ASM)
Bangkok Conference, 16
Asian Theological Seminary (ATS), 217
Assemblies of God (AOG), 180, 186, 207
in Brazil, 4
Australia, 97, 99, 121, 147, 179, 183, 188
Autonomous Pentecostal movements, 4
Azeris, 85

B

Back to Jerusalem International Organization, 38
Back to Jerusalem Movement (BJM), 35
Baguio City, 216–17
Bahrain, 215
Baikdu Mountain, 14
Bali, 132, 148
Balinese, 132
church, 148–49
community, 132, 149
culture, 149
transmigrants, 145
Balinese Protestant Church, 132
Bandhu
Seva Network, 65
Bandung, 142, 147
Banggai, 130
Bangkok, 101, 103–04
Bangladesh, 57
Banten, 122
Baptist, 95, 98, 111, 146, 191, 207
church, 93, 112, 143, 207
convention, 205, 217
group, 94
missionary, 51, 93–94, 104, 207
Barnabas, 192
Basle Missiongesellschaft (BMG), 133
Batak, 146
church, 140
denominations, 142
Karo, 140
land, 140
migrants, 142
people, 140
Toba, 139–40
Batak Protestant Christian Church, 140–41
Batu, 140
Beijing, 36–37
Belgium, 107, 212
Bengal, 51
Bengali, 47
literature, 47
Bengkulu, 139
Bethlehem Church, 101

Bhamaw, 94
Bible, 10, 13, 39–40, 68, 99, 134, 178, 192, 212, 218
  biblical
    basis, 68
    teaching, 26, 219
    training, 97, 187
    values, 5, 149
  Chinese, 13
  King James Version, 10
  Latin, 178
  school, 25, 31, 36, 186
  Scripture, 10, 130–31
  seminaries, 70
  teaching, 178
  training, 107
    center, 109
  translation, 14
Bible Presbyterians (BP), 180
Biblical Seminary of the Philippines (BSOP), 217
BiG Partners/Tent-makers Network, 65
Bihar, 78
Bishop Thoburn, 178–79
Blackmore, Sophia, 179
Blambangan, 124
Bless India Gathering, 5–6
Board of Foreign Missions of the Methodist Episcopal Church, 133
Board Members Network, 65
Bolaang Mongondow, 130
Bolus, Ricardo, 212
Bonifacio, Andres, 199
Boo, Tan See, 177
Borneo, 133
Boxer Rebellion, 13
Bradley, 101
Brant, Howard, 195
Brazil, 4, 147–48, 158
Brazil for Christ, 4
Brethren Assemblies, 178, 181
British, 59, 92–93, 126, 176, 181
  Army, 178
  colonialism, 175
  government, 13, 48, 139
  mission, 139
  Parliament, 10
  raj, 58
  rule, 59, 114
Brother
  Cheng, 34
  Chou, 35
  Guo, 34
  Hsu, 34–35
  Huang, 35
  Jing, 35
  Liu, 35
  Miao, 35
  Shen, 34
  Soon, 35
  Wang, 34–35
  Yu, 34
  Zhang, 34
Brown, Dame Edith, 52
Bru tribal groups, 107
Bruckner, 127, 134–35
Brunei, 158
Buddhism, 149
Burckhardt, Jacob, 7
Burgoz, Jose, 200
Burma, 51–52, 91–96, 104, 107, 114
  Burmese, 113
    Buddhist, 114
    church, 93, 95–96
    provinces, 93
Burma Baptist Convention, 93
Byu, Ko Tha, 93

C

Cagoco-Guiam, Rufa, 205
California, 11, 96, 108, 112, 147, 156, 205
Calvinism, 126
Cambodia, 91, 96–100, 112–13, 183, 187
  Cambodian, 97–99, 113
    Christian, 99
    church, 96–99

evangelist, 98–100
expatriate, 98
immigrant, 104
missionary, 98
refugee, 99
Cambodian Christian Reformed Church (CCRFC), 99
Cambodian Evangelical Church, 96, 98
Cambodian New Life Ministries (CNLM), 99
Campus Crusade for Christ (CCC), 61, 98, 161, 182, 215
Korea, 166
campus ministries, 215
Campus Missions International, 161
Canada, 99, 147, 213, 215
Captain Hawkins, 53
Carey, William, 10, 47, 177
Castillo, Met, 208, 210
Cell for Assistance and Relief to Evangelists (CARE/IMA), 63, 65–66, 70, 75
Center for Evangelism and Missions (SCEM), 184
Central Asia, 4, 30, 37, 85, 153
Central Pacific Railway, 11
Central Party, 32
Central Sulawesi, 130–31, 145
Central Sulawesi Christian Church, 131
Ceylon, 51
Chan Fong, 186
ChangFeng Church, 34
Chanh, Le Quoc, 111
ChangZhi Church, 34
Chanwittakoun, Susan, 105
Chanwittakoun, Vicha, 105
Charter, Ternate, 125
Chengdu, 37
Chiang Mai, 101, 104, 114
Chiang Rai, 102
Chiang Rung, 104
children, 14, 54, 63, 73–75, 129, 179–82, 218
Children's Network, 65
Chin, 94–96, 114
Chin Baptist Convention, 93, 95
China, 2, 10–13, 21–28, 30, 32–40, 91, 94, 104–05, 108, 139, 146, 148, 156–57, 163, 166–68, 176–77, 179, 183, 187, 196
Chinese, 11–12, 25, 100, 102–05, 132–33, 138–40, 143, 147, 156, 175, 188, 190, 213–14
believer, 139
Bible. *See* Bible.
Christian, 139, 177, 180, 190
church, 26, 105, 139, 144, 146–47, 157, 177
culture, 22
diaspora, 213
evangelist, 136
government, 32–33, 38
immigration, 11
language, 156
lifestyle, 13
literature, 176
mission
organization, 37
pastor, 10, 22
society, 39
Three-Self Churches, 2
workers, 11
church, 21–25, 27–31, 34–36, 38–40
history, 22
leader, 25
mission. *See* mission.
China Christian Literature Society (CCLS), 40
China Gospel Fellowship, 34
China Inland Mission, 13, 183
Chinese Congress on World Evangelization (CCOWE), 213
Chinese Phenomenon, 146
Cho, David J., 166
Choi, Kwan-Heul, 156
Chongqing, 35
Chongshin University, 166–67
Christendom, 1–2, 9–10, 56

Christian
activities, 32, 191
Bible-believing, 2
intellectual, 21, 38–39
literature, 21, 39–41, 51, 61
magazine, 40
school, 25, 52
Christian Aid, 66
Christian and Missionary Alliance (C&MA), 96, 98, 133, 143, 202
in Canada, 213
in the Philippines (CAMACOP), 205, 207
Christian Literature Crusade (CLC), 61
Christian Medical Association of India (CMAI), 65
Christian Messenger, 168–69
Christianity, 1–3, 5, 8, 12, 17, 48, 53–56, 58–59, 70–72, 91–93, 97, 100–01, 103, 106, 110, 115, 122–24, 126, 130, 135–37, 141, 145, 148–49, 175, 195–98, 201, 206
new, 1–2
Christianity Today, 154
church
church planting, 6, 14, 32, 37, 70, 94–95, 98, 100, 102, 105, 107–08, 116, 143–44, 147, 178, 180, 184–86, 210
handbook, 31
home, 12, 157
house, 2, 21, 25–28, 32–33, 40, 111
independent, 3, 122, 136, 204
institutionalized, 2
local, 23, 35, 70, 84, 108, 115, 145, 164, 170–71, 184, 186, 190–91, 208–11, 218
rural, 21, 28–30
sending, 84, 153–54, 206
Three-Self, 21, 24–27, 39
Chinese. *See* China.
underground, 26, 39
urban, 21, 28–30
Church Growth Missionary Movement (CGMM), 62
Church Growth Studies, 142
Church Mission Society (CMS), 178
Church of Christ, 180
in Thailand (CCT), 100
Church Planting, 210
Clark, Robert, 210
clinical, 9
Colonial East India Company, 59
colonial power, 58, 91
colonialism, 9, 58, 175–76
Comity Agreement, 46, 63, 81–82, 203
Communism
Communist, 22, 26, 109, 144, 183
coup, 144–46
Party, 28, 31–32, 144, 146
revolution, 144, 157
competitive, 170
Confucius, 156, 166
Congregational, 202
Congregational Church to China, 13
Conquistadors, 197, 199
contextual mission, 148, 150
contextualization, 70–71, 73
continuity, 60
Convent of the Holy Infant Jesus (CHIJ), 178
Convention of the Philippine Baptist Churches (CPBC), 208
conversion, 46, 77–78, 92–93, 98, 103, 107, 128–31, 142, 145, 180
Cooke, Sophia, 179
Coolen, 135
cooperation, 21, 28, 63, 69, 105, 170, 202, 204, 208, 210, 213, 217
Corpuz, Rey, 209
Council On National Service (CONS), 66
Creative Access Nations (CAN), 187
Cromwell, Oliver, 10
cross-cultural
church, 102
involvement, 187

ministry, 94, 102, 104, 184
mission, 36–38, 80, 92–93, 98, 101–02, 104, 110, 121–22, 143, 164, 209
works, 35, 95
training, 37–38, 209
work, 103
Crying Church, 34
cultural
adjustment, 116
anthropology, 16
background, 122
baggage, 71
changes, 56
environment, 17
gap, 116
norms, 148
sensitivity, 150
similarities, 116
training, 27
culture, 5, 7–8, 13–17, 22, 54, 56–58, 71–72, 92, 98, 116, 121, 128, 130, 149, 156, 170, 186
curriculum, 16, 27, 35–36, 84, 188
Cyprus, 213

D

Daejon University, 167
Dayak, 133, 143–44, 147
De Bruyn, van Troostenburg, 131
de Legazpi, Miguel Lopez, 198
de San Bernardino, Martha, 196
de Valderrama, Pedro, 197
de-Westernization, 2–3, 17, 72
Deats, Richard L., 200
Denmark, 215, 219
denominational missions, 62, 164
diaspora, 70, 108
African. *See* African.
communities, 213–15
congregation, 219
Filipino. *See* Filipino.
Indian. *See* Indian.
Indochina. *See* Indochina.
Karen. *See* Karen.
Korean. *See* Korean.
leaders, 212–13
organizations, 213
Thai. *See* Thai.
Vietnamese. *See* Vietnamese.
Discipling A Whole Nation (DAWN), 66
discontinuity, 60, 71
Dominican, 124
order, 124
Dongxiang, 37
Doulos, 185
Dutch, 122, 124–26, 128, 130–31, 133, 135, 137–38, 140, 198
Calvinism, 126
government, 126–27, 132–33, 141
Dutch Bible Society, 130–31
Dutch East India Company (VOC), 122–23, 125–27, 129, 134

E

East Asia, 153
East India Company, 9–10, 59, 122–23, 125
East Java Church, 132
East-West Center for Missions Research and Development (EWCMRD), 7
Eastern, 12
East, 1, 9
economic growth, 21, 33, 158, 169
Edinburgh, 168
Ehwa University, 14
El Shaddai, 3
Emmanuel Church, 104
Emmanuel Hospital Association (EHA), 65
Emperor Akbar, 53
Emperor Jehangir, 53
Enggano, 140
England, 9–10, 54, 212
English, 47–48, 51, 53–54, 179, 187, 190
Esser, 131–32

Ethiopia, 158
Ethne Movement, 209
EURONET TRUST (E-TRUST), 211–12
Europe, 2, 4, 96, 126, 144, 147, 176, 188, 206, 209, 211–13
European, 123, 126, 134, 138, 211
  church, 134, 136
  dress, 54
  evangelist, 139
  laywoman, 137
  masters, 55
  mission, 11
  navigator, 195
  politics, 126
Evangelical Church of Vietnam (ECVN), 109–11
Evangelical Fellowship
  of Cambodia, 98
  of India (EFI), 63
  of India Commission on Relief (EFICOR), 66
  of Thailand, 100
Evangelical Free, 180
Evangelical Literature Fellowship of India (ELFI), 65–66
Evangelical Trust Association of North India (ETANI), 65
Evangelical Trust Association of South India (ETASI), 65
Evangelical Union, 203
evangelism, 32, 34, 46, 49, 57, 62–63, 65, 67, 69–70, 73, 81, 93, 107, 111, 122, 125, 127–28, 135, 137, 140, 142, 145–46, 177–78, 180, 182–85, 190, 204–05
Every Home Crusade (EHC), 61
Ewha Women's University, 166–67
exclusivism, 57
Eyes, 40
Ezemadu, Reuden, 6

F

Faith Missions, 62
FangCheng, 34
Far East, 157, 188, 198
Federation of Evangelical Churches of India (FECI), 65
fellowship, 31–32, 63, 79, 96, 108, 136, 204, 211
Fellowship for Neighbours, 79
Filipino, 197, 199–206, 209–11, 213–16, 219–20
  diaspora, 209, 219
  missionary, 196, 207–08, 210–11, 214–15
  missionary movement. *See* missionary.
  priest, 196, 200
Filipino International Network (FIN), 211–12
Filipino Sending Church, 206
Finnish Pentecostal, 180
First Christian Reformed Church, 99
Fisher, Fred B., 48
Five-Year Revival Movement, 22
Flores, 124, 132
Food for the Hungry International, 106
  Korea, 161
foreign funds, 76
Foreign Missionary Societies, 113, 116, 123, 126
foreign missions, 61, 92, 133, 157
FORUM for Evangelism and Missions (NFEM), 66
Four Square Church, 4
France, 97, 99, 126
  French, 48, 91, 96, 103, 109
Francis Xavier, 71
Franciscans, 124
Frankfurt, 212
Friends Missionary Prayer Band (FMPB), 62
Frontiers Movement International, 209
fulfillment theory, 72
Full Gospel Mission, 161
Fuller Theological Seminary, 186

G

Ganan, 94
Gandhi, Indira, 48
Gandhi, Mahatma, 48, 54, 78
Gandhiji, 48
Gauran, Johani, 210
Gaw-ra-hka, 94
General Assembly of the Presbyterian Church of Korea, 166
General Central Representatives Meeting, 31–32
Gereformeerde Zendingsbond (GZB), 131
German Rheinische Missionsgesellschaft (RMG), 133, 139
Germany, 7, 212
Get Involved, 210
Gillquist, Peter E., 68
Giron, Rudy, 84
Glad Tidings Church, 186, 189
Global Consultation On World Evangelism (GCOWE), 72
Global Indian Missionaries, 85
Global Mapping International, 64
Global Mission Society, 160, 164
Global Missionary Fellowship, 166
Global Partners, 164
Glory Presbyterian, 177
God is Love Church, 4
God's Foot Soldiers, 210
Golden Lampstand, 40
Gomez, Mariano, 200
Gorontalo, 130
Gospel Echoing Missionary Society (GEMS), 62
Goudie, William, 50
Grace Baptist Church, 111
Grace Singapore Chinese Christian Church, 186
Grass Roots Church Planters Training Network (GRCP), 66
Great Command, 189, 191
Great Commission, 5–6, 82, 86, 169, 181, 189, 191, 212–13
Great Commission Magazine, 40
Great Revival Movement, 165
Greensboro, 112–13
Guangzhou, 36
Guinea Bissau, 148
Gujarat, 78

H

Halmahera, 125, 128
Halmahera Evangelical Christian Church, 128
Hampton, John, 10
Han, Suk-Jin, 156
Harvest Campus Ministry, 113
Hawaii, 168, 205
Henan, 24, 34
Higher Purpose for Your Overseas Job, 210, 216
Hindu, 49, 58–59, 65, 69, 125, 132
    culture, 56
    custom, 56
    philosophy, 50
    reformation, 47
    widow, 47
Hinduism, 57, 79, 149, 182
Hindustanis, 2
Hmong, 106, 108, 111, 114, 116
    church, 106
    shaman, 105
    tribe, 105
Hodge, J. Z., 51
Hoezoo, W., 137
holistic gospel, 69
Holy Spirit, 159, 165, 171, 219
Homogenous Unit Principle (HUP), 77
Homonhon, 197
Hong Kong, 24, 26, 105, 148, 158, 211, 215
Houghton, Graham, 57–58, 78
House church. *See* church.
HuaiBei Church, 34
Hume, Allan Octavian, 48

HuoQiu Church, 34
Huria Kristen Protestant Batak Church, 140

I

Ibarra, Antonio, 212
Iglesia Evangelica, 201, 203
ill-gotten wealth, 14
Iloilo, 207
inadequate salary, 46, 74
independent, 2–3, 60, 62, 72, 122, 132, 136, 141, 171, 177, 191, 204
India, 2, 5–6, 9–10, 45, 47–54, 57–61, 63–65, 69–72, 75–80, 82, 85–86, 91, 148, 178, 182–83, 187–88
  Indian, 46, 53, 57–60, 70, 72–73, 79, 82, 180, 182, 188, 190, 213–14, 216
    church, 54, 60, 62, 76, 85
      growth, 49
    civil rights movement, 49
    diaspora, 85
    disciples, 49
    dress, 54
    freedom movement, 48
    independence, 51, 60
    indigenous, 60, 67, 74
    leadership, 60–61
    life, 56
    literacy, 50
    literature, 50
    migrants, 175
    mission movement. *See* mission.
    missionary, 45–46, 58, 64, 73, 75, 81, 85
    missions, 45, 60, 67, 76, 80, 82
    worker, 55, 58, 80
  secular, 47
India Association of (Itinerant) Evangelists (IAE), 65
India Missions Association (IMA), 63–64
Indian Christian Media Association (ICMA), 65
Indian Evangelical Mission (IEM), 62
Indian Missionary Society (IMS), 60
Indian Missions, 83–84
Indian National Congress, 48
indigenous mission, 6, 60–61, 74, 183
  missionary movement, 2, 6, 17
    spontaneous, 4
  Marthoma Church, 60
  organizations, 67
Indochina, 91–92, 100, 112–13, 115–16
  diaspora, 112
  Indochinese, 91–92
Indonesia, 6–7, 105, 121–27, 129, 131–32, 134, 138–50, 158, 183, 186, 188, 207–08, 215
  Indonesian, 6, 121–23, 126–28, 133, 143, 147–48, 150, 188, 190
    church, 121–22, 141–42, 144, 147–49
    evangelist, 137
    government, 144–45
    migrants, 147
    mission, 144
    missionary, 143, 148, 150
Indonesia Missionary Fellowship (IMF), 6
Indonesia Muria Christian Church, 139
Inner Mongolia, 35
Inter-Fellowship of Evangelical Students (IFES), 190
Institute of Christian Management (ICM), 83
Institute of Diaspora Studies, 213
integration, 46, 78, 84, 86
InterCP, 161–62, 164
interdenominational, 62, 176, 183
International Missionary Council (IMC), 1, 168
International School of Leaders, 217

Inter-School Christian Fellowship (ISCF), 182
Inter-Varsity, 215
Islam, 123–24, 128, 133–34, 137, 139, 149
Item, Silvanus, 129
Ivory Coast, 148

J

Jailolo, 128
Jakarta, 122, 125–28, 131, 134, 138, 142
James, G D, 182
Japan, 71, 99, 156–58, 163–65, 167, 211, 215
  Japanese, 180–81
    colonial rule, 155–57, 167
Jarai, 98
Jaro, 207
Java Island, 7, 122, 132, 138, 134–40, 143–45, 147
  Javanese, 124–25, 134–37, 139, 143–45
    evangelist, 132, 136, 138
    Hindu, 125
    language, 134
    Muslim, 134
    translation, 135
Jayaprakash, Joshi, 70
Jebasingh, Emil, 5
Jehangir, 53
Jeju Island, 155–56, 165–66, 168
Jellesma, J. E., 135–36
Jericho, 68
Jerusalem Meeting, 28
Jesuit, 53, 71, 124, 199
  emissaries, 12
Jesus Christ, 22, 25, 28, 50, 68, 70, 135, 181, 191–92, 203, 208
Jesus Family, 35
Jogjakarta, 142
Johnson, Andrew, 11
Johnstone, Patrick, 121, 143
Jones, John P., 49, 55, 72
Jones, Stanley, 48, 54
Joon Gon Kim, 166
Joshua Project, 185
Judson, Adoniram, 92–93

K

Kachin, 94, 96, 114
  converts, 94
  evangelist, 94
  language, 96
  missionary, 94
Kachin Baptist
  church, 94
  Convention, 93–94
Kadu, 94
Kairos Prayer Movers, 209
Kalimantan Island, 6, 133, 143–45, 147
Kam, Joseph, 127, 129, 135
Kampuchea, 96
Kampuchea for Christ (KfC), 98, 100
Karen, 93–96, 102, 114
  Baptist
    churches, 102
    Convention, 93, 95
  church, 93, 95, 101
  diaspora, 95
  evangelist, 93–94
  immigrants, 95
  missionary, 94–95
  refugees, 95–96
  tribes, 94
  village, 102
Kawilorot, 101
Kayah, 94
Kazaks, 85
Keasberry, Benjamin, 177
Kediri, 142
Kellogg, S. H., 51
Kengtung, 104
Kenya, 6, 195
Kerala, 60, 79
Khen, Nai, 106
Khmer, 98–99, 108
Khmer Rouge, 97, 99

Khmu, 103, 106, 114
  church, 103
  tribe, 103
  work, 103
Kil, Sun-Choo, 166
Kim, Helen, 166
Kim, John E., 166
King Joao III, 123
kingdom of God, 28, 159, 170–71, 177, 187, 192
Korea, 3, 5, 7, 13–14, 154–58, 164, 166–69, 172, 215, 217
  Korean, 14–15, 36, 153, 156, 167, 169, 190
    church, 36, 153–60, 165–67, 169–71
      leaders, 215
    diaspora, 169
    emigrants, 156, 168
    immigrants, 156, 164
    mission, 154, 159, 163, 165–67, 169–70
      organization, 160, 164
      strengths, 154, 169
      weaknesses, 154, 169
    missionary, 4, 36, 153–54, 157–60, 163–67, 169–70, 217
    student, 156, 166, 168
Korea Baptist Church, 161
Korea Evangelical Holiness Church, 161
Korea International Mission, Inc. (KIM), 6
Korea Methodist Church, 161
Korea World Mission Association (KWMA), 4, 154, 159, 167
Korea World Mission Council (KWMC), 166
Korean Assembly of God, 161
Korean Mission Field, 156, 168
Krishtagraha movement, 48
Kruger, Muller, 123, 127
Kruyt, Albert C., 130
Kumar, Ashok, 79
Kupang, 131
Kuwait, 215
Kwee, Gan, 139
Kyong-In Railroad and Telephone Company, 14
Kyrgyz, 37, 85
Kyrgyzstan, 148

L

La Iglesia Filipina Independiente, 201
Lahu, 102–03
Lambert, Tony, 24
Lampang Church, 101–03
Lamphun, 102
Lao Foreign Outreach, 107
Laos, 91, 101–08, 114
Larnaca, 213
Covenant, 213
Latin America, 1–4, 15, 163
Lausanne Committee for World Evangelization (LCWE), 215
lay
  believer, 138
  charismatic group, 4
  evangelists, 79
  individual, 136
  leader, 215, 217
  missionary, 162–63
  people, 46, 80, 171, 201
  woman, 137
Lazarus, Sam, 61
Le Jolle, 137
Lee, Setan, 100
Lee, William, 186
Legazpi, Miguel Lopez de, 198
legitimate borrowing theory, 71
Lewis, Jonathan, 210
Leyte, 197
Life Magazine, 40
Lighthouse Baptist Church, 107
Lim, David, 210, 216
Limasawa Island, 197
Limited Access Nations, 213–14
Lin, Savang Rojratanakiat, 105
LinFeng Church, 35

Living Fields Ministry, 99
Logos I, 185
London Missionary Society, 126, 176
Long Koom village, 101
Lopez, Robert, 209–10, 216
Los Angeles, 112
Louisiana, 112–13
Louisiana State University, 113
Luang Prabang, 103, 106, 114
Lucknow Christian College, 51
Ludhiana, 52
Lund, Eric, 208
Lutheran, 180–81
Luwuk, 130
Luzon, 217
Lyman, 139

M

Macau, 196
Madurai, 49
Mae Dok Daeng Church, 101
Magellan, Ferdinand, 197–98
Maharashtra, 78
Majowarno, 135–36
Makassar, 126
Malacca, 25
Malacca Strait, 25
Malay, 103, 127, 175, 177
Malayalee, 60
Malaysia, 104, 176, 179, 182–83, 215
Maluku Islands, 122, 124–25, 127–28, 142
  North, 124–25, 128
Manchuria, 156, 168
Manchurian dynasty, 22
Mandryk, Jason, 121
Mangalwadi, Vishal, 59
Manikan, Braulio, 207
Manila, 213, 216–17, 219
Manila Bay, 199
Manshardt, Clifford, 48
Manzano, Glicerio, 210
Marathi, 51
Marcos, Ferdinand, 207
Marshman, Hannah, 52
Marthoma Church of Kerala, 60
Marthoma Evangelistic Association, 60
martial law, 207
Mason, Caroline Atwater, 51
mass movement, 72, 77–78
Mastra, I. Wayan, 148
McGavran, Donald, 77
McGilvary, Daniel, 101–03
McKinley, William, 199
Medan, 140
Medical Services International (MSI), 187
Mekong Bible Seminary, 107
Mekong Evangelical Mission (MEM), 107
member care, 75
Member Care Network, 65
Mencius, 156, 166
Mennonite Mission, 137, 139
Mentawai, 140
Methodist, 13–14, 168, 178, 191, 202
  bishop, 48
  church, 3
  denomination, 3
  Scottish, 50
  work, 179
Methodist Gospel School, 140
Methodist Mission Board, 12
Mexico, 113, 156, 158, 168
Middle East, 5, 30, 35, 37, 153, 163, 206, 209, 213, 215–16
Milne, William, 177
Milton, John, 10
Minahasa, 129–30, 142, 146
  church, 129
Minahasa Evangelical Christian Church, 127, 142
Mindanao, 205, 217
Ming dynasty, 22
ministry, 22, 26, 29, 31, 36, 41, 51, 84, 94, 100, 102, 104–07, 128, 132, 136–38, 155, 179, 182, 184, 211, 215
  effective, 172

leadership training, 219
sending, 21, 36
skills, 84
Ministry of Education (MOE), 179
Ministry to Muslims (M2M), 209
mobilization, 209
missiologist,
Asian, 17
Western, 3, 16
mission
awareness, 21, 34, 36, 84, 209
China, 21, 23–25, 30–34, 36, 38–39, 41
ten affecting factors, 21
conference, 22, 167, 172, 185
continuity, 60
denominational, 62, 164
discontinuity, 60
education, 46, 63
foreign. *See* foreign missions.
history, 7–10, 15, 17–18, 86, 169
of Indochina, 91–92
of Indonesian church, 121, 148
of Korean church, 155
in affluence, 158
interdenominational, 176
long-term, 80, 210, 216
movement, 22–23, 127, 213
Indian, 45
Korean, 167, 169
short-term, 46, 80, 108, 162, 171, 216
strategies, 17, 76, 217
theology, 170–71, 218
to Shantung, 156–57
training, 21, 36–38, 84, 211, 216–17
world, 1, 45, 207
Mission at the Cross Roads, 72
Mission Korea (MK), 167
missionary , 12–14, 47–48, 50–52, 54–55, 57–59, 63, 74–75, 80, 82, 84, 92, 102–03, 105–06, 110–11, 113–16, 126–27, 135, 137, 139, 155–59, 166–70, 172, 184, 189, 195–98, 202–08, 210–12, 217–20
activity, 8, 92, 219
agency, 110, 115
candidate, 7, 217
career, 162, 170, 184, 192
conference, 81
leader, 16, 104, 217
movement, 2, 4–5, 7, 15, 154, 164, 167, 171, 176, 185, 195, 197, 206
Filipino, 195–97, 204, 214–15, 218, 220
in Singapore, 175, 189
Indian, 6
of the Korean church, 153, 157–58, 163, 65–66, 168, 171
organization, 61
sending
church, 84, 153–54
country, 45
service, 8
training, 77, 84, 216–17
visa, 61
welfare, 46, 73
Missionary Conspiracy, 59
Missionary Convention, 93
Missionary Training Network, 65, 209
Missionary Upholders Family (MUF), 66
Missionary Upholders Trust (MUT), 66
Mitrichit Charoen Krung Church, 105
Mitrichit Chinese Baptist Church (MCBC), 104
Mizoram, 60, 62
modernization,
policy, 26, 28, 38
theory, 31
Moffett, Samuel, 14
Moghul dynasty, 53
Mongolia, 156
Mongolian, 37

monocultural, 170, 190–91
perspective, 169
Mons, 94
Montagnard, 111, 114
Morrison, Robert, 10, 25
Movement for African National Initiative (MANI), 6
Mua Yia, 105–06
Mudites, 68–69
anti-Mudites, 68–69
Mun, Wang 102
Munson, 139
Muslim, 37, 48, 69, 79, 98, 103, 121, 124–27, 130, 133–34, 136, 141–42, 145, 149–50, 198, 201, 205, 216
Muslim, Macapado A., 205
Muslim Neighbours' Network, 65
Myanmar, 91–93, 183, 188

N

Naaman, 196
Nahuway, Jacob, 7
Nagaland Missionary Movement, 62
Nairobi, 6
Nakon Srithamarat, 103
Nan Inta, 101
Nashville, 107
National Association for Christian Social Concerns (NACSC), 65, 67
National Christian Council (NCC), 203
of India, Burma, and Ceylon, 51
National Council of Churches in India (NCCI), 65
National Council of Churches in the Philippines (NCCP), 203–04
National Missionary Society (NMS), 60
National Youth Missions Movement, 209, 215
nationalism, 1, 181, 199–200
nautch, 51
Nava Jeevan Seva Mandal (NSM), 66
Navigators, 182, 215
Ne Win regime, 95
Nederlands Gereformeerde Zendingsvereeniging (NGZV), 132, 136
Nederlands Zendeling Genootschap (NZG), 126–27, 129–31, 134–35
Nehru, Jawaharlal, 10, 48
Neill, Stephen, 49, 53–55, 59, 72
Nepal, 148, 158, 183
Nepalese, 213, 216
Nestorian, 22
Netherland, 125–26, 137, 215, 219
church, 125
networks, 63, 65–67, 107, 209, 211, 213
New Delhi, 1
New England, 99
New Vision Church, 105
New York, 147
New York Times, 153
New Zealand, 97, 99
Newbigin, Lesslie, 55–56
Ng, Andrew, 184
Ngoro, 135
Nias, 140
Nichols, Doug, 215
Niger, 184
Ninan, George, 82
No Empty Village Mission Strategy, 29
Nommensen, L. J., 139–40
non-patriotism, 57
Norris, Frederick W., 71
North America, 4, 6, 142–43, 188, 206, 211, 213
North Carolina, 112
North Eastern States of India, 78
North India, 66, 80
North India Harvest Network, 66
North Vietnam, 108–09, 111, 117
Northeast Asia, 4, 163

Northeast Thailand, 107–08
Northern Buru, 128
Norway, 215, 219
Nussabaum, Stan, 64

O

Okinawa, 158
Oldham, William, 179
Olympic Games, 33, 169
One Sending Body (OSB), 217
Oostrom-Philips, 136
Operation Mobilization (OM), 61, 185
Orange County, 112
ordination, 31, 215
Overseas Contract Workers (OCW), 206
  Filipino skilled workers, 214
Overseas Foreign Workers (OFW), 214, 216
Overseas Workers' Network, 65

P

Padang, 126, 139
Padroado, 123
Paik, George L., 155
Pakistan, 78, 158, 213
Palaung, 94
Palembang, 140, 142
Panarukan, 124
Pancasila, 149
Pang, Hwa-Chung, 156
Papua, 122, 128–29, 143, 145, 147
parachurch, 182–83
Parshall, Phil, 57
Partners International/Christian National Evangelism Commission (CNEC), 66
partnerships, 6–7, 46, 76, 82, 84, 86, 142, 144, 157–58, 167, 171, 177, 215, 217
Paul, Rajaiah D., 52, 55
Paul Mission, 161, 164
Paulus Khow Tek San, 136
Payao Bible College, 104
Pei Suen, 26
Peking, 11, 22, 156
Pentecostal, 3–4, 62, 101, 146, 180, 204, 207
Pentecostal Fellowship of India (PFI), 65
Perspectives in the World Christian Movement, 61
Phelan, John Leddy, 198
Philippine Baptist Theological Seminary (PBTS), 217
Philippine Council of Evangelical Churches (PCEC), 203–04, 208, 210
Philippine Federation of Christian Churches (PFCC), 203
Philippine Missions Association (PMA), 208–11, 215
Philippine Missions Mobilization Movement, 209
Philippine Partnership for Global Community (PPGC), 217
Philips-Stevens, 135
Phillips, Charles, 178
Phnom Penh, 97
Phnong, 98
Pickett, Waskom, 48–49, 79
PingYuen Church, 35
Pol Pot, 97
political Padri, 59
Pope, 123
Portland, 213
Portugal
  Portuguese, 53, 122–25, 197
Portuguese Suzerainty, 123
position of weakness, 157–58, 165
Prarthana Samaj, 55
Presbyterian, 3, 13–14, 100–03, 113–14, 116, 157, 202
  Korean, 15, 155–57, 166, 168
  Presbytery of Korea, 155
Presbyterian Church of Korea
  Daeshin, 161
  Hapjung, 161
  Hapshin, 161
  Koshin, 161

Tonghap, 160–61
Presbyterian Synod of Mizoram, 62
Presbyterian Theological Seminary (PTS), 217
Prince Sihanouk, 96
Prinsep Street Presbyterian, 177
Protestant, 4, 10, 13–14, 22, 45, 47, 49, 52–53, 91–92, 96–97, 100–01, 109, 122, 125–27, 129, 131–32, 134–35, 140–42, 146, 149, 155, 175, 178, 196–97, 199, 201–07, 216
Protestant Church of Maluku, 127, 142
Protestant Church of Western Indonesia, 127
Protestant Churches Coordinating Committee, 101
Punjab, 52, 78
Punjabi, 51
Purworejo, 136
Pyongyang, 13, 155, 165

Q

Qatar, 215
Qingdao, 36–7
Queen Elizabeth, 9
Quelpart, 155, 168
Qunming, 36–37

R

radical displacement, 71
radio broadcast, 82, 108
Raffles, Thomas Stanford, 126, 139, 175
Rakhine, 94
Ramachandra, Vinod, 190
receptivity, 114
Reformation Age, 9
relativistic syncretism, 72
religion, 1, 7–8, 12, 54, 71–72, 115, 124–26, 130, 138, 140, 149, 180, 186, 198, 217
Renminbi (RMB), 33
Research Network, 65
retirement, 46, 63, 73–75
revival, 108, 110, 113, 165, 171
Reynolds, William D., 155
Rheinische Missiongesellschaft (RMG), 133, 139
Ricci, Mateo, 22
Richard, H. L., 57–58
Richardson, Don, 129
Rizal, Jose, 199
Roe, Thomas, 53
Roman Catholic, 4, 53, 91, 100, 122–26, 129–30, 132, 146, 149, 175, 178, 180, 195–96, 201–02, 205–06
monks, 22
Roman Empire, 9
Roman government, 67
Roti, 131
Roy, Ram Mohun
Hindu reformation, 47
Royal British Empire
in China, 13
RuiAn Church, 35
Ruiz-Duremdez, Sharon, 208
Russia, 84, 105

S

Sadoyo, Petrus, 137
Saiyasak, Chansamone, 107
Salatiga, 137
mission, 137
Salt Lake City, 99
Salvation Army, 180
Saly Kounthapanya, 106
Samaj, Prarthana, 55
Samarang, 7
San Francisco Karen Baptist Fellowship, 96
Sangh, Kristanugami, 79
Santos, Francis, 212
Saravan, 107
Sarawak, 104
Saudi Arabia, 214
Saul, 192

Savannakhet, 107
Sawi, 129
Schwartz, Christian Friedrich, 47–48
School of Missions and Evangelism (SOME), 189
Scranton, 14
Scripture Union (SU), 182
Seagrave, Sterling, 12
self-supporting, 110, 149, 155
  organizations, 141
  self governing, 141, 155
Semarang, 18, 126–27, 134, 137, 142, 207–08
seminary, 104
  professor, 14
  training, 27
Sen, Keshab Chandra, 55
Seoul, 3, 7, 169
Serampore, 52
Serfogee Raja, 47–48
Serve-A-Peoples Network, 65
Seventh-day Adventists (SDA), 180, 202
Shakespeare, William, 9
Shandong, 35, 39
Shanghai, 12, 36–37, 156
Shans, 94
Shanxi, 35
Sharon Pentecostal Fellowship, 62
Shourie, Arun, 59
Siam Mission, 101, 103
Siamese, 101
Siberia, 156, 168
Sibolga, 139
Sikhs, 49
Simo, 137
Singapore, 140, 175–92, 211, 215
Singapore Bible College, 188
Singapore Center for Evangelism and Missions, SCEM, 184
Singaporean-Indian Christian, 182
Singh, Khushwant, 49, 54, 72
social
  action, 66–67
  change, 47
  clubs, 80
  environment, 17
  groups, 5
  justice, 69
  movement, 32
  responsibility, 170
  service, 59
  structure, 28, 175
  system, 17
  work, 46, 70, 74, 109, 178
Solina, Joy, 210
Solor, 124
Soltu, 72
South Africa, 72, 78, 148
South America, 6, 147, 211
South Asia, 78, 80, 163
South Asia Institute of Advanced Christian Studies (SAIACS), 78
South India, 51, 54, 76, 80
South Sulawesi, 131
South Vietnam, 109, 111
Southeast Asia, 4, 91, 96, 107–08, 163, 183, 188
Southeast Islands, 122, 124, 127, 131–32, 143
Southern Baptists, 111, 142, 180–81, 208
Southern Methodist Mission Board, 12
Southside Baptist Church, 112
Southwest Fellowship, 35
Spain, 197–99, 212
Spanish, 123, 125, 129, 197–201
Spice Islands, 124, 197
Sri Lanka, 52
Stock, Frederick, 78
Stock, Margaret, 78
Stokes, Samuel Evan Jr., 48
Storying and the Acts Principle, 210
Straits-born, 177
Stream, 40
Sulawesi, 129, 145
Sultan of Ternate, 125, 128–29
Sultan of Tidore, 128
Sumba, 131–32

Summer Institute of World Mission (SIWM), 7
Sundanese, 137–38, 141, 145, 149
Sunday school, 31–32, 178
Supot, 105
Surabaya, 125–26, 134–35, 142
Surabaya Fellowship for Supporting Evangelism, 135
suttee, 10
Suzerainty, 123–24
Swain, Clara, 52
Swedish Baptist missionary, 208
Swie, Ang Boen, 139
Swiss Brethren, 106

T

Taedong River, 13
Tai-Woong Lee, 166
Taiping Rebellion, 11
Tajik, 87
Tamil
  dictionary, 51
  grammar, 51
Tang dynasty, 22
Tanjore, 47–48
Taylor, James Hudson III, 187
Templin, Ralph T., 48
Teng Siu Ping modernization theory, 31
Tennessee, 107
tentmakers, 79–80, 187, 210, 216, 218
Ternate, 124–25, 128–29
Thai-Burma border, 96
Thai-Cambodian border, 104
Thai Church Development, 104
Thai Lu, 104
Thai Maranatha Church, 104
Thailand, 91–92, 95, 97, 100–05, 107–08, 112, 114, 157–58, 168, 186, 188
  Thai, 101–05, 113–14, 116, 188
    diaspora, 105
Thailand Baptist Churches Association, 101
Thailand Overseas Missionary Society, 104
Thailand Protestant Churches Coordinating Committee, 101
thank offering, 156–166
The Peace Child, 129
The Seed, 40
The Shepherd, 40
The Ways, 40
Theological Seminary of Korea (Pyongyang), 155
theology, 67–69, 148, 170–71, 218–19
  liberal, 180
  social, 40
  theological
    belief, 126
    books, 39–40
    education, 27, 31, 219–20
    institution, 215, 217
    teaching, 26
    training, 27, 219
      program, 183
Third Triennial Convention of the Asia Missions Association, 3
Thoburn, Isabella, 52
Thomas, Robert J., 13
Thomas, T. V., 215
Thra Bo Gale, 94
Thra Ka Te, 94
Thra Ne Hta, 94
Thra Shwe Lin, 94
Thra Swa Pe, 94
Three Years Mission Movement, 23
Tiang Kam Foek, 132
Tibet, 148
  Tibetans, 37
Timor Evangelical Christian Church, 127, 142
Tira, Joy Sadiri, 213
Tobelo, 128
Tokyo, 156, 168
Trang province, 103
Tranquebar, 47, 50, 52

Transformation Movement, 66
Transmigrants, transmigration, 131, 145–46
Treaty of Paris, 199
tribal
area, 81
church, 109, 140
leader, 109
group, 93, 95, 102–03, 107, 110–12, 114, 201
people, 30, 35, 37, 68
religions, 124, 130, 140
Trichinopoly, 47
trinity, 191
Tsang, Reginald, 187
Tulasi Raja, 47
Turk, 85
Tyrannus Overseas Mission, 161

U

Ummah Fellowship, 209
unbalanced missions, 169
Underwood, Horace, 13–14
Underwood, Lilias Horton, 14
Union of Evangelical Students in India (Indian IFES), 61
uniqueness theory, 71
United Arab Emirates, 215
United States of America, 2, 11–12, 14, 95–97, 99, 108, 121, 144, 153, 168, 176, 199, 201–02, 206, 208, 215
American, 11–13, 48–50, 92–94, 96, 100–03, 109, 113–14, 116, 128, 140, 157, 178, 198–99, 202, 205–06, 208
anti-American
sentiments, 96
University Bible Fellowship, 161
University Christian Fellowship (UCF), 38
unreached, 22, 69, 93, 95, 106, 115–16, 127, 129, 143–44, 147, 164, 183, 189, 208–10
Urban Ministries Network, 65
Urdaneta, Andres de, 198
Urdu, 51
Urumqi, 37
Utah, 99
Utrechtse Zendingsvereeniging (UZV), 128, 132
Uyghur, 37
Uzbeks, 85

V

Van der Veen, 131
Van Loosdrecht, A. A., 131
Varnashrama Dharma, 50
Vatican II, 178
Vietnam, 91, 108–14, 117, 158, 183, 187
diaspora, 112
Vietnamese, 97–98, 113–14
church, 110–13
missionary, 110–12
refugee, 113
Vietnamese Baptist Church, 112
Vietnamese Hope Baptist Church, 112–13
Visayas, 217
VISION 2020, 5
vision statement, 5
Vladivostock, 156
Vo, Hoa Duc, 112

W

Wan, Enoch, 215
war
American Civil War, 12
Korean War, 157, 165
World War II, 109, 141, 157, 204
Washington, D.C., 12, 105
WEC International Mission Korea Center, 161
WeiFang Church, 35
Wenzhou, 39
Wenzhou City Church, 34
Western

Christendom, 1–2, 9–10
civilization, 54
denominations, 2
de-Westernization. *See* de-Westernization.
forces in missions, 1
non-Western, 1–2, 4, 15, 17, 157
Partisan, 54
Western Seminary, 213
Winslow, Jack C., 54, 58
Winter, Ralph D., 3, 16, 58, 61, 72
Winter, Roberta, 67
Wiung, 134–35
women
churches, 148
college, 52
education, 51
literature rate, 51
university, 14
work, 46
workers, 128
Woonsan, 14
Worker to Witness, 210
World Christian Encyclopedia, 2
World Concern, 106
World Council of Churches, 168
World Evangelical Fellowship, 63, 98
World Korean Missionary Fellowship (WKMF), 167
World Link University (WLU), 84
World Vision, 66
worship, 3, 72, 79, 96–97, 181, 216
WuHai Church, 35
Wulung, Tunggul, 137
Wycliffe Bible Translators, 105, 184

X

Xian, 22, 36
Xichuan, 35
XuChang Church, 34

Y

Yalu River, 14
Yamamori, Ted, 215
Yao tribal group, 102
Yi Dynasty, 13
Yi Ki-Poong, 155
YinShang Church, 34
Yonsei University, 14
Youth For Christ (YFC), 61, 182
Youth Ministries Network, 65
Youth With A Mission (YWAM), 61, 161–62
YueChing Church, 35
Yunnan, 104

Z

Zamora, Jacinto, 200
Zendeling Genootschap (NZG), 127, 129–31, 134–35
Zhejiang, 34–35
Ziegenbalg, 49
Zoram Evangelical Fellowship, 62
Zoram Missionary Fellowship, 60